On Changing the World

On Changing the World

Essays in Political Philosophy, from Karl Marx to Walter Benjamin

Michael Löwy

On Changing the World
Michael Löwy

First Published in India 2016
Reprinted 2025

ISBN 978-93-5002-455-3

Published in agreement with Haymarket Books, Chicago for publication and sale only in South Asia.

Published by
AAKAR BOOKS
28 E Pocket IV, Mayur Vihar Phase I
Delhi 110 091, India
www.aakarbooks.com

Printed at
D.K. Fine Art Press, Delhi

Contents

Acknowledgments

Critique, Glasgow, Scotland

"From the 'Logic' of Hegel to the Finland Station in Petrograd," first published in *Critique* 6 (1976): pp. 5–15.

M. E. Sharpe Publishers, Inc., Armonk, New York

"Fire Alarm: Walter Benjamin's Critique of Technology," first published in Day et al., eds., *Democratic Theory and Technological Society* (M. E. Sharpe, 1988).

Monthly Review Inc.

"The First Revolution of the Twentieth Century," first published in *Monthly Review* (January 1990): pp. 44–50. Copyright © 1990 by Monthly Review Inc. Reprinted by permission of Monthly Review Foundation.

New Left Review, London

"Marxists and the National Question," first published in *NLR* 96: pp. 81–100. (A shorter version of this article first appeared as the concluding essay in Georges Haupt, Michael Löwy, and Claudie Weill, *Les Marxistes et la question nationale: 1848–1914* [anthology] [Paris, 1974].)

"Revolution against 'Progress': Walter Benjamin's Romantic Anarchism," first published in *NLR* 152: pp. 42–59.

"'The Poetry of the Past': Marx and the French Revolution," first published in *NLR* 177: pp. 111–24.

Social Compass, Louvain-la-Neuve, Belgium

"Religion, Utopia, and Counter-Modernity: The Allegory of the Angel of History in Walter Benjamin," first published in *Social Compass* 36, no. 1 (March 1989): pp. 95–104.

Telos, New York

"Marcuse and Benjamin: The Romantic Dilemma," first published in *Telos* (Summer 1980): pp. 25–33.

"Marxism and Revolutionary Romanticism," first published in *Telos* 49 (1981): pp. 83–95.

Preface

Is it still possible to write, in our day, after all that has happened during the last years, about Karl Marx and about socialism? Isn't it true, as a famous thinker wrote, that "Marxism is definitely dead for humanity"?

One can find very similar comments in dozens of recent books and hundreds of recent articles and editorials. However, this particular comment was written by Benedetto Croce in . . . 1907. Could it not be that the present self-fulfilling prophecies will fare no better than those so confidently proclaimed eighty years ago?

Of course, no one can deny that the demise of the Soviet Union opens a new historical period. What is the meaning of such events? Is it true, as we are being told by experts, columnists, and academicians, that "socialism is dead"?

It is not possible to die before being born. Socialism is not dead for the good reason that it is not yet born. What the Western media called "the Communist states" and the Eastern official ideology "really existing socialism," were neither. At best, one could consider them as a set of noncapitalist societies, where the private property of the main means of production was abolished; but they were very far from *socialism*—that is, from a society where the associated producers are the masters of the process of production; a society based on the largest economic, social, and political democracy; a commonwealth liberated from all class, ethnic, and gender exploitation and oppression. Whatever their economic and social achievements or failures, these "really existing" societies had one basic common shortcoming: the lack of democracy, the exclusion of the workers and of the whole society from any real participation in political power.

The democratic rights—freedom of expression and organization, universal suffrage, political pluralism—are not "bourgeois institutions" but hard-won conquests of the labor movement. Their curtailment in the name of socialism leads to bureaucratic despotism. As Rosa Luxemburg (who actively supported the October Revolution) had already warned in her fraternal criticism of the Bolsheviks in 1918: "Without general elections, without a free struggle of opinion, life dies out in every public institution, becomes a mere semblance of life, in which only the bureaucracy remains an active element." Although some aspects of pluralism and workers' democracy still existed during the years 1918–23, increasingly authoritarian measures were taken. This mistake—together with the dramatic objective situation of the Soviet Union during these years: backwardness, civil war, famine, foreign intervention—created favorable conditions for the appearance of the bureaucratic malignant growth which, under the form of Stalinism, destroyed the Bolshevik party and its historical leadership, and produced some of the worst political mass murders of this century.

What the conservative or liberal media call "the death of socialism" is in fact the decomposition and dissolution of the authoritarian and bureaucratic system of noncapitalist industrial development, which came out of the Stalinist model established in the Soviet Union in the twenties and thirties, on the ashes of the October Revolution; a model that had already been criticized and rejected during the twenties and thirties, in the name of Marxism, by a whole generation of radicals. What is dead in Eastern Europe and the Soviet Union is not "socialism" but its bureaucratic caricature: the monopoly of power by the *nomenklatura*, the dictatorship over needs, the command economy.

There seems to exist a sort of consensus today among Eastern European leaders that the only way out is "the market economy." However, there is no reason to accept the contention, presented as a kind of self-evident truth by a unanimous chorus of (Eastern and Western) establishment economists, neoliberal ideologists, competitive businessmen, and mainstream press editorialists, that the market economy, capitalism, and the profit system are the only possible alternatives for the failure of the totalitarian command economy which existed in the noncapitalist countries—an economy where a small group of (incompetent) technocrats decided what to produce and to consume and despotically imposed their decisions on the society. *Tertium datur*: there exists another road, the democratic planning of economy by society itself, where the people themselves decide, after a pluralist and open debate, the main economic choices, the priorities of investment, and the great lines of the economic policy—that is, socialist democracy.

The crimes committed in the name of communism and socialism by the bureaucratic regimes—since the bloody purges of the thirties until the invasion of Czechoslovakia in 1968—have deeply injured the idea itself of a socialist future and paved the way for liberal/conservative ideologies among large sections of the population, both in the East and the West. However, the aspirations for a free and egalitarian society, for social and economic democracy, for the protection of nature, and for self-administration and control from below are deeply rooted among significant parts of the working class and of youth, on both sides of the border between the former blocs. From this standpoint, socialism, not as a supposedly "existing" state, but as a program that has inspired for one and a half centuries the emancipatory struggles of the victims of capitalism and imperialism, not only is not "dead" but will remain alive as long as exploitation and oppression exist.

Understandably, in the present situation of crisis, one can find, among many leftists, a deep state of ideological confusion, disarray, and perplexity. Even those who are not yet ready to give away the whole Marxist heritage are preparing themselves for a retreat in good order. The dominant tendency in the left, both East and West, is the one that argues for the need of "modernizing" Marxism, adapting it to the ruling ideas, to liberalism, to individualism, to positivism—and above all to the new religion of the market, with its idols, its rituals, and its infallible dogmas. For this view of things the failure of "really existing socialism" has its origins in the attempt of the October Revolution to break away (at least partially) from the model of capitalist civilization, from the world market; the modernization of Marxism would therefore imply a certain return to the canons of the Western social and economic system.

What is being thrown away is not only the (extremely) dirty water—the antidemocratic, bureaucratic, often totalitarian nature of the noncapitalist societies and of their system of centralized planning—but also the "baby": the idea itself of moving beyond capitalism, towards collective forms of economy. What is being forwarded in this attempt at "reconciliation with reality" (to use a venerable Hegelian formula) is not above all the universal values negated or perverted by Stalinism—democracy, human rights, freedom of expression, social equality, solidarity—but those publicized ever since by the Western elites and their ideologists: "free competition," "free enterprise," monetarism, market-fetishism.

There is no doubt that Marxism needs to be questioned, criticized, and renewed, but in our view this should be done *exactly for the opposite reason*: because its break with the productivist pattern of industrial capitalism and with the foundations of the modern bourgeois civilization was not sufficiently radical. The Marxists (if not Marx himself) have often moved into the footsteps of the ideology of progress typical of the eighteenth and nineteenth centuries, particularly in presenting the development of productive forces as the objective foundation of the revolution and as the main argument for legitimating the need for socialism. In certain forms of vulgar Marxism the supreme aim of the social revolution is not a fraternal and egalitarian reorganization of society—that is, a "utopia" implying a new way of producing and living, with productive forces of a qualitatively different nature—but simply to remove the relations of production that are an obstacle for the free development of the productive forces. Many Marxists followed the bourgeois/positivist model, based on the arbitrary extension to the historical sphere of the epistemological paradigm of the natural sciences, with its "laws," its determinism, its purely objective "prediction," its linear evolutionism—a tendency pushed to its last consequences by a certain kind of "orthodox Marxism," from Plekhanov to Louis Althusser.

Happily, the main content of Marxism is elsewhere: in the philosophy of praxis and the dialectical/materialist method, in the analysis of commodity fetishism and of capitalist alienation, in the perspective of the workers' revolutionary self-emancipation, and in the utopia of a classless and stateless society. This is the reason why Marxism holds an extraordinary potential for critical and subversive thought (and action). The renewal of Marxism must start with this humanist/democratic and revolutionary/dialectical heritage to be found in Marx himself and in some of his followers, like Rosa Luxemburg, Trotsky, and Gramsci (to cite only these three)—a tradition that was defeated during the twenties and the thirties by counterrevolution, Stalinism, and fascism.

Moreover, in order to *radicalize its rupture with bourgeois civilization* Marxism must be able to integrate the practical and theoretical challenges raised by contemporary social movements like ecology and feminism. This requires the vision of a new civilization, which would not be just a more "progressive" version of the Western industrial/capitalist paradigm, grounded on a state-controlled development of the same productive forces—but a new way of life, based on use value and democratic planning, renewable energies and ecological production, race and gender equality, and free community and international solidarity.

Today, more than ever, Marxism must be "the pitiless criticism of all that exists" (Marx, 1843). Rejecting the "modernist" apologies for the established order, the "realistic" discourses legitimating the capitalist market or bureaucratic despotism, it represents the Principle of Hope (Bloch), the concrete utopia of an emancipated society.

The essays collected in this volume deal with the history of Marxism as a *political philosophy*. "Politics" does not mean here only questions relating to power and state but the broad range of issues concerning human common life in the polis. And "philosophy" refers to basic theoretical, methodological, or ethical interrogations.

However, as Marx wrote in his famous "Thesis XI on Feuerbach," it is a political philosophy that aims not only at interpreting but above all at *changing the world*. This is the reason why the concept of *revolution*—in its various historical and social dimensions—is the central theme in most of these essays. Other issues are also discussed here, but always in relation to the revolutionary perspective: the national question, religion, utopia—cultural, "spiritual," or ethical dimensions that have been systematically neglected by the economistic tendency dominant in much Marxist literature.

The interpretation of Marxism offered here is quite unorthodox; in many aspects it is *poles* apart from what used to be considered as "scientific socialism" for large sections of the left. It is also very different from several recent currents like structuralist Marxism, poststructuralist (or postmodern) Marxism, and analytical Marxism. It takes its inspiration from the dialectical, historicist, humanist, antipositivist, and anti-evolutionist tradition in Marxist theory. And it tries to bring into the forefront *the hidden romantic moment* in Marxist political philosophy.

Romanticism is not just a literary or artistic school from the nineteenth century but one of the fundamental *worldviews* in modern culture, from the end of the eighteenth century until now: its essence is the protest against the industrial/bourgeois civilization in the name of precapitalist values. Usually ignored, romanticism is one of the key sources of the Marxist critique of capitalist civilization, and an important component of the Marxist utopia. The attempt to highlight the romantic aspect in the writings of Marx himself and of several other Marxist figures is probably one of the most polemical aspects of this book.

The authors discussed here—after Marx and Engels, Lenin, Rosa Luxemburg, Lukács, Gramsci, Marcuse, and Walter Benjamin—are far from being "homogeneous." Their diversity is also part of the vitality of the development of Marxist theory. The approach proposed in these essays—sometimes focusing on one aspect only of a complex body of writings, on a specific moment in their political and intellectual evolution—underlines some common features: the romantic/revolutionary dimension, an "open" view of history ("socialism *or* barbarism"), a dialectical approach (of Hegelian inspiration) to social reality, and a utopian horizon.

These essays were written at different moments from the seventies until today.* They correspond to a certain extent to an evolution in my own spheres of interest: from Marx and Rosa Luxemburg to Lukács, and then to romanticism, religion, and Walter Benjamin. I became interested in romanticism while doing research on Lukács for my doctoral thesis. At that time I still believed that Marxism and romanticism were somehow contradictory. In a (friendly) review of my book, Raymond Williams criticized this assumption and thus helped me to supersede it and to open a new area of research: the romantic impulse in the Marxist political culture. It was also while studying Lukács's early writings that I first observed the surprising *elective affinities* between revolutionary utopia and heretical forms of religiosity—a question that I tried to examine more systematically in my work on Walter Benjamin and the Jewish-German messianic culture and in my present research on Latin American liberation theology.

However, this is a personal evolution that remains deeply rooted in the soil of Marxist political philosophy. It has become fashionable for radical intellectuals (both in the United States and in Europe) to recant their former leftist views, their Marxist writings, and their utopian hopes of changing the world. Readers expecting such signs of repentance or contrition in this book will be disappointed, I'm afraid. I'm as convinced now as in 1968 that the present state of the world is inhuman, unjust, and deserves to be radically changed—the main difference being that I now understand much better than twenty-five years ago the danger of ecological catastrophe and therefore the threat for the survival of the human species represented by the "system."

---

* This book was originally published in the 1990s. This is a revised and enlarged edition.

In the title "From Karl Marx to Walter Benjamin" there is at the same time an element of continuity and of change. The new problems, authors, and issues do not replace, erase, or negate the former ones, but present, in my eyes, the possibility of an enrichment, an enlargment, and an opening of perspectives. Walter Benjamin has too often been reduced, by modern (and postmodern) interpreters, to a literary critic or a renewer of aesthetics; he was all that but much more: one of the most important and original revolutionary philosophers of the twentieth century; by his critique of technology, of the ideology of progress, and of the "really existing modernity," he opens a new chapter in the history of Marxist thought and stimulates a new reading, a new (critical) interpretation of Marx himself. The same can be said, in a different context, about Rosa Luxemburg or Lukács.

Of course these essays have only a fragmentary character and do not at all present a systematic picture of this pluralist growth of the Marxist political philosophy or of its dialectical (contradictory) development. Their aim is not to propose a set of ready-made answers to some controversial questions, nor to replace an old and outworn orthodoxy by a new one. But rather to revisit some high moments of the revolutionary tradition—1789, 1905, 1917—and then follow some small mountain roads, like that steep path in the Pyrenees leading to the French/Spanish border, where in 1940 Walter Benjamin committed suicide, rather than being delivered into the hands of the Gestapo.

One of the reasons to study Walter Benjamin precisely now, at this strange beginning of the twenty-first centruy, is that he was a great master in a precious but difficult art that is more than ever necessary to learn today: the art of rowing against the stream.

1

Marxism and Revolutionary Romanticism

Is romanticism an essentially conservative and reactionary movement? Or does it also contain revolutionary potential by virtue of its opposition to capitalism and bourgeois society? The first difficulty in dealing with these questions is the ambiguity of the romantic phenomenon. Notwithstanding this, however, one of the most fundamental traits of romanticism as a sociopolitical movement (though inseparable from its cultural and literary manifestations) is *the nostalgia for precapitalist societies and a cultural critique of capitalism*.

Etymologically, the term "romantic" contains this reference to the past: to the Romance language literature of the Middle Ages. If so, why extend the concept of romantic nostalgia to the entire gamut of precapitalist formations? This objection is all the more justified since for "classical" German romanticism the lost paradise is simply feudal society. Yet, romanticism can and must be defined within a broader frame of reference for the following reasons: a) In Rousseau, who is incontestably the great forerunner of romanticism, there is no sympathy at all for feudalism. The same is true in the nineteenth century of those eminent representatives of economic romanticism, the Russian populists, and others. b) The reference to the Middle Ages is ambiguous, since medieval society contains several different social structures: on the one hand, of course, some hierarchical institutions such as knighthood, religious orders, etc.; on the other, some relics of the egalitarian and collectivist rural *gens* community. c) Various precapitalist societies, despite their undeniable differences, contain common traits distinguishing them from the capitalist mode of production. As Lefort stresses, "it is in regard to capitalism . . . that all other social formations reveal their affinity."[1]

In the romantic view of the world the precapitalist past is endowed with a series of (real, partially real, or imaginary) virtues, such as the predominance of qualitative values (use values or ethical, aesthetic, and religious values), organic community among members, or else the essential role of affective ties—in contrast to modern capitalist civilization, based on quantity, prices, money, commodities, profits, and atomization. When this nostalgia becomes the central axis structuring the whole worldview, the result is a romantic idea in the strict sense, as in Germany at the beginning of the nineteenth century. When it is a matter of just one element among others in a more complex politico-cultural whole, it is more properly a *romantic dimension* (as in Lukács in 1922–23).

Most intellectual historians agree in attributing dual paternity to nineteenth-century romanticism: Rousseau and Burke[2]—the most eminent precursor of 1789 and the most implacable enemy of the Great Revolution! Although in "classical" German romanticism of the beginning of the nineteenth century the reaction against the French Revolution is the dominant tendency, in their youth authors such as Kleist, Schlegel, and others sympathized with the Revolution, and Hölderlin never renounced his Jacobinism. Because of this, authors such as Carl Schmitt have hastily concluded that "romanticism dissolved into the simple principle of a subjectivized occasionalism, and the mysterious contradictions of diverse political orientations of so-called political romanticism can be explained by the moral inadequacy of a lyricism for which any content can be the occasion of an aesthetic interest."[3] This interpretation is not only unable to explain strictly political romantic thinkers such as Adam Müller, whose aesthetic dimension is very limited—but also ignores the fact that a solid nucleus lies behind romanticism: the idealized reference to the precapitalist past and an angry critique of some aspects of bourgeois society. Other authors, such as Droz, end up reducing the phenomenon to its conservative and counterrevolutionary aspect.[4] This interpretation tends to dismiss the republican sympathies of the young Schlegel and Kleist as irrelevant biographical episodes and excludes Hölderlin altogether.

In reality, this ambiguity can be rediscovered in late nineteenth-century romanticism, for example, in the astonishing journey of Lukács's friend, the writer Paul Ernst, who went from the most extreme wing of the Socialist party to an ultraconservative worldview, close to fascism. The same thing happens to the sociologist Robert Michels, a member of the Max Weber circle in Heidelberg who went from a revolutionary socialist before the war to an avowed partisan of Italian fascism.[5]

These surprising political metamorphoses and heterogeneity are just different paths of possible development from the common romantic matrix: nostalgia for precapitalist societies. This politico-cultural puzzle can be clarified by developing a tentative typology of the main political patterns of romanticism: a) *"Past-oriented" or "retrograde" romanticism*, which seeks to reestablish an earlier social state. These terms are preferable to "reactionary," which is too restrictive because of its tie to the reaction against the French Revolution. For this school, of which Novalis is perhaps the most coherent representative, it is not a matter of *conserving* the status quo, but of returning to the Catholic Middle Ages, before the Reformation, the Renaissance, and the development of bourgeois society. b) *Conservative romanticism*, which, unlike the previous one, simply wants to *maintain* things as they are, untouched by the French Revolution (England and Germany at the end of the eighteenth century), and to reestablish what existed in France prior to 1789, which already entails a specific articulation of capitalist and precapitalist forms. Burke and his *Considerations on the French Revolution* (1798) represent the first great representatives of this school. c) "*Disenchanted*" *romanticism*, for which it is impossible to go back to precapitalist societies. Despite its faults and cultural decline, industrial capitalism is seen as an irreversible phenomenon. This is the position of turn-of-the-century German sociologists such as Tönnies and even Weber to a certain extent. d) *Revolutionary romanticism*, which refuses both the illusion of returning to the communities of the past and reconciliation with the capitalist present, seeking a solution in the future. In this school, which includes many socialist thinkers, such as Fourier, Landauer, and Bloch, nostalgia for the past does not disappear but is projected toward a postcapitalist future.

Revolutionary romanticism also differs from other romantic schools by the precapitalist society it chooses as its frame of reference. It is not the feudal system and its institutions (nobility, monarchy, church, etc.). The precapitalist Golden Age varies according to authors, but it is not the one advocated by past-oriented or conservative romantics. For Rousseau and Fourier it is a mythical "state of nature"; for Moses Hess, ancient Judaism; for Hölderlin, the young Lukács, and many others, Greek antiquity; for the Peruvian Marxist José Carlos Mariategui, "Inca communism"; for Russian populists and Landauer, traditional rural communities.

In relation to Landauer, Buber explained the spirit of this type of romanticism as follows: "What he has in mind is . . . a revolutionary conservation: the revolutionary selection of elements of social existence worth conserving and using for a new construction."[6] Yet, these elements no longer exist, and what is at issue is not conservation but a *renaissance*. The essential thing is this: the revolution must reappropriate certain aspects and qualities of precapitalist communities. This subtle dialectic between the past and the future frequently passes through a passionate rejection of present capitalist and industrial society. In this context, what is the relation between Marxism and revolutionary romanticism?

At first sight, Marx seems not to have been affected by romanticism. Thus, I have argued that "Marx's socialism had nothing in common, either socially or ideologically, with anti-capitalist romanticism. Its root lay in a quite different sector of the petty bourgeoisie—the Jacobin, enlightened, democratic-revolutionary, anti-feudal, and "Francophile" section—whose brilliant literary representative was Heinrich Heine, an intransigent enemy of romanticism."[7] This has been criticized by Breines and Herf, who have emphasized the importance of romantic roots in Marx's thinking.[8] On close examination, I agree with them that there is in Marx an undeniable romantic dimension. According to Breines, Marx "achieved a fusion of romantic and enlightenment-utilitarian currents of social criticism." This seems to be quite accurate, but instead of fusion, it would be more precise to speak of a dialectical overcoming (*Aufhebung*).* At any rate, to claim that Marx is antiromantic because he is a Jacobin and close to Heine is itself contradictory. Inspired by Rousseau, Jacobinism already contains an essential romantic component. And Heinrich Heine, a friend of Marx and an implacable adversary of conservative romanticism, also had a romantic streak: "Despite the war to the death I have waged against romanticism, I nonetheless myself remained a romantic all my life, and more than I myself supposed."[9]

Even if Heine could not be really considered a romantic, other writers who influenced Marx and Engels were decidedly romantics. This is the case, for example, with Carlyle, whose biting critique of capitalism had a profound impact on the thinking of Marx and Engels. In 1844, Engels wrote an enthusiastic review of *Past and Present*, whose diatribe against "mammonism"—the worship of the god of greed, Mammon, who allegedly ruled England—he quoted approvingly. Though critical of its author's conservative options, Engels recognized a decisive link between them and the value of the work. "Carlyle is first and foremost a Tory. . . . Certainly, a Whig could never have written a book half as humane as *Past and Present*."[10] As for Marx, in 1845 he read Carlyle's little book on Chartism, taking numerous notes such as this marvelously romantic image of industrial capitalism: "If men have lost belief in God, their only recourse against a blind non-God of necessity and mechanism, against a terrible world steam engine that imprisons them in its iron stomach like a monstrous Phaloris bull would be, with or without hope—*revolt*."[11] In an 1850 article, Engels returned to Carlyle. While irrevocably rejecting his most recent writing, he sketched an analysis of his earlier 1840s works, which is very enlightening: "Carlyle has the merit of having (in his writings) taken a stand against the

---

* *Aufheben* is a German word that the philosopher Hegel converted into an important category in his dialectics. As he pointed out, "this word has two meanings; it means to 'keep' or 'preserve' as well as to 'put a stop to' . . ." (G. W. F. Hegel, *Science of Logic*, quoted in Henri Lefebvre, *Dialectical Materialism* [London: Jonathan Cape, 1968], p. 35). It implies transcending or overcoming—but also preserving—a thought or reality in a higher synthesis.—Ed.

bourgeoisie in an epoch when the latter's conceptions, tastes and ideas entirely dominated official English literature, and that in a way which at times was even *revolutionary*. For example, in his history of the French revolution, in his apology of Cromwell, in his pamphlet on Chartism, in *Past and Present*. But in all these writings, the critique of the present is *closely connected* with an extraordinarily unhistorical apotheosis of the Middle Ages, incidentally also very frequent among the English *revolutionaries*, for example, Cobbett and some of the Chartists."[12] This remark contains two propositions fundamental for a Marxist approach to romanticism: a) the romantic critique of the capitalist present is "closely connected" with nostalgia for the past; and b) this critique can in some cases acquire an authentically revolutionary link in the worldview of revolutionary romanticism between nostalgia for the past and the future.

Even more important than Carlyle's influence was that of the most unrelenting romantic critic of capitalist civilization: Honoré de Balzac—from whom Engels admits having learned "more than from all the professional historians, economists, and statisticians of the period."[13] Of course, their reading of Carlyle and Balzac was highly selective: both Engels and Marx categorically rejected the past-oriented illusions of the two writers. But they unhesitatingly appropriated their romantic critique of capitalism—a critique deeply charged with ethical and cultural values.

Gouldner is thus right in insisting on the "important romantic *components*" in Marx's thought. So is Fisher, in stressing that Marx integrated into his work "the romantic revolt against a world which turned everything into a commodity and degraded man to the status of an object."[14] This component is found, for example, in the *Communist Manifesto*, where, though classifying the anticapitalist romantic trends as "reactionary," Marx and Engels insist on the value of their social critique. Even "feudal socialism," this mixture sui generis of "echoes from the past" and "rumblings of the future," despite its "total inability to understand the march of modern history," has the indisputable merit of "striking at the heart of the bourgeoisie with a bitter and spiritually trenchant critique." As for "petit-bourgeois socialism" (Sismondi and his school), despite its limitations, it must be noted that it "analyzed with great perspicacity the contradictions inherent in the modern conditions of production. It unmasked the hypocritical apologies of the economists. It demonstrated irrefutably the destructive effects of mechanization and of landed property, overproduction, crises, the relentless elimination of the petit-bourgeois and small farmers, the misery of the proletariat, the anarchy of production, the glaring disproportions in the distribution of wealth," etc.[15] An impressive acknowledgment of an intellectual debt! In reality, all anticapitalist critiques of this "petit-bourgeois" romanticism were integrated by Marx and Engels into their view of bourgeois society—even if they unequivocally rejected as utopian and reactionary the positive solutions they advanced. Moreover, Marx and Engels are not skimpy in their admiration of the "eminently revolutionary" historical role of the conquering bourgeoisie and its economic successes, which are superior to the pyramids of Egypt and the Roman aqueducts—realizations that in their eyes prepared the material conditions for the proletarian revolution.[16]

Starting in the 1860s, Marx and Engels became increasingly interested in certain precapitalist social formations. The works of Maurer (the historian of the ancient Germanic communities) and later of Morgan stimulated their evaluation of the past. Thanks to these authors, they discovered an exemplary precapitalist formation, distinct from the feudal system exalted by classical romantics: the primitive community. Marx pointed to this *political choice* of a different past in a letter to Engels dated March 25, 1868, in which he wrote about Maurer's book: "The first reaction against the French Revolution and the Enlightenment philosophy connected with it was, of course, to see [it] from a medieval, romantic perspective, and even some people such as Grimm are not exempt from this. The second reaction—and it corresponds to the socialist orientation, although these scholars do not at all suspect that they are connected with it—consists in plunging beyond the Middle Ages to the primitive epoch of each nation. And these people are very surprised to discover the most modern reality in the most ancient time, including even egalitarians to a degree that would thrill Proudhon."[17]

Engels was also struck by Maurer's discoveries, which inspired him to write among other things the little essay on the old Teutonic rural community—an essay that proposes, as a socialist program for the countryside, a renaissance of that type of community.[18] He even went beyond Maurer, who appeared excessively tainted by Enlightenment evolutionism. In a letter to Marx dated September 15, 1882, he complained of the persistence in Maurer of Enlightenment philosophy's prejudice, which asserts that "starting with the Dark Ages constant progress took place; this prevents him not only from seeing the antagonistic character of real progress, but also several setbacks."[19] This passage synthesizes Engels's and Marx's position on this problem: a) a rejection of the linear and naive (if not apologistic) "progressivism" which considers bourgeois society universally superior to prior social forms; b) an understanding of the contradictoriness of capitalist progress; and c) the recognition that from a human viewpoint and compared with the communities of the past, industrial capitalist civilization is in some respects a decline.[20]

A radically antiromantic Marxism was born only in the struggle against Russian populism with Plekhanov. Evolutionist and admiring capitalist industrial progress, this tendency is based on some texts by Marx and

Engels, but nothing is more revealing of the difference between this deromanticized Marxism and Marx's own thinking than the study of the writings of the author of *Capital* on the Russian rural community. Without sharing all the presuppositions of the Narodniki, Marx shared their beliefs in the future socialist role of the traditional Russian commune (*obshchina*). As he wrote in a letter of March 8, 1881, to Vera Zasulich, "this commune is the fulcrum for the social regeneration of Russia, but in order to function as such it would first be necessary to eliminate the deleterious influences which assail it from all sides and then to assure it of normal conditions for a spontaneous development."[21] The romantic revolutionary problematic of the union between the precapitalist past and the socialist future mediated by the rejection of the capitalist present is obvious here—even if Marx insists on the necessity for the Russian rural community to appropriate the technical conquests of European industrial civilization.

The rough draft of the letter to Zasulich also discusses precapitalist rural communities in India, which reveals Marx's own intellectual development since the 1850s. In 1853, Marx defined the role of English colonization in India as both monstrously destructive as well as progressive (by the introduction of railroads, etc.)—progress assuming the form of "this hideous pagan idol which stores nectar only in the skulls of the slain."[22] In the 1881 letter, however, Marx wrote: "As for the East Indies, for example, everyone except Sir H. Maine and the likes of him knows that over there the suppression of common ownership of the land was just an English act of violence, *pushing the native people not ahead but backwards.*"[23] Here the emphasis is on the (humanly) *regressive* aspect of capitalism.

Of course, for Marx and Engels industrial capitalism as a world system had played a progressive role, not only by developing the productive forces on an unprecedented scale, but by their partial socialization (through cooperation, the world market, etc.)—two conditions that create the objective possibility for a socialist transformation of the economy. The anticapitalist romantic dimension is articulated and intermingled with the other resolutely modernist and passionately antifeudal perspective leading to the *Aufhebung* of both the precapitalist past and the bourgeois present.

At the end of the nineteenth century and the beginning of the twentieth, the romantic-revolutionary dimension of Marxism tends to disappear not only from Russian Marxism but from that of the Second International as well.[24] A rare exception here is Luxemburg, who took up Marx and Engels's preoccupations with the primitive community.

The central theme of her *Introduction to Political Economy* (unpublished in her lifetime but brought out by Paul Levi in 1925) was the analysis of this community—which she called the *primitive communist society*—and the critique of capitalist mercantile society. Like Engels and Marx, she passionately studied Maurer's writings and marveled at the democratic and egalitarian functioning of the German village community and its *social transparency*: "Nothing more simple and more harmonious can be imagined than this economic system of the ancient Germanic Marches. The whole mechanism of social life is out in the open. A rigorous plan, a robust organization here encloses each person's activity and integrates him as an element of the whole. The immediate needs of daily life and their equal satisfaction for all is the point of departure and the culmination of this organization. All work together for all and decide everything for all."[25] She insists on the *universality* of agrarian communism as the general form of human society at a certain stage of its development, which is found not only among Germanic and Slavic peoples but also among Indians, Incas, Kabyles, and Hindus.[26]

In this perspective, the European colonization of one third of the world was a socially destructive, barbaric, and inhumane enterprise.[27] This is the basis for her solidarity with anticolonial struggles in which she saw the tenacious resistance of old communist traditions to profit and capitalist "Europeanization." There seems to be an alliance here between anticolonial and anticapitalist struggles as a revolutionary convergence between the old and the new communism.[28]

Contrary to Luxemburg (or to Marx and Engels), the precapitalist reference in the young Lukács is not primitive communism nor a determinate *economic* formation but rather certain *cultural* configurations: the Homeric Greek universe; Russian (literary and religious) spirituality; and Christian, Hindu, or Jewish mysticism. Here and there one can also find mention of medieval Catholicism—notably in regard to the art of Giotto or Cimabue—but it is not central. On the other hand, Lukács was much closer to classical German romanticism—especially the early twentieth-century neoromanticism of Paul Ernst, Simmel, etc.

This romantic dimension did not disappear when he joined the Hungarian Communist party in December 1918. He simply combined it with the Marxist worldview in an original ideological synthesis.[29] For Lukács in 1919, communist society reestablished the continuity broken by capitalism: the new culture brought by the proletarian anticapitalist revolution is intimately bound with the ancient culture of precapitalist societies. The future throws a bridge toward the past, over the gaping abyss of capitalist nonculture. This typically romantic-revolutionary problematic reappears in different guises in a 1919 lecture on the changing function of historical materialism. Starting with the Hegelian distinction between *objective spirit* (social relations, law, the state, etc.) and *absolute spirit* (philosophy, art, religion), Lukács stressed that precapitalist societies are characterized by the decisive role of absolute spirit. On the contrary, under capitalism, all active social forces exist only as manifestations of objective spirit. Religion itself becomes a social institution like all others (the Church), comparable to the state, the army, or schools. With communism a period will begin in which absolute spirit—that is, philosophy, culture, science—once again will dominate economic and social life.[30] In *History and Class Consciousness* (1923), there is less emphasis on the romantic dimension, yet it remains one of the leitmotivs of Lukács's theoretical universe.

Toward the end of the 1920s, Lukács's thinking turned against romanticism. For some forty years his soul was torn between an Enlightenment outlook and an "anti-capitalist romantic demon," from which he would not free himself. The first is dominant, but occasionally the second resurfaced.

In 1928, Lukács wrote a very positive review of Carl Schmitt's book, whose thesis he accepted without reservation: absence of political content in romantic thought.[31] Following Schmitt, he discusses the romantics' "incoherence," the "insignificance of their political activity, their anti-scientific subjectivism, their exaggerated aestheticism, etc." This antiromanticism reappears in 1931 in an article in which he condemns Dostoyevski who had been the main inspiration of his romantic-messianic period up to 1918. Dostoyevski is seen as a "reactionary" and as a representative "of a section of the anti-capitalist romantic intellectual petit-bourgeois opposition" for which "a wide avenue opens toward the right, toward reaction (today toward fascism) and on the other hand a narrow and difficult path toward the left, toward revolution."[32]

A few years later, however, in another article on Dostoyevski, Lukács not only "rehabilitated" the great Russian writer but also developed a particularly brilliant and penetrating analysis of the *revolutionary* dimension of anticapitalist romanticism. All of Dostoyevski's work, he wrote, manifests "a revolt against the moral and spiritual deformation of man that results from the development of capitalism." To this degradation, he opposes the nostalgia for a Golden Age characterized by harmony among men. "This dream is the authentic core . . . of Dostoyevsky's utopia, a world in which . . . culture and civilization will not be an obstacle to the development of the human soul. The spontaneous, savage and blind revolt of Dostoyevsky's characters takes place in the name of this Golden Age, and whatever the content of the spiritual experience, it always has an unconscious relation to this Golden Age. This revolt is the poetic and historically progressive grandeur of Dostoyevsky; here a light truly rose in the darkness of the misery of St. Petersburg; a light which illuminated the roads for the future of humanity."[33] *The Golden Age of the past which lights the road toward the future*: one could hardly imagine a more striking formula to capture the romantic-revolutionary worldview, for which Lukács here shows undeniable sympathy.[34]

It is tempting to attribute Lukács's warm reevaluation of anticapitalist romanticism in 1939–41 to the political context: the German-Soviet pact and the open hostility of the Soviet Union towards "capitalist democracies." Some references to current affairs in the text confirm this hypothesis. Thus, Lukács accuses his adversaries of not having overcome the ideology of the Popular Front. Yet, this would be inaccurate. Whatever the case, after the war Lukács again disassociated himself from romanticism by developing a series of analyses that sometimes astonishingly resemble a sophisticated version of the mythical struggle between the "bourgeois angel of Enlightenment" and the "black feudal demon" he spoke of ironically in 1941. For example, in 1945, in the essay on Mann, he described the plot of *The Magic Mountain* as "the intellectual duel between the representatives of light and darkness, between the Italian humanist-democrat Settembrini and the Jewish pupil of the Jesuits Naphta, propagator of a Catholic-oriented system prefiguring fascism," thus grossly reducing the paradoxical romantic ideology of Naphta to a "reactionary and anti-capitalist demagoguery."[35] During the same period (1946), in his *Short History of German Literature*, Lukács stressed the obscurantist and "unhealthy" nature of romanticism, notably in Novalis, and insisted that "the critique of romanticism is one of the most pressing tasks of the history of German literature. This critique could never be rigorous enough."[36] This narrow conception runs through all of Lukács's postwar writings, reaching its peak with *The Destruction of Reason* (1953), which presents the history of German thought from Schelling to Tönnies and from Dilthey to Simmel as an immense confrontation between "reaction" and "reason," and all romantic currents "from the historical school of law to Carlyle" as leading necessarily to a "general irrationalization of history" and, later, to fascist ideology.[37]

Only much later, during the last years of his life, did Lukács return to a more nuanced and open approach to romanticism. This is true especially in his 1967 preface to the second edition of *History and Class Consciousness*, where he recognized that "ethical idealism with all its anti-capitalist romantic elements," had given him "something positive," and that these elements "with multiple and profound modification" were integrated into his new (Marxist) view of the world.[38] This tortuous and contradictory itinerary, which shows Lukács's thinking to resemble that of Hans Castorp, the hero of *The Magic Mountain*, oscillating constantly between two poles—a "progressive Settembrini" or a "revolutionary Naphta"—proves how difficult it was for Lukács to overcome the antinomies of his own thinking and to take up the romantic challenge.

Lukács and Luxemburg are two particularly significant but different examples of the integration of certain revolutionary romantic themes into a Marxist context. The interest in these attempts is far from purely historical.

Herbert Spencer, the prolific and polygraphic sycophant of capitalist industry, wrote a century ago that the future of industrial society would necessarily and inevitably produce the disappearance of militarism and wars. Today, after two world catastrophes, after Auschwitz and Hiroshima, the traditional link between technical development and "progress" seems very problematic, and it is becoming difficult to deny that some aspects in some precapitalist formations were superior to capitalist industrial civilization.

Today, thanks to "technical progress," not only does humanity find itself under the permanent menace of an atomic holocaust, but we are also rapidly approaching a catastrophic rupture of the planet's ecological equilibrium. As for the so-called "socialist" states (the Soviet Union and China), they appear less and less like a real alternative to this civilization and, on the contrary, they seek to imitate as faithfully as possible the methods of production and forms of consumption of capitalist societies. This explains the importance of rediscovering the romantic-revolutionary dimension of Marxism and enriching the socialist perspective of the future with the lost heritage of the precapitalist past, with the precious treasure of communal, cultural, ethical, and social qualitative values, submerged since the advent of capitalism in the "glacial waters of egoist calculation."

In an essay written in 1920s, Thomas Mann proposed a pact between the romantic conception of culture and revolutionary social ideas—Greece and Moscow, Hölderlin and Marx.[39] Moscow is no longer the hearth of the revolution, but this proposition, in its general spirit, seems to open a fertile, still relatively unexplored terrain for a renewal of Marxist thought and revolutionary imagination.

—Trans. by David J. Parent

Notes

1. Claude Lefort, "Marx d'une vision de l'histoire à l'autre," in *Les formes de l'histoire, essais d'anthropologie politique* (Paris, 1978), p. 210.
2. Cf. for example, John Bowle, "The Romantic Reaction: Rousseau and Burke," in *Western Political Thought*, vol. 3 (London, 1961). Chap. 3.
3. Carl Schmitt, *Politische Romantik*, 2d ed. (Munich, 1925), p. 227.
4. Cf. Jacques Droz, *Le romantisme allemand et l'Etat* (Paris, 1966), pp. 294ff.
5. Of course, some people went in the opposite direction. For an analysis of anticapitalist romanticism and of its socio-historical roots in Germany, see my book, *Georg Lukács—From Romanticism to Bolshevism* (London, 1971), pp. 1, 3.
6. Martin Buber, *Pfade in Utopia* (Heidelberg, 1950).
7. Löwy, *Georg Lukács*, p. 25.
8. Paul Breines, "Marxism, Romanticism, and the Case of Georg Lukács: Notes on Some Recent Sources and Situations," *Studies in Romanticism* 16 (Fall 1977):

pp. 475–76; and Jeffrey Herf, "Review of Löwy, *Pour une sociologie des intellectuels*," *Telos* 37 (Fall 1978): p. 228. Breines's analysis of the *Manifesto* is very pertinent: "In the *Manifesto* and Marx's previous writings, the capitalist industrial revolution and the entire world of objectified relations it creates are grasped as simultaneously liberating and oppressive. . . . The Enlightenment and its utilitarian progeny stressed the former side of the picture; the romantic current the latter. Marx stood alone in transforming both into a single critical vision." Yet, Breines is wrong in affirming that in Marx's and Engels's writings in the second half of the nineteenth century only the Enlightenment-utilitarian root blossomed while the romantic one withered.

9. Quoted by Lukács, "Heine et la révolution de 1848," *Europe* (May–June 1956): p. 54. Lukács stresses that we find in Heine's works "a constant dialectical interpenetration, full of contradictions, of romantic tendencies and of tendencies for a definitive overcoming of romanticism."
10. Friedrich Engels, "Die Lage Englands," 1844, in Karl Marx and Friedrich Engels, *Werke*, vol. 1 (Berlin, 1961), p. 528.
11. Thomas Carlyle, *Chartism* (London, 1840). Noted by Marx in *Excerpthefte* B35AD89a. This unpublished booklet is located in the Marx-Engels Archive at the International Institute of Social History in Amsterdam.
12. Marx and Engels, *Werke*, vol. 7, p. 255. Italics added.
13. Friedrich Engels, "Letter to Miss Harkness," April 1888, in Karl Marx and Friedrich Engels, *Briefwechsel* (Berlin, 1953), p. 481. The term "romantic" does not here designate a literary genre, but Balzac's social and political *view of the world.*
14. Alvin Gouldner, *For Sociology* (London, 1973), p. 339; and Ernst Fisher, *The Essential Marx* (New York, 1970), p. 15.
15. Karl Marx and Friedrich Engels, *Le manifeste communiste* (Costes, 1953), pp. 99, 102–3.
16. Marx and Engels's remarks on Sismondi pose an important problem: the possibility for thinkers operating from the viewpoint of the past to attain a knowledge of the present deeper in some regards than that of those who identify directly and critically with this present. Marx will return to this question several times, notably in *The Theories of Surplus Value.*
17. Supplement to Friedrich Engels, *L'origine de la famille, de la propriété privée et de l'Etat* (Paris, 1975), pp. 328–29.
18. Engels, of course, added: "not in its ancient aspect, which has had its day, but under a rejuvenated form." Friedrich Engels, "La Marche," 1882, in *L'origine de la famille*, p. 323.
19. Marx and Engels, *Briefwechsel*, p. 425.
20. This became one of the leitmotivs of *L'origine de la famille.* Everywhere in Morgan's studies on the gens, Engels insisted on the *regression* of "civilization" when compared to the primitive community: "What an admirable constitution this *gens* organization is! Without soldiers, gendarmes or police, without nobility, without kings or governors, without prefects or judges, without prisons, without trials, everything runs its regular course. . . . All are equal and free—including women. . . . And if we compare their situation with that of the immense majority of the civilized men of our time, the distance between the proletarian or small farmer today and the ancient free member of the *gens* is enormous" (Engels, *L'origine de la famille*, p. 105). Engels hastens to add: "That is

one of the aspects of the thing. But let us not forget that this organization was doomed to destruction."

21. Marx and Engels, *Briefwechsel*, p. 408.
22. Karl Marx, "The Future Results of the British Rule in India," 1853, in *On Colonialism* (London, 1971), p. 90.
23. Supplement to *L'origine de la famille*, p. 333. Italics added.
24. Russian Marxism took an antiromantic direction as a result of the antipopulist polemics. This is especially noticeable at the end of the nineteenth century, when the ideological struggle with the Narodniki was at its peak. See, for example, Lenin's famous brochure *Characteristics of Economic Romanticism—Sismondi and our National Sismondians*, 1897.
25. Rosa Luxemburg, *Introduction à l'économie politique* (Paris, 1970), p. 138.
26. As with Engels in his *L'origine de la famille*, Luxemburg is also inspired by Morgan. Using him as a point of departure, she develops a grandiose view of history: an innovative conception of the millennarian evolution of humanity in which contemporary civilization "with its private property, its class domination, its male domination, its state, and its constraining marriage" appears as a mere parenthesis, a transition between primitive communist society and the communist society of the future. The romantic-revolutionary link between the past and the future appears here even more explicitly than in Marx and Engels: "The noble tradition of the remote past thus extended its hand to the revolutionary aspirations of the future, the circle of knowledge closed back harmoniously and, in this perspective, the current world of class domination and exploitation, which claimed to be the *ne plus ultra* of civilization, the supreme end of universal history, was just a minuscule transitory stage on humanity's long march ahead." Luxemburg, *Introduction*, p. 91.
27. In *The Accumulation of Capital*, she examined again the historical role of English colonialism and was indignant at the criminal contempt of European conquerors toward the ancient system of irrigation: capital, in its blind voracity, "is incapable of seeing far enough to recognize the value of the economic monuments of a more ancient civilization"; colonial policy produces the decline of this traditional system, and consequently famine begins, starting in 1867, to make millions of victims in India. Cf. Rosa Luxemburg, *The Accumulation of Capital* (London, 1951), p. 376.
28. Luxemburg, *Introduction*, p. 92. On the subject of the Russian rural commune, however, Luxemburg has a much more critical view than Marx. Based on Engels's analyses, which at the end of the nineteenth century registered the degeneration of the *obshchina*, she shows the *historical limits* of the traditional community and the necessity of overcoming it. Her gaze turns resolutely toward the future, and here she parts ways with economic romanticism in general and with Russian populism in particular, insisting on "the fundamental difference between the world socialist economy of the future and the primitive communist groups of pre-history." Ibid., p. 133.
29. The best expression of this is the essay on "The Old Culture and the New Culture," published at the time of the triumph of the Hungarian workers' council revolution (1919). The thread running through this work is the contrast between the culture of past society and the "non-culture" of capitalism. Lukács here does not distinguish between the different modes of precapitalist production and refers to precapitalist epochs as a whole that share common characteristics.

First of all, an "artistic spirit" dominated all productive activity: from the viewpoint of creation, printing a book was not, in essence, different from writing it; or painting a picture from finishing a table. Secondly, culture was born from a slow and organic growth in the compost of social existence, and this organicity gave it a harmonious and grandiose character. With the arrival of capitalism, "everything ceased being evaluated for itself, for its intrinsic (e.g., artistic or ethical) value and has value only as a saleable or purchasable commodity on the market." This general mercantilization destroyed all possibility of culture in the true sense of the word. Of course, in precapitalist epochs culture was reserved for the dominant classes. But under capitalism even they are subject to the movement of the commodity and incapable of authentic cultural creation. Communism offers, for the first time, a culture open to all: a "new culture" that Lukács sees primarily as a *cultural restoration*. Thanks to the abolition of capitalism, organic development "becomes possible again," social activities lose their commodity function, and their own human finality "is returned to them." Cf. Georg Lukács, "The Old Culture and the New Culture," *Telos* 5 (Spring 1970).

30. Georg Lukács, "Die Funktionswechsel des historischen Materialismus," 1919, in *Taktik und Ethik* (Neuwied: Luchterhand, 1975), pp. 116–22. The version of this essay published in 1923 in *History and Class Consciousness* is significantly altered. Still, it is interesting to compare Lukács's idea with Bahro's thesis concerning artistic and politico-philosophical practice as the decisive dimension of an authentic communist society and as the indispensable condition for ending domination. Cf. Rudolf Bahro, *L'alternative: Pour une critique du socialisme existant réellement* (Paris, 1979), pp. 268–69.
31. Georg Lukács, "Rezension: Carl Schmitt, politische Romantik," 1928, in *Geschichte und Klassenbewusstsein* (Neuwied, 1968), pp. 695–96.
32. Georg Lukács, "Über den Dostojevski Nachlass," *Moskauer Rundschau* (March 1931). Lukács compares Dostoyevski's journey from revolutionary conspiracy to orthodox religion and tsarism with Schlegel's shift from republican romanticism to Metternich and the Catholic church. This article provides for the first time an analysis that reappears in most of Lukács's later works on anticapitalist romanticism. On the one hand, there is the recognition of the contradictoriness of the phenomenon, while on the other, a sometimes excessive tendency to consider the reactionary and even prefascist predisposition as the dominant pole. Not by chance, this essay aroused the indignation of his friend, Ernst Bloch, and led to a cooling of their relations—followed some years later by their polemics about expressionism (1934), which is actually a polemic about romanticism.
33. Georg Lukács, "Dostojevski," in *Russische Revolution, Russische Literatur* (Rohwolt, 1969), pp. 148–49. In this edition the article is dated 1943, but in reality it had already been published in Russian in the journal *Literaturniy Kritik* 9 (1936).
34. This sympathy reappears in a series of articles Lukács wrote in Moscow in 1939–41, which have remained unpublished until recently. His point of departure is some of Marx's and Engels's texts on anticapitalist romanticism: the passage on feudal socialism in the *Manifesto*, the articles on Carlyle, etc. He insists on the *merits* the two authors recognize in this movement's critique of capitalism and analyzes in this light and works of writers such as Balzac, Tolstoy, Scott, etc. Against some Soviet literary critics (Kirpotin, Knipovich), who contrast "progressive" bourgeois thought with Balzac's "reactionary"

conceptions, Lukács rejects what he considers a liberal-bourgeois ideological tradition: "the mythology of a struggle between 'reason' and 'reaction,'" or, in another variant, the myth of the struggle of "the bright angel of bourgeois progress . . . with the black demon of feudalism." For him, Balzac's (or Carlyle's) relentless critique of capitalism is *profoundly clairvoyant*, particularly in regard to its culture-*destructive* role. Cf. Georg Lukács, *Ecrits de Moscou* (Paris, 1974), pp. 243, 257.

35. Georg Lukács, "A la recherche du bourgeois," 1945, in *Thomas Mann* (Paris, 1976), p. 37.
36. Georg Lukács, *Brève histoire de la litterature allemande*, 1946 (Paris, 1949), p. 94.
37. Lukács, *Die Zerstörung der Vernunft* (Berlin, 1955), p. 105.
38. Georg Lukács, "Vorwort," 1967, in *Geschichte und Klassenbewusstsein*, pp. 12–13.
39. Thomas Mann, "Kultur und Sozialismus," in *Die Forderung des Tages* (Berlin, 1930), p. 196.

2

Marxism and Utopian Vision

The "Crisis of Marxism" is more a journalistic catchphrase than a theoretical concept. In certain advanced capitalist countries, much of the left intelligentsia with origins in Stalinism and/or Maoism (with a few isolated exceptions, like Castoriadis) has been deeply affected by the simultaneous unfolding of dissidence in the Soviet Union and Eastern Europe (particularly the revelations in Solzhenitsyn's *Gulag Archipelago*) and the crisis of Maoism in China.

They have undergone a severe demoralization and disorientation, whose main form, especially since the 1970s, is a rejection of Marxism as a "totalitarian doctrine." In many cases, this sudden revulsion has gone even further and has led former leftists into the ranks of the old right, the new right, or the very new, modern right.

It is not accidental that this crisis has been most profound in those countries where Stalinism and/or Maoism exercised pervasive influence among intellectuals—France and Italy. (By contrast, in the past fifteen years British Marxism has known an astonishing development on the social, cultural, and scientific levels.)

Exploited ad nauseam by the mass media in their most superficial form, "new" philosophy and the "new" ideologues of anti-Marxism are basically the opposite side of the Stalinist coin. Incapable in the past of distinguishing Marxism from its lamentable bureaucratic caricature, these doctrinairists are now simply serving up their old positions with a negative sign lazily attached.

Nevertheless, the anxiety and confusion exhibited by large numbers of these former left intellectuals is a manifestation of a deeper problem: *the challenge to Marxism posed by the paradox of its transformation in postcapitalist societies into a state ideology serving an oppressive and exploitative order.*

Stalinism in all its varieties is not a "theoretical deviation" (Althusser), but is one of the most decisive political phenomena in the history of the twentieth century. It is the formulation, in societies that have abolished capitalism (in some cases through genuine social revolutions—the Soviet Union and China), of authoritarian, totalitarian states through the use of terrorism.

In these societies, power is monopolized by a social layer—the bureaucracy—with its own interests distinct from and opposed to those of the workers. Rather than a class or a caste, this layer resembles an "estate" (the *Stand* of Marx and Max Weber), a clerical and parasitic social order structured through an institution of the politico-ideological type. In the postcapitalist societies, the ideology of this dominant layer originating in the workers' movement is a caricature of Marxism.

The bureaucracy empties Marxism of its critico-revolutionary content and reduces it to a petrified and hollow shell which it then fills with its own conservative, mystifying, and self-serving content.

To explain this bureaucratic degeneration of the postcapitalist states as the product of Marx's theoretical conceptions is about as useful and enlightening as saying that the Inquisition was the result of the principles of the Gospel, that the Vietnam War (fought in the name of democracy) was the fruit of the ideas of Thomas Jefferson, or that the German Third Reich was the application of the nationalism of Fichte (or the irrationalism of Schelling or the statism of Hegel).

A serious and respectable critique of Marxist authoritarianism *does* exist. But the capitalist mass media, which has praised the insignificant "new" philosophers to the skies, has never paid any attention to it. It is the critique which anarchists, anarcho-syndicalists, and libertarian communists have been presenting for the past one hundred years. We can reject these arguments because they are wrong (which I do), but they are genuine *arguments* and not publicity stunts.

In my opinion, one of the main contributions brought by Marx to the domain of political thought is precisely the perspective of an *antiauthoritarian* revolution.

In the first half of the nineteenth century, an authoritarian and *substitutionist* conception of the revolution predominated among the revolutionary currents of the nascent communist movement (Jacobino-Babeuvism, Blanquism). The revolution was conceived as the action of a tiny group, a revolutionary elite, which took upon itself the mission of saving the people from slavery and oppression.

These currents based themselves on the essential premise of the metaphysical materialism of the eighteenth century: people were the product of circumstance and, if their circumstance was oppression and obscurantism, the mass of people were condemned to ignorance. The proletariat was thus considered incapable of assuring its own emancipation. Liberation would have to come to it from the outside, from above, at the hands of a small minority which, as the exception, had succeeded in attaining enlightenment.

This group would now play the role that eighteenth-century materialist philosophers had attributed to the enlightened despot: to destroy *from above* the circular and self-perpetuating mechanisms of the social conditions and thereby enable the majority of people to have access to knowledge, reason, and freedom.

In his *Theses on Feuerbach* and in *The German Ideology*, Marx broke with the premises of mechanical materialism and formulated the seed of *a new vision of this world*. Within this vision were the methodological bases for *a new theory of revolution* drawn from the most advanced experiences of the workers' movement of his epoch (English Chartism, the revolt of the Silesian weavers in 1844, etc.)

By rejecting both the old materialism of the philosophy of Enlightenment (change the circumstances to liberate the people) and neo-Hegelian idealism (liberate human consciousness to change society), Marx cut the Gordian knot of the philosophy of his time. His third thesis on Feuerbach asserts that in revolutionary praxis altering conditions and transforming consciousness go hand in hand. His new conception of revolution (presented for the first time in *The German Ideology*) flows from this basic premise with rigor and logical coherence. It is only through their own experience in the course of *their own revolutionary praxis* that the exploited and oppressed masses can overcome both the external circumstances that chain them (capital, the state) and their previous mystified consciousness.

In other words, *the only genuine form of emancipation is self-emancipation*. As Marx would later write in the founding declaration of the First International: "the emancipation of the workers is the task of the workers themselves." The revolution has to be self-liberation. It is defined at one and the same time by radical changes in economic, political, and social structures and the achieving of consciousness by the laboring masses about their real interests, their discovery of new, radical, and emancipatory aspirations, values, and ideas.

The framework for a vision of the revolution obviously relates not only to the "seizure of power," but also to an entire historical period of uninterrupted social transformation. In Marx's vision there is no room for any kind of enlightened despot, whether individual or collective, no Caesar or Tribune of the People.

If, as we believe, Marxism is the "intellectual horizon of our epoch" (Sartre), all attempts to "go beyond" it only end up in regression to inferior levels of thought, not beyond but *behind* Marx. Within this "crisis of Marxism," bourgeois neoliberalism, positivism, metaphysical idealism or vulgar materialism, social biology, and reactionary obscurantism are flourishing. Only the actualization of Marxism can open the way for a new critique with genuine powers of emancipation.

In our opinion, this process must begin from Marx's own point of departure in 1843 when, in a letter to Ruge, he defined his approach as *the ruthless criticism of all that exists*. It is a question of utilizing the Marxist method, which he defined in his prologue to *Capital* as "a rational dialectic . . . critical and revolutionary," his radical humanist historicism and his philosophy of praxis in order to understand, interpret, and change the world in which we live.

This method should be used to understand new phenomena that did not exist in Marx's time, to correct and dialectically overcome his many errors, limitations, and weaknesses. In particular, it should be employed to criticize both the regimes and societies under capitalist domination and also the postrevolutionary states that illegitimately lay claim to his thought—all with the perspective of their revolutionary abolition.

This renovation necessarily includes the enrichment of Marxism with the contributions of the new social movements, above all the feminist movement (but also the movements around ecology, pacifism, etc.). The integration of feminism as an essential and permanent dimension of the Marxist program—and not a separate chapter tacked on from "the outside"—is a decisive condition for Marxism to achieve a universal and radically emancipating character whose purpose is the abolition of not one but *all forms of social oppression*.

The actualization of Marxism also requires its enrichment through the most advanced and most productive forms of non-Marxist theoretical thought—from Max Weber to Freud, from Mannheim to Piaget—as well as the integration of the limited but useful output of the various branches of academic social science. Inspiration for this should be drawn from Marx himself, who knew how to make good use of the work of philosophy and science in his day—not only Hegel, Feuerbach, and Ricardo, but also Quesnay, Ferguson, Sismondi, J. Steuart, Hodgskin, Maurer, Morgan, Lorenz, von Stein, Flora Tristan, Saint-Simon, Fourier, etc.

Marx's use of these sources did not diminish in the slightest the unity and theoretical coherence of his work. The claim that Marxism holds an exclusive monopoly on science, condemning all other currents of thought and investigation, has nothing to do with Marx's concept of the conflictive articulation of his theory with contemporary scientific production.

Finally, the creative development of Marxism and the overcoming of its current "crisis" demands the reestablishment of *its utopian dimension*. An irreconcilable and thoroughgoing critique of the present forms of late capitalism and postcapitalist bureaucratic societies is necessary but insufficient. The credibility of the project of a revolutionary transformation of the world requires the existence of models of an alternative society, visions of a radically different future, and horizons of a humanity that is truly free.

Scientific socialism must once again become utopian by drawing its inspiration from the "Principle of Hope" (Bloch) that resides in the struggles, dreams, and aspirations of millions of oppressed and exploited, "the defeated of history," from Jan Hus and Thomas Münzer up to the soviets of 1917–19 in Europe and the 1936–37 collectives in Barcelona. On this level it is even more indispensable to open the door of Marxist thought wide to the gamut of intuitions about the future, from the utopian socialists of yesterday to the romantic critics of industrial civilization and from the dreams of Fourier to the libertarian ideals of anarchism.

Marx deliberately set severe limits on himself when it came to a utopian vision. He was convinced that preoccupation with the problems associated with the realization of socialism should be left to future generations. But our generation cannot adopt this posture. We are confronted with postcapitalist bureaucratic societies that claim to be the concretization of "socialism" and even "communism." We have an imperative need for alternative models of a genuine *free association of producers* (Marx).

We need a *Marxist utopia*—a heretical concept, but without heresy how could Marxism have developed? A utopia presents in the most concrete way possible an imaginary liberated enclave not yet in existence (u-topos, nowhere) in which the exploitation of workers, the oppression of women, alienation, reification, the state, and capital are all abolished. Without abandoning for an instant the realistic preoccupation with revolutionary strategy and tactics and the very material problems of the transition to socialism, at the same time free rein must be given to creative imagination, daydreams, active hope, and the red visionary spirit.

Socialism does not exist in the present reality; it must be reinvented as the final outcome of the struggle for the future. This means encouraging far-ranging discussion without limits or taboos on the possibilities for democratic socialism based on self-management, real democratic planning (in which use values once again predominate over exchange values), nonalienated relations between the sexes, the reestablishment of the balance between humanity and nature, and the ecological equilibrium of the planet.

The goal is not to turn out abstract speculation. It is to conceptualize a humane *Gemeinschaft* that qualitatively differs from the existing state of affairs, beginning with the objective possibilities created by the contradictions inherent in industrial civilization, by the simultaneous crisis of contemporary capitalism and of so-called "really existing socialism."

Among the utopian elements that should be further explored one could mention for instance:

- A new productive and technological system, exploring the development and reliance on renewable energy sources, especially those which do not endanger human life or harm the natural environment. The rule under which socialism cannot first take possession of the bourgeois state apparatus and use it for its own purposes, but has to destroy the old structure and build a new one, applies also, although in a different form, to the existing technical and productive apparatus. The present form of industrial machinism is not the only possible one. It can and should be radically transformed—replaced by more advanced and less destructive methods of production.
- The emancipation of labor, not only by the expropriation of the private owners and the control over the process of production by the producers themselves, but also by thorough change in the very nature of labor. This means the abolition of the sexual division of labor and of the traditional separation between manual and intellectual activity, as well as the reestablishment of the qualitative, *artistic* dimension of labor. Marx criticized industrial capitalism (in the *Grundrisse*) for its degradation of work: "labor loses all the characteristics of art . . . [and] becomes more and more a purely abstract activity, a purely mechanical activity." A socialist reorganization of the work process would require, therefore, the restitution to human labor of its "characteristics of art."
- The free distribution of an increasing number of goods and services, corresponding to the basic material and cultural needs, and the parallel decline in the role of the market, commodity production, and money.
- Truly equal, nonhierarchical and nonoppressive gender relations, and the universalization to the whole of society human values so far restricted to (and imposed on) women: peacefulness, nurturance, altruism, etc.
- A democratic and decentralized organization of economic, social, and political life, where self-administration and direct control by the workers and the population gradually replace the kind of repressive and bureaucratic structure known as the "state." Even the proletarian, revolutionary state should eventually "wither away" (Engels), its indispensable functions being progressively absorbed by civil society. Planning on a world scale, based on regional and local units, would substitute for the present system of rival nation-states, with their borders, armies, customs, etc.

Independent of polemics with the utopian socialists of his age, Marx's works contain, even if in a fragmentary way, a utopian-revolutionary dimension for which he has always been denounced in the name of "realism" by his academic and reformist critics. One of the characteristics of the social democratic, Stalinist, and post-Stalinist impoverishment of twentieth-century Marxism was precisely the abandonment of its "messianic" dimension in favor of a restricted and narrow conception of social change. To paraphrase an old formulation of Lenin's, today we could say that *without revolutionary utopia there will be no revolutionary practice.*

In the struggle to recover the explosive charge of Marxist utopia, we must rely on the underground currents, the heretical and subversive tradition hidden or disowned by the bureaucracy: Rosa Luxemburg, Trotsky, Lenin of *State and Revolution* and *Philosophical Notebooks*, the young Lukács, Gramsci, Walter Benjamin.

Lukács's *History and Class Consciousness* (1923) was the most advanced philosophical expression of the principles of the October Revolution. The ideas of Benjamin may well be a source of inspiration for the revolts and revolutions to come.

The starting point and the final conclusion of Benjamin's work—inspired by German romanticism's cultural critique of bourgeois industrial civilization, but going beyond it from a revolutionary viewpoint—is a critical reflection on *progress.* His *Theses on the Philosophy of History*, one of the most important contributions to Marxist thought and revolutionary theory since the *Theses on Feuerbach* in 1845, stresses that historical materialism must understand progress in a different way. The technical and industrial development of capitalism, the increasing domination over nature, the blind development of production is not a stream flowing in a naturally inevitable direction (in which we can swim) toward socialism. It is instead a road that can lead to catastrophe, to the destruction of human culture.

A few years after Benjamin wrote his theses (1940), Auschwitz and Hiroshima provided confirmation of the correctness of his warning beyond anything he could have imagined. In 1986 in a world unceasingly threatened by an irreversible breaking of the balance of nature and by nuclear holocaust, Benjamin's ideas have lost none of their pertinence.

For Benjamin, the revolution is not "progress," improving the established order, perfecting the existing economic and social mechanisms. It is a "messianic" interruption of the course of history, of its *continuum.* Rather than the locomotive of history, the socialist revolution is the emergency brake that brings to a stop the headlong rush of the train toward the abyss.

The agent of this revolutionary interruption, the proletariat, carries in its collective consciousness, as a historical memory and as a motivation for its revolt, the ageless struggle of the oppressed and defeated. The proletariat is their inheritor and the executor of their estate.

—Trans. by Joanna Misnik

3

Marxism and Religion: The Challenge of Liberation Theology

The involvement of Christians in revolutionary struggles is not a new phenomenon, at least in Latin America. "Traditional" Marxism has reacted with an analysis counterposing Christian workers, supporters of the revolution, to the Church (the "clerics"), a thoroughly reactionary body. The death of the cleric, Camillo Torres, a Colombian guerrilla fighter, killed in a skirmish with the army, could be considered an exceptional case. But the growing commitment of Christians and priests to mass struggles and their massive involvement in the Sandinista revolution clearly requires us to revise this simplistic analysis.

Counterposing the base of the Church to its conservative hierarchy is no longer sufficient when a large number of bishops have declared their solidarity with popular movements. This commitment has occasionally cost them their lives as was the case with Monsignor Oscar Romero, archbishop of San Salvador, assassinated by the death squads in March 1980. Marxists who are disconcerted or confused by these developments still resort to the distinction between these Christians' valid social practice and a religious ideology defined as necessarily regressive and idealist. However, with liberation theology we have seen the emergence of religious thinking using Marxist concepts and inspiring social liberation struggles.

It is time Marxists realized something *new* is happening. Its importance is *world historic.* A significant sector of "God's people" and its Church (Christian) is in the process of changing its position in the field of the class struggle, going over with arms (spiritual) and supplies (material resources) to the side of working people.

This new phenomenon has little connection with the former "dialogue" between Christians and Marxists—conceived as two separate camps—and even less to do with the dull, diplomatic negotiations between bureaucratic apparatuses. The caricatural example of the latter was the recent Budapest "meeting between Christians and Marxists"—that is, between representatives of the Vatican and the East European states. What is happening in Latin America (and elsewhere) around the theology of liberation is something quite different: *we are seeing a new fraternity between revolutionaries who believe in God and those who do not,* within an emancipatory dynamic which is outside the control of both Rome and Moscow.

Undoubtedly this all signifies a challenge to the "classic" Marxist conception of religion—especially in its vulgarized version, reduced to the materialism and anticlericalism of the eighteenth-century bourgeois philosophers. Nevertheless, we can find in Marx and Engels's writings—and in those of some modern Marxists—concepts and analyses that can help us understand today's rather surprising reality.

THE OPIATE OF THE PEOPLE?

We can begin with the celebrated phrase "religion is the opiate of the people," which seems to summarize the Marxist conception of the religious phenomenon in the eyes of most of its supporters and adversaries. First of all we should remember that this statement is not specifically Marxist. The same phrase can be found, in various contexts, in the writing of Kant, Herder, Feuerbach, Bruno Bauer, and Heine. A careful reading of the text from Marx shows he is more nuanced than one may have believed. He took into account the *dual* character of the phenomenon:

> Religious distress is at the same time the expression of real distress and the protest against real distress. Religion is the sigh of the oppressed creature, the heart of a heartless world, just as it is the spirit of an unspiritual situation. It is the opiate of the people.[1]

This analysis owes more to a left neo-Hegelianism, seeing religion as the *alienation of the human essence,* rather than to Enlightenment philosophy (religion as a clerical conspiracy): In fact when Marx wrote the above passage he was still a disciple of Feuerbach, a neo-Hegelian. His analysis of religion was therefore "pre-Marxist." But it is nevertheless dialectical since it grasps the *contradictory* character of the religious phenomenon: sometimes a *justification* of existing society and sometimes a protest against it. It was only later—particularly with *The German Ideology* (1846)—that the strictly Marxist study of religion as a *social and historical reality* began. In other words an analysis of religion as one of the many forms of ideology, of the *spiritual production* of a people, the production of ideas, representations, and consciousness—necessarily conditioned by material production and the corresponding social relations.[2]

Friedrich Engels showed a much greater interest than Marx in religious phenomena and their historic role. Engels's main contribution to the Marxist study of religions is his analysis of the relationship of religious representations to the *class struggle.* Over and beyond the philosophical polemic (materialism against idealism) he tried to understand and explain concrete social expressions of religions. Christianity no longer appeared as a timeless "essence," but as a cultural form undergoing transformations in different historical periods: first as a religion of the slaves, then as the state ideology of the Roman Empire, then tailored to feudal hierarchy, and finally adapted to bourgeois society. It thus appears as a symbolic space disputed over by antagonistic social forces: feudal theology, bourgeois protestantism, and plebian heresies. Occasionally this analysis tends towards a narrowly utilitarian, instrumental vision of the problem:

> . . . each of the different classes uses its own appropriate religion . . . and it makes little difference whether these gentlemen believe in their respective religions or not.[3]

Engels seems to only find the "religious disguise" of class interests in the different forms of belief.

However, thanks to his class struggle method, Engels realized—unlike the Enlightenment philosophers—that the conflict between materialism and religion is not always identical to the struggle between revolution and reaction. For example, in England seventeenth-century materialism in the figure of Hobbes defended absolute monarchy while Protestant sects used religion as their banner in the revolutionary struggle against the Stuarts. . . .[4] In the same way, far from seeing the Church as a socially homogenous whole, he makes a remarkable analysis showing how in certain historical conjunctures it divides according to its class composition. Thus during the Reformation, on the one side there was the high clergy, the feudal summit of the ecclesiastical hierarchy, and on the other side there was the lower clergy, which supplied the ideologues of the Reformation and of the revolutionary peasant movement.[5]

While being a materialist, an atheist, and an irreconcilable enemy of religion, Engels nevertheless grasped, like the young Marx, the dual character of the phenomenon: its role in legitimizing established order, but also, according to social circumstances, its critical, protest, and even revolutionary role. Furthermore, most of the concrete studies he wrote concentrated on this second aspect. First of all with regard to *primitive Christianity*, the religion of the slaves, the banished, the damned, the persecuted, and the oppressed.[6] The first Christians came from the lowest levels of society—apart from the slaves this also meant those free men who had been deprived of their rights and small peasants who were crippled by debts.

Engels even went so far as to draw up an astonishing parallel between this primitive Christianity and modern socialism: a) the two great movements are not made by chiefs and prophets—but are mass movements; b) both are movements of the oppressed, suffering persecution, their numbers are proscribed and hunted down by the ruling authorities; c) both preach an imminent liberation from slavery and misery. To embellish his comparison Engels, somewhat provocatively, quoted something Renan said:

> If you want to get an idea of what the first Christian communities were like take a look at a local branch of the International Workingmen's Association.

The essential difference being of course that the primitive Christians transposed deliverance to the hereafter whereas socialism places it in this world.[7]

Is this difference as clear-cut as it appears at first sight? In his study of the second great Christian protest movement—the medieval heresies and the Peasant Wars in Germany—it seems to become blurred: Thomas Münzer, the theologian and leader of the revolutionary peasants and plebians of the sixteenth century, wanted the immediate establishment *on earth* of the Kingdom of God, of the millenarian Kingdom of the prophets. According to Engels, the Kingdom of God for Münzer was a society without class differences, private property, and state authority independent of, and foreign to, the members of that society. However, Engels still tended once again to reduce religion to a strategem: he speaks of Münzer's Christian phraseology and his biblical cloak.[8] The specifically religious dimension of Münzerian millenarianism, its spiritual and moral force, its authentically experienced mystical depth, seemed to escape him.

Having said this, with his analysis of the religious phenomenon from the point of view of the class struggle Engels brought out the protest potential of the phenomenon and opened the way for a new approach—one distinct from both that of the Enlightenment philosophers and from the German neo-Hegelians—to the relationship between religion and society.

Bloch and Goldman's Contribution

Most of the twentieth-century Marxist studies on religion are limited to developing the ideas sketched out by Marx and Engels, or to applying them to a particular reality. This was the case for example with Karl Kautsky's historical studies on primitive Christianity, the medieval heresies, and Thomas Münzer. While he provides us with interesting details on the social and economic bases of these movements and their communist aspirations, he reduces their religious beliefs to a simple "envelope" (*Hülle*) or "garment" (*Gewand*) that "conceals" social content.[9] As for Lenin, Trotsky, or Rosa Luxemburg's writings, they especially deal with the tactical problems religion posed for the workers' movement—their key idea was that the atheist battle against religion must be *subordinated* to the concrete necessities of the class struggle, which demands *unity* between workers who believe in God and those who do not.

Ernst Bloch radically changed the framework of the Marxist approach to religion. In a similar way to Engels he distinguished two socially opposed currents: the theocratic religion of the official churches, opium to the people, a mystifying apparatus in the pay of the powerful, and the underground, subversive religion of the Cathars, the Hussites, Joachim Flore, Thomas Münzer, Baader, Weitling, and Tolstoy. However, unlike Engels, Bloch refuses to see religion uniquely as a "cloak" of class interest (he explicitly criticizes this thesis but attributes it to Kautsky . . .). In its protest movement forms religion is one of the most significant forms of *utopian consciousness*, one of the richest expressions of the *"hope" principle*. Through its capacity of creative anticipation, Judeo-Christian eschatology—Bloch's preferred religious universe—marks out the imaginary space of *not-yet-being*.[10]

Basing himself on these presuppositions, Bloch develops a heterodox and iconoclast interpretation of the Bible—both the Old and New Testaments—drawing out the *Biblia pauperum*, that denounces the pharaohs and calls on everyone to choose *aut Cesar aut Christus* (either Caesar or Christ).

A religious atheist—according to him only an atheist can be a good Christian, and vice versa—and a theologian of the revolution, Bloch not only produced a Marxist reading of millenarianism (following Engels in this) but also—and this was new—a *millenarian interpretation of Marxism*. The eschatological and collectivist heresies of the past are not for him simply "precursors of socialism" (the title of Kautsky's book)—a closed chapter of the past—but a *present-day* subversive heritage.

Of course Bloch, like the young Marx of the famous 1844 quotation, recognized the dual character of the religious phenomenon, its oppressive aspect and its potential for revolt. The first requires the use of what he called Marxism's "breath of cold air," the relentless materialist analysis of ideologies, idol, and idolatries. The second on the other hand calls for Marxism's "inviting warmth" seeking to save religions' *utopian cultural surplus*, their critical and anticipatory force. Beyond any "dialogue," Bloch dreamed of an authentic *union* between Christianity and revolution, like in the period of the Peasant Wars.

Lucien Goldmann's work is another interesting and original attempt at the Marxist study of religion. In his book *The Hidden God* (1955) (London: Routledge and Kegan Paul, 1964) he compared (without assimilating one to the other) *religious faith* and *Marxist faith*: both have in common an opposition to individualism (rationalist or empiricist) and believe in transindividual values—God for religion, the human community for socialism. A similar analogy exists between the Pascalian gamble on the existence of God and the Marxist gamble on the liberated historical future: both presuppose risk, the danger of failure, and the hope of success. Both come down to a question of *faith* and are not demonstrable on the exclusive level of factual judgments. What separates them is of course the supernatural or superhistorical character of religious transcendence. Without wanting in any way to "Christianize Marxism," Lucien Goldmann brought a fresh approach to the conflictual relationship between religious belief and Marxist atheism.

Marx and Engels thought religion's subversive role was a thing of the past, which no longer had any significance in the epoch of modern class struggle. This forecast has been more or less historically confirmed (with a few important exceptions) for a century. But to understand what has been happening for more than twenty years in Latin America—as well as in the Philippines and to a lesser extent here and there in Europe—we need to integrate into our analysis the intuitions of Bloch (and Goldmann) on the utopian potential of the Judeo-Christian tradition.

What Is Liberation Theology?

What is liberation theology? Why does it cause concern not only in the Vatican but also in the Pentagon, not only for the cardinals of the Holy See but also for Reagan's advisors? Quite clearly because the stakes involved go considerably beyond the framework of traditional ideological debates: for the supporters of both clerical and social established order it is a question of a challenge in practice to their power.

As Leonardo Boff has stated, liberation theology is a reflection of, and reflects on, a preexisting praxis. More precisely it is the expression and legitimation of a huge social movement that emerged at the beginning of the 1960s—well before the new theological writings. It involved significant sectors of the Church (bishop, priest, religious orders), lay religious movements (Catholic Action, Christian University youth, young Christian workers), popularly based pastoral interventions (among workers, in urban communities and among peasants), and ecclesiastical "base" communities. Without this movement (one could call it "Christians for liberation") we cannot understand social phenomena as important as the rise of the revolution in Central America or the emergence of a new workers' movement in Brazil.

This movement (here we will examine only the Catholic version of it, but it also exists in the Protestant milieu) is vigorously opposed by the Vatican and by the Church hierarchy in Latin America—the Latin American Bishop's Conference (CELAM) led by the Colombian bishop Alfonso Lopez Trujillo. Can we say there is a class struggle inside the Church? Yes and no. Yes, to the extent that certain positions tend to correspond to the interests of the ruling classes or to those of the oppressed. No, to the extent that bishops, Jesuits, or priests who head the "Church of the Poor" are not themselves poor. Their rallying to the cause of the exploited is motivated by spiritual and moral reasons inspired by their religious culture, Christian faith, and Catholic tradition. Furthermore, this moral and religious dimension is an essential factor in the motivations of thousands of Christian activists in the trade unions, the neighborhood associations, the base communities, and the revolutionary fronts. Poor people become conscious of their condition and organize to struggle as Christians, belonging to a Church and inspired by a faith. If we consider this faith and religious identity, deeply rooted in popular culture, as a simple "envelope" or "cloak" of social and economic interests we fall into a sort of reductionist approach that prevents us from understanding the richness and authenticity of the real movement.

Liberation theology is the spiritual product—the term spiritual production comes, as we know, from Marx in the *German Ideology*—of this social movement, but in legitimizing it, in providing it with a coherent religious doctrine, it has enormously contributed to its extension and strengthening. Even if the Christian/liberation current is still a minority and the majority of the Latin American Church remains moderate or conservative (with its notoriously reactionary strongholds in Colombia and Argentina), its influence is far from negligible—particularly in Peru and Brazil, where the Episcopal Conferences, despite insistent pressure from the Vatican, have refused to condemn liberation theology.

Marxism and Liberation Theology

Why does liberation theology so disturb Vatican orthodoxy? Of all the sins that Rome attributes to the new theologians there is one that is far and away the most dangerous, the most worrying: the sin of Marxism. According to Monsignor Lopez Trujillo (president of CELAM), the representative of the conservative current, the indiscriminate use of Marxist analysis is in the process of getting out of hand and of undermining the ecclesiastical structure.[11]

There is no doubt that Marxism is one of the main bones of contention in the polemic concerning liberation theology. How is it that Roman Catholic theologians have been attracted to such a heretical doctrine? Cardinal Ratzinger (the main Vatican theologian), whose political insight should not be underestimated, had the following the say about it: "(around the 1960s) a definite sense of a vacuum of significance in the Western World developed." In this situation "various forms of neo-Marxism went through a transformation, taking on a moral elan and providing a promise of significance which appeared nearly irresistible to university youth." Furthermore, "the moral challenge of poverty and oppression could no longer be ignored at a time when Europe and North America had reached a level of unheard-of opulence. This challenge obviously required new answers that could not be found in the then existing traditions. The changed theological and philosophical situation directly stimulated the search for answers within a Christianity which was to let itself be guided by Marxist philosophers' apparently scientifically founded models of hope."

The result has been the emergence of liberation theologians who "have adopted a basically Marxist approach." The seriousness of the danger presented by this new doctrine was underestimated "because it did not fit into any previously existing scheme of heresy; its starting point fell outside what could be dealt with by the traditional schemas of discussion." The cardinal recognizes it is undeniable that the new theology, articulating biblical criticism and Marxist analysis, is "seductive, with a near flawless logic"—it seems to respond "both to scientific requirements and to contemporary moral challenges." But this only makes it more formidable: "indeed an error is even more dangerous the bigger its kernel of truth."[12]

We know what came next—a few months later the Sacred Congregation for the Doctrine of the Faith published a document, signed by its "prefect" (Cardinal Ratzinger himself) who, for the first time, officially condemned liberation theology as a "deviation." The main criticism made by this *Instruction on some aspects of "liberation theology"* against the new Latin American theologians is their use "in an insufficiently critical way" of concepts "borrowed from various currents of Marxist thought." As a result of these concepts—particularly that of the class struggle—the Church of the poor in the Christian tradition becomes in liberation theology "a class-based Church, now conscious of the needs of the revolutionary struggle as a stage towards liberation and celebrating this liberation in its liturgy which necessarily leads to calling into question the Church's *sacramental and hierarchical structure. . . .*"[13]

These formulations are obviously polemical, but it is undeniable that liberation theologians have drawn analyses, concepts, and points of view from the Marxist theoretical arsenal which play an important role in their understanding of social reality in Latin America. Liberation theology has profoundly shaken up the political/cultural field merely by referring positively to certain aspects of Marxism—independently of the content of the reference. By this it breaks a taboo and encourages a great number of Christians to take a fresh look, not just at the theory but also at the practice of Marxists. Such an approach could be critical, but it was quite distinct from the traditional anathema against "atheistic Marxism, diabolical enemy of Christian civilisation"—that we can find on the other hand mentioned in the speeches of military dictators, from Videla to Pinochet. . . .

A study of the historical conditions (economic, social, and political) that have permitted this opening of Catholic culture to Marxist ideas goes beyond the scope of this article. We can just note, however, the role of two series of convergent events: the new European theology and the Second Vatican Council, which opened the Church up to new currents of modern thought, and on the other side, the break up of Stalinist monolithism following the Communist Party of the Soviet Union's (CPSU) Twentieth Congress and the Sino-Soviet split. In Latin America you also had the role of the Cuban revolution and the end of the communist parties' hegemony: Marxism ceased to be seen as a closed and rigid system, submitted to the ideological authority of Moscow and became once again a thought in movement, open to various interpretations and therefore accessible to a new Christian interpretation.[14]

It is difficult to present an overall view of liberation theology's attitude and positions on Marxism, because, on the one hand, there is a very wide range of attitudes—going from the prudent use of some elements up to the integral synthesis—and on the other hand, a certain change has taken place between the positions expressed in the more radical period of 1968 to 1980 and today's more reserved stance (following Rome's criticisms). But, on the basis of the writings of the most representative liberation theologians (like Gutierrez and Boff) and of certain episcopal documents, one can identify some essential points of reference.

Certain Latin American theologians (influenced by Althusser) refer to Marxism simply as one (or the) *social science*, to be used in a strictly instrumental way to improve our knowledge of Latin American reality. This is at one and the same time too wide and too narrow a definition. Too wide because Marxism is not the only social science. . . . Too narrow because Marxism is not only a science but is founded on a *practical* chosen option. It aims not just to know the world but to *change* it.

In reality, the interest—many writers speak of the "fascination"—of liberation theologians for Marxism is greater and more profound than the heuristic borrowing of a few analytical concepts.

It also involves *values* (of the community), *ethical/political choices* (solidarity with poor people), and *future utopias* (a society without classes or oppression). Gustavo Gutierrez thinks Marxism does not only provide a scientific analysis but also a utopian aspiration of social change. He criticizes the scientistic vision of Althusser, which "prevents us from seeing the profound unity of Marx's work and consequently from easily understanding its capacity to inspire a radical and permanent revolutionary praxis."[15]

Which sort of Marxism inspires the liberation theologians? Certainly not that of the Soviet *diamat* textbooks nor that of the Latin American communist parties. Rather they are attracted to "Western Marxism"—occasionally dubbed "neo-Marxism" in their documents. In *Liberation Theology: Perspectives*, Gustavo Gutierrez's great inaugural work (1971), the most quoted Marxist writer is Ernst Bloch. There are also references to Althusser, Marcuse, Lukács, Gramsci, Henri Lefebvre, Lucien Goldmann, and . . . Ernest Mandel (counterposed to Althusser for his better understanding of Marx's concept of alienation).

But these European references are less important than the Latin American ones: Mariátegui, as a source of original Marxism, adapted to the reality of the continent, the Cuban revolution, as an event galvanizing the history of Latin America, and finally the theory of dependence: the criticism of dependent capitalism put forward by Fernando Henrique Cardoso, and Gunder Frank, Theotonio Dos Santos, and Aníbal Quijano (all mentioned several times in Gutierrez's book). It goes without saying that Gutierrez and his cothinkers prioritize certain Marxist themes (humanism, alienation, praxis, utopia) and reject others ("materialist ideology," atheism).

The Starting Point Is Poverty

The starting point for this discovery of Marxism is an unavoidable social fact, a brutal mass reality in Latin America: *poverty*. Obviously poverty has existed for centuries on the continent, but with capitalist development in the town and countryside, the rural exodus, unemployment, and the explosive growth of the shantytowns on the periphery of the urban centers, a new, more dramatic and extensive poverty has emerged. In many respects it is worse than in the past. For the liberation theologians Marxism appears to be the most systematic, coherent, and global explanation of the causes of this poverty and as the only sufficiently radical proposition for abolishing it.

Concern for the poor is part of the millenarian tradition within the Church going back to the evangelical sources of Christianity. Latin American theologians place themselves within the continuity of this tradition, which provides them with both reference and inspiration. But on a key point they sharply break with the past: for them poor people are no longer essentially *objects of charity, but subjects of their own liberation*. Paternalist aid or assistance is replaced by solidarity with the poor's struggle for self-emancipation. Here is where the link is made with a fundamental Marxist political principle—*the emancipation of working people will be the work of the workers themselves.* This change is perhaps the liberation theologians' most important new political contribution. It also has the greatest consequences in relation to the Church's social doctrine.

The Vatican accuses Gutierrez and his allies of having replaced the poor of the Christian tradition with the Marxist proletariat. This criticism is not exactly valid. For the Latin American theologians the poor is a concept having moral, biblical, and religious connotations. God her/himself is defined by them as the "God of the Poor," and Christ is reincarnated in today's crucified poor. It is also a socially broader concept than that of the working class: it includes, according to Gutierrez, both the exploited classes and the despised races and marginalized cultures (in his most recent writings he adds women who are doubly exploited).

Some Marxists will no doubt criticize this replacement of the "materialist" concept of the proletariat by such a vague, emotional, and imprecise category. *In reality, this term corresponds to the Latin American situation, where one finds, both in the towns and in the countryside an enormous mass of poor people*—unemployed, semi-employed, seasonal workers, street vendors, marginal people, prostitutes, etc.—who are excluded from the "formal" productive system. The Christian/Marxist trade union activists of El Salvador have invented a term that covers all these components of the oppressed and exploited population: the "pooriat" (*pobresiado*).

The priority option in favor of the poor, adopted by the Puebla Conference of Latin American Bishops (1979) was in practice a compromise formula, interpreted in a traditional (social assistance) sense by the Church's more moderate or conservative currents, and read more radically by the liberation theologians and the more advanced clerical currents—as a commitment to the organization and struggle of poor people for their own liberation. In other words, the Marxist *class struggle*, not only as an "instrument of analysis" but as a *guide for action*, became an essential feature of the new Church of the Poor. As Gustavo Gutierrez states:

> to deny the reality of the class struggle means in practice taking a position in favour of the dominant social sectors. Neutrality on this question is impossible.

What is needed is:

> to eliminate the appropriation by some of the surplus value produced by the work of the great majority, and not lyrical appeals in favour of social harmony. We need to build a socialist society which is more just, more free and more humane and not a society of false conciliation and apparent equality.

This leads to the following *practical* conclusion:

> Building a just society today means necessarily being consciously and actively involved in the class struggle taking place in front of us.[16]

How can this be squared with the Christian obligation of universal love? Gutierrez's answer is distinguished by its great political rigor and moral generosity: we do not hate our oppressors, we want to liberate them too by freeing them from their own alienation, their ambition, their egoism—in a word from their inhuman condition. But to do that we have to resolutely choose the side of the oppressed and concretely and effectively fight the oppressor class. . . .

Liberation Christianity and Revolution

Choosing the side of the poor is not for liberation Christianity a mere literary phrase: it is expressed *in practice* by the commitment of hundreds of thousands of Christians—members of base communities, lay people involved in pastoral work, priests, and members of religious orders. It is seen in the setting up of neighborhood committees in the shantytowns, the formation of class struggle opposition currents in the trade unions, the organization of landless peasant movements, and the defense of political prisoners against torture. It inspires their active participation in workers' and popular struggles throughout the continent, the creation in Brazil of the Workers party, the Sandinista revolution in Nicaragua, and the Farabundo Martí National Liberation Front (FMLN) revolutionary combat in El Salvador.

If this is seen, as by some shortsighted Marxists, just as a "trick" by the Church, a "populist maneuvre" to keep control over the masses or a skilful tactic to hold off communism, then the essential reality is ignored and nothing is understood either of the subjective motivations or the objective significance of the phenomenon. It is not a "trick" but a deep-going spiritual turn, an authentic moral and political *conversion* to the cause of the poor which led the priests Domingo Lain (killed in 1974) and Gasper Garcia Laviana (killed in 1978)—both of Spanish origin—to join the guerrilla fighters in Colombia and Nicaragua. It inspired the Brazilian Jesuit Joao Bosco Penido Burnier (killed in 1976) and the Salvadoran Jesuit Rutilio Grande (killed in 1977) to work in solidarity with the peasants and help their organization. Such a conversion led Monsignor Oscar Romero (killed in 1980), despite having already received death threats from the army, to call on soldiers to refuse to obey their superior officers when told to fire on the people.[17]

To fight effectively against poverty we must understand its causes. This is where liberation theology converges again with Marxism. The great majority's poverty and the obscene wealth of the privileged few are underpinned by the same economic foundation—the *capitalist system*. More precisely in Latin America we are talking about *dependent capitalism* subordinate to the multinational monopolies of the big imperialist centers.

The moral criticism of capitalism's injustices and hostility to its cold and impersonal nature is an old tradition of the Church. Max Weber, the sociologist of religions, already has drawn our attention to the fundamental opposition between Catholicism's ethical rationalism and capitalism's economic rationalism. Of course this did not prevent the Church from becoming reconciled with bourgeois order from the nineteenth century on, but the criticism of "liberal capitalism" remains a component of Catholic culture.

In the 1960s this tradition started to be articulated with the Marxist analysis of capitalism (which also includes a moral condemnation of injustice) specifically in the form of *dependence theory*. The great merit of dependency theorists (notably André Gunder Frank and Aníbal Quijano) was to break with the "developmentalist" illusions that dominated Latin American Marxism in the 1950s (particularly the communist parties' ideology), by showing that the cause of misery, underdevelopment, growing inequality, and military dictatorships was not "feudalism" or insufficient modernization, but the very structure of dependent capitalism. Consequently they argued that some form of socialist transformation could wrest Latin American nations from dependency and poverty. Certain aspects of this analysis were to be integrated not only by the liberation theologians but also by bishops and episcopal conferences, particularly in Brazil.

In May 1980 a group of experts from the U.S. Republican party prepared a document that was to become a basic political "primer" for the party's presidential candidate, Ronald Reagan—the Santa Fe Document. In the second part of the document, entitled "Internal Subversion," proposal No. 3 states:

> United States' foreign policy must begin to confront (and not only react a posteriori to) liberation theology. In Latin America the Church's role is vital for the concept of political liberty. Unfortunately Marxist-Leninist forces have used the Church as a political weapon against private property and the capitalist system of production, infiltrating the religious community with ideas that are more communist than Christian.

On the other hand, if by "communist ideas" the Republican party experts mean those of the communist parties then their analysis completely misses what is basically happening. The Church of the Poor, inspired in the first place by religious and ethical considerations, displays a much more radical, intransigent, and categorical anticapitalism—since it includes the dimension of moral revulsion—than the continent's communist parties, who still believe in the progressive virtues of the industrial bourgeoisie and the historical "antifeudal" role of industrial development (capitalist). Just one example shows this paradox. The Brazilian Communist party explained in its Sixth Congress (1967) resolutions that:

> the socialisation of the means of production does not correspond to the present level of the contradiction between the productive forces and the relations of production.

In other words, industrial capitalism must at first develop the economy and modernize the country. However in 1973 the bishops and religious superiors from the Centre-West region of Brazil published a document (*The Cry of the Churches*) with the following conclusion:

> We must overcome capitalism: it is the greatest evil, an accumulated sin, the rotten roots, the tree which produces all the fruits we know so well—poverty, hunger, illness and death. . . . In order to do this it is necessary to go beyond the private property of the means of production (factories, land, commerce and banks). . . .[18]

Another episcopal document is even more explicit. The *Declaration of the Bishops from the North East of Brazil* (1973) states:

> the injustice produced by this society is the fruit of capitalist relations of production which necessarily create a class society characterised by discrimination and injustice. . . . The oppressed class had no other option for its liberation than to follow the long and difficult road (the journey has already begun) leading to the social ownership of the means of production. This is the principal foundation of the gigantic historical project of the global transformation of present society into a new society in which it becomes possible to create the objective conditions allowing the oppressed to recover the humanity they have been stripped of. . . . The Evangelist calls all Christians and all men of good will to join this prophetic current.

This document was signed by thirteen bishops (including Helder Camara), and by the provincial superiors of the Franciscans, Jesuits, Redemptionists, and the Abbot of St. Benoit monastery in Bahia.[19]

♦

What Model of Socialism?

As we can see with these extracts—and by a lot more that have come out of the Christian/liberation current—solidarity with the poor leads to a condemnation of capitalism and then to a desire to socialism. What sort of socialism? There is a more or less generalized and explicit criticism of "presently existing" models of socialism among revolutionary Christians and liberation theologians. As for Gutierrez, he insists that the oppressed people of Latin America must leave the previously adopted paths to socialism and *creatively seek its own road to socialism.* His approach is inspired by Mariátegui's writings, for whom socialism in Latin America cannot be a "pure imitation" or "copy" of other experiences but a "heroic creation": "we must give birth, through our own reality, our own language, to an Indo-American socialism."[20] It goes without saying that, for the liberation theologians, socialism, or any form of human emancipation, is only a preparation or *anticipation of total salvation*, of the coming of the Kingdom of God on earth.

We should not deduce from all this that the liberation theologians purely and simply support Marxism. As Leonardo and Clodovis Boff emphasize in their answer to Cardinal Ratzinger, Marxism is used as a *mediation* for the propagation of the faith:

> . . . it has helped clarify and enrich certain major theological notions: people, poor, history and even praxis and politics. That does not mean to say that we have reduced the theological content of these notions to the limits of the Marxist form. On the contrary, we have used the valid theoretical content (which conforms to the truth) of Marxist notions within the theological horizon.[21]

Critique of the Church

Among those aspects of Marxism they reject are, as one might expect, *materialist philosophy, atheist ideology, and the characterization of religion as the "opium of the people."* However, they do not reject Marxist criticism of the Church and "presently existing" religious practices. As Gustavo Gutierrez has said, the Latin American Church has contributed to giving a sacred character to established order:

> The protection it receives from the social class that benefits from and defends capitalist society that dominates Latin America, has made the institutionalized Church a part of the system, and the Christian message a component of the ruling ideology.[22]

This severe judgment is shared by a sector of the Latin American bishops. For example, the Peruvian bishops in a declaration adopted by their Thirty-sixth Episcopal Assembly (1969), stated:

> Above all we Christians should recognise that through lack of faith we have contributed in our words and actions, by our silence and omissions, to the present situation of injustice.

One of the most interesting documents on this question is a resolution adopted by the CELAM Department of Education towards the end of the 1960s:

> The Christian religion has been used and is still used as an ideology justifying the domination of the powerful. Christianity in Latin America has been a functional religion for the system. Its rites, its churches and its work have contributed to channelling popular dissatisfaction towards the beyond, totally disconnected to the present world. Thus Christianity has held back popular protest against an unjust and oppressive system.[23]

Of course this criticism is made in the name of an authentic evangelical Christianity, in solidarity with the poor and oppressed, and has nothing in common with a materialist questioning of religion as such.

Undoubtedly among all the liberation theologians Leonardo Boff has formulated the most systematic and radical criticism of the authoritarian structures of the Catholic Church, from Constantine to today. In his opinion these structures reflect a Roman and feudal model of authority: pyramid hierarchy, making obedience sacred, refusal of any internal criticism, and papal personality cult. Boff's "irreverence" goes so far as to compare (quoting from the writings of a left-wing Brazilian Christian, Marcio Moreira Alves) the institutional and bureaucratic structure of the Church with that of the Communist party of the Soviet Union: "The parallels in their structures and practices reveal the logic of any centralizing power."

This type of analysis certainly did not please the Vatican, because following the publication of his book Boff was condemned by the Roman ecclesiastical authorities to a year of silence. Having said this, we should note that Boff does not reject the Church as such. He demands its profound transformation, its refoundation from the periphery to the center, by the poor, by those who live in "*basements of humanity.*"[24]

CHRISTIANS IN THE REVOLUTIONARY MOVEMENT

As these extracts from the theologians' writings and the bishops' conferences show, a significant but minority sector of the Latin American Church has integrated certain basic Marxist ideas into its new understanding of Christianity. Some Christian trade unionists, Christians who are members of left-wing organizations or certain more radicalized movements like Christians for Socialism have a more direct approach of accepting a *synthesis* or *fusion* between Christianity and Marxism. Here we are talking about a Christian current inside the revolutionary movement. Indeed in many countries it is one of the main components of the revolutionary movement.

More or less direct links exist between this current and liberation theology, but it would be a mistake to confuse them. One of the best known representatives of this radical consciousness is the Brazilian Dominican priest, Frei Betto, a leader of the base communities movement who has become famous through his dialogue on religion with Fidel Castro.

While liberation theologians have learned a lot from Marxism, do Marxists have anything to learn from them? Certain interesting questions can be posed, both from the theoretical and practical point of view. For example:

1. Should one still consider—as most "Textbooks of Marxism-Leninism" do—the opposition between "materialism" and "idealism" as the fundamental question of philosophy? Is it still possible to contend, as does the *Concise Philosophical Dictionary*, that dialectical materialism was superior to metaphysical materialism which was undeveloped, dead, crude, and "idiotic"?[25] Isn't it true that the revolutionary idealism of the liberation theologians is superior to the idiotic materialism of the bourgeois economists and even of certain Stalinist "Marxists"? Particularly since this theological idealism has been shown to be perfectly compatible with a historical materialist approach to social reality.

2. Why can't liberation theology help us combat the reductionist, economist, and vulgar materialist tendencies that exist within the Marxist tradition? We have to take into consideration the role of moral and "spiritual" motivations if we want to understand why a whole layer of middle-class intellectuals and individuals (the radicalized clergy) broke with their class and now support the cause of the oppressed. In the same way, to explain why the Christian masses shrug off their apathy and rise up against their oppressors we have to examine not just their objective social condition, but also their subjectivity, culture, beliefs, and their new way of living their religion. Linking up again with the intuitions of Latin American Marxists like José Carlos Mariátegui, the liberation theologians also help us to reevaluate certain precapitalist communal traditions, kept alive in popular tradition (particularly among the peasants) and to distrust the blinkered culture of "economic progress," capitalist modernization, and the "development of the productive forces" as such. Revolutionary Christians have been more aware of the social consequences of the "development of underdevelopment" under the multinationals' domination than many Marxists enmeshed in the chains of a purely economistic "developmentist" logic.

3. In revolt against the Church's authoritarianism, the Christians for liberation are wary of political authoritarianism in the trade unions and political parties. Their "basism" or "rank and filism" occasionally takes on naive and excessive forms but is an understandable reaction against the antidemocratic, corrupt, or manipulative practices of the populist or Stalinist apparatuses. Correctly formulated, isn't this antiauthoritarian sensibility,

this aspiration to democracy, at the base a vital contribution to the self-organization of the oppressed and to an antibureaucratic recomposition of the workers' movement?

4. Liberation theologians stimulate us to reflect on the moral dimension of revolutionary commitment, of the struggle against social injustice, and the building of a new society. The Jesuits were deemed in the eyes of their enemies to support the amoral maxim "the end justifies any means." Trotsky in *Their Morals and Ours* defends them from this accusation and notes that such a doctrine, taken in the strict sense of the term, would be "internally contradictory and psychologically absurd."[26] In any case the new revolutionary Jesuits, like Ernesto and Fernando Cardenal, Sandinista government members, have little in common with this type of Machiavellianism: their political commitment is inseparable from certain ethical values. To a large extent it is due to the role of the Sandinista Christians that the Nicaraguan revolution is the first authentic social revolution, since 1789, to have abolished the death penalty. An example to be followed!

5. Finally liberation theology forces Marxists to reexamine their traditional thinking about religion: if this has played and continues to play in many places the role of the "opium of the people," can it not also act as the *tocsin of the people*, as a call galvanizing the oppressed from their lassitude, their passivity, and their fatalism and make them conscious of their rights, their strength, and their future?

WITH CHRISTIANS OR NOT AT ALL!

What then are the criticisms we can raise with the liberation theologians? The most urgent discussions to have with the Christians for liberation are not debates on materialism, religious alienation, or the history of the Church (and even less on the existence of God), but on the eminently practical and burning questions of the day: for example, divorce, abortion, contraception, and the right of women to control their bodies. In fact it is a debate that concerns the whole of the Latin American workers' movement, and it is far from having a coherent line in this area. It is difficult to foresee what will be the outcome of the conflict between the Vatican and liberation theology, between the conservative Church and the Church of the Poor. In any event we can be reasonably sure about one thing—the revolution in Latin America will be made with the Christians, or it will not take place.

Notes

1. Karl Marx, "Toward the Critique of Hegel's Philosophy of Right," 1844, in *Marx and Engels, Basic Writings on Politics and Philosophy*, ed. Lewis S. Feuer (London: Collins Fontana, 1969), p. 304.
2. Karl Marx, *German Ideology*, 1846 (London: Lawrence and Wishart, 1974).
3. Friedrich Engels, "Ludwig Feuerbach and the End of Classical German Philosophy," in Feuer, ed., *Marx and Engels, Basic Writings*, p. 281.
4. Friedrich Engels, "On Materialism," in Feuer, ed., *Marx and Engels, Basic Writings*, p. 99.
5. Friedrich Engels, "The Peasant War in Germany," 1850, in Feuer, ed., *Marx and Engels, Basic Writings*, pp. 452–75.
6. Friedrich Engels, *Anti-Dühring* (London: Lawrence and Wishart, 1969), pp. 121–22, 407.
7. Friedrich Engels, "Contribution to a History of Primitive Christianity," in *Marx and Engels, "On Religion"* (London: Lawrence and Wishart).
8. Engels, "The Peasant War in Germany," p. 464.
9. Karl Kautsky, *Vorläufer des neueren Sozialismus*, vol. 1: *Kommunistische bewegungen im Mittelalter* (Stuttgart: Dietz Verlag, 1913), pp. 170, 198.
10. Ernst Bloch, *Le principe espérance* (Paris: Gallimard, 1976) and *L'atheisme dans le christianisme* (Paris: Gallimard, 1978).
11. A. Lopez Trujillo, *Théologies de la libération* (Paris: Cert, 1985), p. 113.
12. Cardinal Ratzinger, "Les consequences fondamentales d'une option marxiste," in Trujillo, *Théologies*, pp. 122–30.
13. "Instruction on Some Aspects of 'Liberation Theology,'" 1984, in Trujillo, *Théologies*, pp. 156, 171–74. This document was followed in 1985 by a more conciliatory and "positive," "Instruction of Christian Liberty and Liberation."
14. On this see the excellent study by Guy Petitdemange, "Théologie(s) de la liberation et marxisme(s)" in *Pourquoi la théologie de la libération? Cahiers de l'actualité religieuse et sociale* (1985), supplement to No. 307. For a historical study of this process also see the interesting essay by Enrique Dussel, "Encuentros de cristianos y marxistas en America Latina," *Cristianismo y sociedad* 74 (1982).
15. Gustavo Gutierrez, *Théologie de la libération—Perspectives* (Brussels: Lumen Vitae, 1974), p. 244. However in 1984, following criticism from the Vatican, Gutierrez seemed to retreat to a less exposed position, limiting the convergence with Marxism to a link up between theology and social sciences. See Gutierrez, "Theologie et sciences sociales," 1984, in Trujillo, *Théologies*, pp. 189–93.
16. Gutierrez, *Théologie*, pp. 276–77.
17. For an impressive list of Christians victimized as a result of their commitment to the struggle, see *La Sangre por el Pueblo: Nuevos martires de America Latina* (Managua: Jesuits of the Instituto Historico Centroamericano de Managua, 1983).
18. "Documentos de Partido Comunista Brasileiro" (Lisboa: Ed Avante, 1976), p. 71. *Los obispos Latinoamericanos entre Medellin y Puebla* (San Salvador: Universidad Centroamericana, 1978), p. 71.
19. "I have heard the cries of my people" (Exod. 3:7). Document adopted by the bishops and religious superiors of northeast Brazil, *Entraide et fraternité* (Brussels, 1973), pp. 42–43.

20. Gutierrez, *Théologie*, pp. 102, 320. The quote from Mariátegui is taken from *Ideologia y politica* (Lima), p. 249.
21. Leonardo Boff and Clodovis Boff, "The Cry of Poverty," 1984, in Trujillo, *Théologies*, p. 139.
22. Quoted by Gutierrez, *Théologie*, pp. 117–18. In a note, Gutierrez mentions several other Latin American Episcopal documents which take a similar line.
23. *Juventud y cristianismo en America Latina*, quoted in ibid., p. 266.
24. Leonardo Boff, *Igreja, carisma e poder* (Petrópolis: Vozes, 1982), pp. 70–72, 91–93. (Published as *Church, Charisma, and Power* [London: SCM Press, 1985]).
25. Iudin and Rosenthal, *Concise Philosophical Dictionary* (Moscow, 1955), pp. 256, 360.
26. Leon Trotsky, *Their Morals and Ours* (London: New Park Publications, 1986), p. 10.

4

Weber against Marx? The Polemic with Historical Materialism in *The Protestant Ethic*

The relationship between Weber and Marx has been the object of innumerable debates and controversies, dealing with several aspects of their theories. However, from the beginning of the century up to the present, one set of questions has always been given special attention: the opposition between the Weberian and the Marxist method in historical sociology, and more specifically, the role of religious or economic factors in the origins of capitalism. The aim of this paper is to "revisit" this classic debate, by focusing on Weber's methodological and historical arguments in *The Protestant Ethic and the Spirit of Capitalism.*

It is usually said that Weber's *Protestant Ethic* is a polemical dialogue with the ghost of Marx, that is, a refutation of historical materialism. Marx's and Weber's positions are summarized as follows: for Marx, every attempt to explain Western rationalism must, recognizing the fundamental importance of the economic factor, above all take account of economic conditions; for Weber, on the other hand, the spirit of capitalism could only have arisen as the result of certain effects of the Protestant Reformation.

The problem seems clear and the difference between the two theses is obvious. There is, however, a small detail that spoils the clarity of the picture: the above "summary" of Marx's conception is actually a literal quotation from . . . Max Weber! In his introduction to the *Gesammelte Aufsätze zur Religionssoziologie* (1920)—the first volume of which includes *The Protestant Ethic*—Weber writes: "It is hence our first concern to work out and explain genetically the special peculiarity of Occidental rationalism, and within this field that of the modern Occidental form. Every such attempt at explanation must, recognizing the fundamental importance of the economic factor, above all [*vor allem*] take account of the economic conditions."[1] And this is not all: the above "summary" of Weber's views is actually a position that he considered both "foolish" and "doctrinaire"! He insisted that ". . . we have no intention whatever of maintaining such a foolish and doctrinaire thesis as that the spirit of capitalism (in the provisional sense of the term explained above), could only have arisen as the result of certain effects of the Reformation, or even that capitalism as an economic system is a creation of the Reformation."[2]

The fact is that Weber is very careful *not* to present his work as a spiritualist causal interpretation of history; in the above mentioned introduction to his collected essays on the sociology of religion, he recognizes that "we treat here only one side of the causal chain," and in the last page of *The Protestant Ethic* he acknowledges that "it would also further be necessary to investigate how Protestant Asceticism was in turn influenced in its development and its character by the totality of social conditions, especially economic."[3] Referring to this passage in a polemical article written in 1908, Weber ironically observed: "It is well possible that if I ever complete my investigation, I will be as angrily accused of capitulation to historical materialism as now of (capitulation to) ideology."[4] He was also wary of the attempts by conservative historians to use his essay in the struggle against Marxism: in an "anti-critical" article from 1910, he complains of people like Hans Delbruck, who "trumpet too much" (*viel zu sehr in die Trompete gestossen*) about his work, presenting it in a one-sided way as "a 'refutation' of the materialist conception of history."[5]

How is it then possible to explain that Weber's *Protestant Ethic* has been so often and so consistently presented as the classical example of a methodological alternative to Marxism in the social sciences? Or as the scientific refutation ("falsification") of historical materialism? Or as the demonstration that "ideas" can be *the* determining factor in social and economic transformation? The most influential representative of this line in interpretation has been Talcott Parsons, starting in 1937 with *The Structure of Social Action*[6] and then in his later writings. For instance, in his introduction (from 1974) to Weber's *Theory of Social and Economic Organization*, he writes: "Weber's earlier development took a course which brought him into close contact with the Marxian position. But he soon recoiled from this, becoming convinced of the indispensability of an important role of 'ideas' in the explanation of great historical processes. The first document of his new conviction was the study of the Protestant Ethic as an element in the genesis of modern capitalism."[7] As a recent study has shown, this paradigm for the interpretation of Weber's historical sociology became dominant and influenced several other social scientists such as H. R. Trevor-Roper, Werner

Sombart, Pitirim Sorokin, and Reinhard Bendix. For all of them, "Weber came to be regarded as a theorist of values, especially spriritual values, and the emphasis on Weber's sociology of religion brought Weber into sharp contrast with Marx on the grounds that Weber saw values as the primary mechanism of social change as opposed to interests."[8]

As we have already seen, this kind of paradigm hardly corresponds to Weber's own views. Is it then a pure and simple misunderstanding (or manipulation) of his writings? This is not entirely the case, because *there are* certain passages in *The Protestant Ethic* that clearly and unambiguously challenge historical materialism and try to present a "spiritualist" causal relation. These are mainly two passages on America and Benjamin Franklin where he presents some historical facts that show, in his opinion, the fallacy of "naive historical materialism." We will briefly examine the way these pages fit into the general pattern of the book, and then, in greater detail, attempt to check the facts by using Weber's own sources. Our thesis is, in a nutshell, that these passages are both untypical in relation to the general orientation of the book and quite problematic from the standpoint of the factual evidence.

What is actually the general pattern of *The Protestant Ethic*? This is not easy to answer. Sometimes Weber openly acknowledges the primacy of economic over religious changes. For example, in this passage on the origins of Protestantism in Germany: "A number of those sections of the old Empire which were most highly developed economically and most favoured by natural resources and situation, in particular a majority of the wealthy towns, went over to Protestantism in the sixteenth century. . . . There arises thus the historical question: why were the districts of highest economic development at the same time particularly favourable to a revolution in the Church?"[9] Whatever may be the answer to this historical question, this paragraph implies that in Germany capitalists became Protestants and not Protestants capitalists. In another passage, Weber suggests that Protestantism provided moral support for an *already existing* historical trend: "The idea of a man's duty to his possessions, to which he subordinates himself as an obedient steward, or even as an acquisitive machine, bears with chilling weight on his life. . . . The origin of this type of life also extends in certain roots, like so many aspects of the spirit of capitalism, back into the Middle Ages. But it was in the ethic of ascetic Protestantism that it first found a consistent ethical foundation."[10] In a similar vein, Weber writes that modern capitalism needed the support of religious forces as it needed the power of the State: modern capitalism could destroy the old medieval regulation of economic life "only in alliance with the growing power of the modern State; the same, we may say provisionally, may have been the case in its relations with religious forces."[11]

But the general methodological pattern of the book lies elsewhere: in its brilliant, thorough, and profound study of the "elective affinity," the inner relationship between these two cultural structures—the Protestant ethic and the spirit of capitalism—leaving open the question of *primacy*. The concept of "elective affinity" (*Wahlverwandtschaft*) is one of Weber's most fruitful methodological contributions to the sociology of culture. The term has its origins in alchemy and was used by Goethe as the title of a well-known novel. For Weber it designates the kind of active relationship (based on a certain structural analogy) between two social or cultural configurations, leading to mutual attraction, mutual influence, and mutual reinforcement. One of the reasons why this concept has not been given sufficient consideration in the Anglo-American debate on Weber is that the term *Wahlverwandtschaft* from the German edition[12] was translated into English by Parsons as "certain correlations" (or, in another passage, "those relationships").[13] While the Weberian concept implies a rich and meaningful inner link between the two forms, and a powerful reciprocal interaction, the Parsonian translation replaces it by a banal external relationship (or correlation) emptied of any cultural content. As it appears in *The Protestant Ethic*, the concept of elective affinity is not at all contradictory with historical materialism and can be perfectly integrated into a Marxist analysis of religion.

There remain nonetheless the two passages on America and Benjamin Franklin, which cannot be considered a mere turn of phrase, and which state, clearly and straightforwardly, the *causal primacy* of the "spiritual factor." We shall now attempt to analyze and check these passages, using *exclusively* Weber's own sources, that is, the books he himself quoted to support his thesis.

The first passage is as follows:

> Concerning the doctrine of the more naive historical materialism, that such ideas originate as a reflection or super-structure of economic situation, we shall speak more in detail below. At this point it will suffice for our purpose to call attention to the fact that *without doubt* in the country of Benjamin Franklin's birth (Massachussetts), the spirit of capitalism (in the sense we have attached to it) was present before the capitalistic order. There were complaints of a peculiarly calculating sort of profit-seeking in New-England, as distinguished from other parts of America, as early as 1632. It is further undoubted that capitalism remained far less developed in some of the neighbouring colonies, the later Southern States of the USA. . . . In this case the causal relationship is *certainly* the reverse of that suggested by the materialistic standpoint. [Emphasis added.][14]

First of all, it should be noted that even this polemical passage is not so much directed against Marx as against "the more naive historical materialism." Weber does not explain—either in *The Protestant Ethic* or elsewhere—who these "naive materialists" are, but very probably he is referring to the leading figures of Second International Marxism: Kautsky, Plekhanov, etc. If this is so, his criticism would not be entirely unjustified. For instance, in his historical study of the German Reformation (first published in 1895), Kautsky ironically dismissed those who waste their time examining the "theological squabbles" (*theologische Zänkerungen*) between Protestantism and Catholicism, instead of "deducing the struggles of these times from the contradictions of material interests"—the method of historical materialism."[15]

However, Weber attempts to oppose this "materialistic standpoint" with a kind of "spiritualistic" explanation, by suggesting, or rather stating, that the spirit of capitalism in Massachussetts at the beginning of colonization was not the consequence of a "capitalistic order," but of the Puritan ethics of the settlers. Is this really so "certain" and "without doubt"? Could there not be other reasons, beside religious ones, for the capitalistic spirit of the New Englanders?

Weber frequently quotes the historian J. A. Doyle, who "clearly brought out" the differences between the Puritan North, with its ascetic compulsion to save, and the South. Indeed, Doyle mentions among the causes that made the New England settler into a trader the fact that the Puritans "had lost the capacity for luxurious expenditure." But this same Doyle, whose "discerning eye" is praised by Weber, also saw other causes for the economic differences between the North and the South; not only heavenly causes, but quite early ones, and in particular the most earthly of all, namely, *land*. According to Doyle:

> The natural tendencies of a colony where land is plentiful and population scanty is to confine itself to agriculture, and to depend for manufactured goods on imports. That tendency is displayed to the full in the Southern colonies. In New England it was kept in check partly by material, partly by moral causes. The supply of fertile land was limited by nature; it was practically yet more limited by that strong desire for cohesion which the political and ecclesiastical institutions of the country and the pressure of the savages begot and kept alive. . . . The prosperous New Englander, who already farmed as much land as he could personally supervise, must keep his money in a strong box or else employ it in trade. And if this were true of the surplus capital of the farmer, much more was it true of the accumulation of the merchant. In a community like New England, trade, once started, must ever be seeking fresh outlets.

It must be added that for Doyle Puritanism was also to a certain extent an *obstacle* that had to be overcome in order to permit trade to develop fully: "The presence of the sea, its promise of wealth, of adventure, of variety in life, did battle against the rigid discipline of Puritanism, just as it did battle against the exclusiveness of the Greek city state. As might have been expected, Massachussetts, richer, more enterprising, and more densely populated, quickly outran Plymouth in trade."[16] To summarize: for Doyle, limited fertile land, dense population, ocean harbors, etc., are, *besides* Puritanism and sometimes *against* Puritanism, among the factors that fostered trade and manufacture in New England.

Now let us turn to the complaints of a "peculiarly calculating sort of profit-seeking in New England," "as early as 1632," mentioned by Weber. In this passage there is no reference, but in a footnote to page 174 he again mentions these complaints of 1632 and gives as a reference Weeden, *Economic and Social History of New England*, I, page 125. Let us turn to page 125 in Weeden's book: "In 1632 there are many indications that trade is increasing. . . . The Rev. John White, of Dorchester, bewailing the spiritual condition of the land, shows that temporal affairs have been pursued with sufficient energy. Great and fundamental errors have been committed, 'profit being the chief aim and not the propagation of religion.'" In other words: this complaint of 1632 suggests that profit making was not a consequence of people being religious but of their not being religious enough. The Puritan reverend did not see profit seeking as a blessed calling but as something *opposed* to true religiosity. This may or may not be true; but this complaint can hardly be quoted, as Weber did, to sustain a thesis that the Puritan religion was the main cause of this "peculiar profit-seeking" in New England.[17]

Another problem arises from this document from 1632: did this capitalistic spirit really arise suddenly, ex nihilo, or rather, *ex puritanismus*, in America, only twelve years after the landing of the *Mayflower*? Is it not much more reasonable to suppose that this spirit was not mysteriously born in America but that the settlers *brought it with them from England*? In other words, could it not be that the profit-seeking mind of the New Englanders in 1632 did not fall from the heavens of Puritanism in America but grew in the fertile soil of England, at that time *the most capitalistic country in the world*? Is it not possible that the immigrants brought in their luggage not only Protestantism but also capitalism? Not only the Bible ("the Good Book"), but also good accounting books? This hypothesis is even reinforced if we accept Weber's theory of the *elective affinity* between capitalism and Puritanism in England. If the Puritans were already capitalist-minded in England, there is no reason why they should not continue to be so in New England.

The same reasoning applies to the concrete development of handicrafts in New England. According to Weber, "the existence of iron works (1643), weaving for the market (1659), and also the high development of the handicrafts in New England in the first generation after the foundation of the colonies, are, from a purely economic view-point, astounding."[18] Again we must ask: are these handicrafts the product of the Protestant ethic or of the highly developed crafts in *England* (transported to America)? In relation to Weber's two examples, iron works and weaving for the market, we can bring to bear the following: a) The iron works of 1643 were organized by John Winthrop, Jr., using English labor and know-how. According to Doyle, "in 1643, having satisfied himself of the existence of iron, he *returned to England*, formed a company, engaged workmen, and procured all things necessary for establishing works." b) Weaving for the market did not start in 1659, but, according to Doyle, much earlier, by *English clothiers* who immigrated: "In 1639 a number of clothiers from Yorkshire settled to the north of Ipswich, naming their town after their native place, Rowley. There they set up a fulling mill and brought up their children to the craft of weaving and spinning." This was not an isolated phenomenon and involved relatively large and prosperous enterprises, as we learn from a letter by Lord Maynard to Archbishop Laud (March 17, 1638) complaining of "the intention of divers clothiers of great trading to go suddenly into New England" (quoted by Weeden).[19]

Of course, the above remarks do not pretend to offer a "materialistic historical" explanation of the origins of American capitalism, or to deny that Puritanism played a role (although an ambiguous one) in this process; I only want to suggest that, according to Weber's own sources, it is neither "certain" nor "without doubt" that "in this case the causal relationship is . . . the reverse of that suggested by the materialistic standpoint."

I will now turn to Weber's second passage against historical materialism, which deals with America and Benjamin Franklin:

> . . . In the backwoods small bourgeois circumstances of Pennsylvania in the XVIIIth century, where business threatened for simple lack of money to fall back into barter, where there was hardly a sign of large enterprise, where only the earliest beginnings of banking were to be found, the same thing [activity directed to acquisition for its own sake] was considered the essence of moral conduct, even commanded in the name of duty. To speak here of reflection of material conditions in the ideal superstructure would be patent nonsense. What was the background of ideas which could account for the sort of activity apparently directed towards profit alone as a calling toward which the individual feels himself to have an ethical obligation? For it was this idea which gave the way of life of the new entrepreneur its ethical foundation and justification.[20]

Weber is comparing here the capitalist Florence of the fourteenth and fifteenth centuries, which only tolerated ethically the capitalist attitude, and "the backwoods of Pennsylvania," which produced a prototype of the capitalist spirit, Benjamin Franklin. Leaving aside the problem of Florence (there is an important debate on the issue among Weber, Sombart, and Keller, and the whole question is highly controversial), we will focus our attention on Benjamin Franklin. First of all, it should be mentioned that

Franklin did not live in the "backwoods of Pennsylvania" but in *Philadelphia*, the second or third largest and most prosperous city in America in the eighteenth century, according to all records. Secondly, he was born and reared in *Boston* (until the age of seventeen), America's first city and the most capitalist-minded of all. Thirdly, he lived for many years in *London*, at that time probably the greatest capitalist center in the entire world.

So much for the "backwoods of Pennsylvania." But let us examine more closely Franklin's capitalist credo as quoted by Weber. The essence of this thought can be summarized in one word: Money (with a capital "M"). How to acquire money. How to save money. How to make money out of money. How to make money out of man. But why? What for? Weber answers by quoting Franklin's autobiography:

> If we thus ask, *why* should "money be made out of men," Benjamin Franklin himself, although he was a colourless deist, answers in his autobiography with a quotation from the Bible, which his strict Calvinistic father drummed into him again and again in his youth: "Seest thou a man diligent in his business? He shall stand before kings" (Prov. XXII 29). The earning of money within the modern economic order is, so long as it is done legally, the result and the expression of virtue and proficiency in a calling; and this virtue and proficiency are, as it is now not difficult to see, the real Alpha and Omega of Franklin's ethic, as expressed in the passages we have quoted, as well as in all his works without exception.[21]

According to Weber, in other words, the calling is for Franklin, as for his Calvinist father, *a moral end in itself*. However, the overwhelming impression given by Franklin's passages quoted by Weber is that *money* is the end in itself, the summum bonum. For instance:

> Remember that *time* is money. He that can earn ten shillings a day by his labour, and goes abroad, or sits idle, one half of that day, though he spends but sixpence during his diversion or idleness, ought not to reckon *that* the only expense; he has really spent, or rather thrown away, five shillings besides. . . . Remember, that money is of the prolific, generating nature. Money can beget money, and its offsprings can beget more, and so on. . . . He that kills a breeding-sow, destroys all her offspring to the thousandth generation. He that murders a crown, destroys all that it might have produced, even scores of pounds.[22]

Could it not be that for him the calling is only a *means* of attaining other ends, namely, wealth? Weber recognized that Franklin's moral admonitions are colored with utilitarianism, and that for him frugality and industry are virtues only because they are useful in making money. He believes nevertheless that Franklin "expresses a type of feeling which is closely connected with certain religious ideas." The only evidence he can provide for this assertion is the above-mentioned passage from Franklin's autobiography, where the Bible is quoted in order to justify diligence and proficiency in a calling.[23] But in fact, what Franklin writes in this passage shows precisely that for him industriousness is only praised as a *means* for enrichment:

> . . . my father having, among his instructions to me when a boy, frequently repeated a proverb of Salomon, "Seest thou a man diligent in his calling, he shall stand before kings, he shall not stand before mean men," I from thence *considered industry as a means of obtaining wealth and distinction* which encouraged me, tho' I did not think that I should ever literally stand before kings, which however, has since happened; for I have stood before five and even had the honour of sitting down with one, the King of Denmark, to dinner. [Emphasis added.][24]

The calling is here considered as a sure way of obtaining wealth and distinction, under the guidance of ancient wisdom (Salomon).

Social distinction, in the sense of upward social mobility, independence, equality with the rich and powerful, appears clearly as the aim of industry and money-making in many of Franklin's writings. For instance, in a passage from *The Way to Make Money Plenty in Every Man's Pocket*, Franklin recommends honesty, industry, and thrift as a means of becoming rich and independent, and he adds: "Then shalt thou be a man and not hide thy face at the approach of the rich, nor suffer the pain of feeling little when the sons of fortune walk at thy right hand . . . nor stoop to the silken wretch because he hath riches, nor pocket an abuse because the hand which offers it wears a ring set with diamonds."[25]

On the other hand, there is no doubt that wealth is for Franklin not only a means for obtaining social distinction but also an end in itself. We must therefore return to Weber's question: why should money be made out of men? Weber's argument is that making of money, acquisition as the ultimate purpose of life, is (from a hedonistic point of view) completely irrational, and cannot be explained except by the influence of religious ideas—the calling as a moral end in itself—the best example being Benjamin Franklin himself.[26] It seems to me that Franklin's autobiography does not sustain this explanation. Moreover, why can we not suppose that a specific economic behavior is in itself simply not rational (in hedonistic terms), without the need of religious inspiration? Weber himself admits that *today* capitalism and its (irrational) spirit of money-making as an absolute end "functions" without the need of religion. Why would this not be true from the beginning? In fact, it was perhaps more rational (in utilitarian terms) for a small craftsman of the seventeenth century to be industrious and thrifty as a *means* of social mobility, than today for a wealthy capitalist to be obsessed with money-making.

Marx analyzed in his writings this irrational character of capitalism, and presented it as a form of *alienation* similar in its structure to *religious* alienation. In both cases human beings are dominated by their own products—Capital and God. The capitalist, writes Marx, "insofar therefore as his acts or omissions are only a function of the capital personified in him with consciousness and will, considers his own private consumption as a theft against the accumulation of capital, as in Italian bookkeeping, where each private spending appears as a debit of the capitalist in favour of his capital."[27] A similar argument appears earlier, in the *Manuscripts of 1844*, as a sharp indictment of capitalist alienation and its inhuman possessiveness: "The less you eat, drink, buy books, go to the theatre or to balls, or to the public house . . . the more you will be able to save and the *greater* will become your treasure which neither moth nor rust will corrupt, your *capital*. The less you *are*, the less you express your life, the more you *have*, the greater is your *alienated* life and the greater is the saving of your alienated being."[28]

This alienation of the capitalist, this "acquisitive impulse and avarice as absolute passions" are, in Marx's view, particularly characteristic of the historical origins of the capitalist mode of production. But even in contemporary capitalism, according to Marx, the capitalist is to a large extent dominated by the "absolute impulse to acquire" (*absoluten Bereichungstrieb*), this being not an individual mania, but the expression of an alienated social mechanism, of which the capitalist is only a cog. On the other hand, of course, the capitalist is forced by the laws of competition to accumulate and continually to enlarge his capital.[29]

Marx is, like Weber, convinced of the inherent irrationality of the capitalist spirit. But he considers this irrationality (which has, of course, its own inner coherence and rationality) as being an intrinsic, immanent, and essential character of the capitalist mode of production (as an alienated social process), and not, as Weber suggests, the product of external, noneconomic, religious forces.

Marx did not study the influence of capitalism on Puritan ethics (this was done later by historians like Tawney, H. M. Robertson, etc.). Although he considers religion to be the expression of social and historical conditions, he does not "reduce" it to the economy, or deny its historical efficacy. On the contrary, he admits that religion may in certain periods—for instance in the Middle Ages—play the main role in social life.[30] Moreover, he notices the *affinity* between Puritanism and capitalism and mentions it in the *Grundrisse*—a work that was only published in 1939 and was therefore unknown to Weber. After quoting a passage from the economist William Petty on the immortal qualities of money, Marx writes: "The cult of money has its asceticism, its self-denial, its self-sacrifice—economy and frugality, contempt for mundane, temporal and fleeting pleasures; the chase after the *eternal* treasure. Hence the connection [*Zusammenhang*] between English Puritanism or Dutch Protestantism and money-making [*Geldmachen*]."[31]

In conclusion: Weber was perfectly justified in speaking of a *Wahlverwandtschaft* between the Protestant ethic and the spirit of capitalism and in showing the importance of religion in legitimating and reinforcing certain forms of economic behavior. What is much more open to question are his polemical attempts at "refuting" historical materialism in *The Protestant Ethic*. For his own historical sources seem to suggest that a) his thesis that early American capitalism and Benjamin Franklin's typically capitalist mind are primarily the product of religious causes is neither "certain" nor "without doubt"; and conversely, that b) an attempt to explain these historical facts by socioeconomic causes is not necessarily "patent nonsense."

Notes

1. Max Weber, *The Protestant Ethic and the Spirit of Capitalism* (London: Unwin University Books, 1967), p. 26; Max Weber, *Gesammelte Aufsätze zur Religionssoziologie*, vol. 1 (Tübingen: J. C. B. Mohr, 1920), p. 12.
2. Weber, *The Protestant Ethic*, p. 91.
3. Ibid., pp. 27, 183.
4. Max Weber, "Bemerkungen zu der vostehenden 'Replik'," 1908, in *Die protestantische Ethik II: Kritiken und Antikritiken*, ed. J. Winckelmann (Gütersloh: GTB, 1978), p. 56.
5. Max Weber, "Antikritisches Schlusswort zum 'Geist des Kapitalismus'," (1910), in *Die protestantische Ethik II*, p. 326.
6. Talcott Parsons, *The Structure of Social Action* (New York: Free Press, 1966), p. 510.
7. Talcott Parsons, "Introduction," in Max Weber, *The Theory of Social and Economic Organization* (New York: Free Press, 1964), p. 6. "Recoil" has several meanings in English, the most usual one being "to shrink mentally, in fear, or horror, or disgust" (*Oxford Concise Dictionary* [London: Oxford University Press, 1987], p. 866). This may describe Parsons's feelings in relation to Marxism, but it hardly fits Weber's own attitude.
8. Bryan S. Turner, "Marx, Weber and the Coherence of Capitalism: The Problem of Ideology" in *The Marx-Weber Debate*, ed. Norbert Wiley (Newbury Park: Sage Publications, 1987), pp. 169–70.
9. Weber, *The Protestant Ethic*, p. 36.
10. Ibid., p. 170. There are other passages where Weber refers to the Protestant ethic as providing "justification," "legalisation," etc., to capitalist practices (ibid., pp. 163, 178).
11. Ibid., p. 72.
12. Weber, *Gesammelte Aufsätze*, p. 83.
13. Weber, *The Protestant Ethic*, pp. 91–92.
14. Ibid., pp. 55–56.

15. Karl Kautsky, *Vorläufer des neueren Sozialismus*, vol. 2: *Der Kommunismus in der deutschen Reformation* (Stuttgart: J. W. Dietz, 1921), p. 3.
16. Weber, *The Protestant Ethic*, pp. 172, 278; J. A. Doyle, *The English in America*, vol. 2 (London: Longman, Green, and Co., 1887), pp. 33, 34, 35.
17. Weber, *The Protestant Ethic*, pp. 55, 174, 379; William B. Weeden, *Economic and Social History of New England*, 1620–1789, vol. 1 (Boston: Houghton Mifflin, 1890), p. 125.
18. Weber, *The Protestant Ethic*, p. 278.
19. Doyle, *The English in America*, pp. 37, 40, emphasis added; Weeden, *Economic and Social History of New England*, p. 165.
20. Weber, *The Protestant Ethic*, p. 75.
21. Ibid., pp. 53–54.
22. Ibid., pp. 48–49. The passages quoted by Weber are from Benjamin Franklin's book *Necessary Hints to Those That Would Be Rich* (1756). Weber himself admits that "the earning of more and more money" is "the *summum bonum* of this ethic" (ibid., p. 53).
23. Ibid., pp. 51–54.
24. Benjamin Franklin, *Autobiography* (London: Dent and Sons, 1931), p. 95.
25. Benjamin Franklin, *The Life and Works of Benjamin Franklin* (London: Brightly and Childs, n.d.), pp. 183–84.
26. Weber, *The Protestant Ethic*, p. 53.
27. Karl Marx, *Das Kapital*, vol. 1, in Karl Marx and Friedrich Engels, *Werke*, vol. 23 (Berlin: Dietz Verlag, 1962), p. 619.
28. Karl Marx, *Economic and Philosophical Manuscripts*, in Erich Fromm, *Marx's Concept of Man* (New York: F. Ungar, 1961), p. 144.
29. Marx, *Das Kapital*, pp. 618–21.
30. Ibid., p. 96.
31. Karl Marx, *Grundrisse, Foundations of the Critique of Political Economy (Rough Draft)* (Middlesex: Penguin Books, 1973), p. 252; Karl Marx, *Grundrisse der Kritik der politischen Ökonomie* (Berlin: Dietz Verlag, 1953), p. 143.

5

Marxists and the National Question

The aim of this essay is to isolate certain key theoretical and methodological aspects of the classic Marxist debate on the national question: a debate that had its starting point in the relatively imprecise positions developed by Marx and Engels themselves in their writings and that was carried on vigorously in the Second International before the First World War, culminating in Lenin's formulation of a realistic theory of the right of nations to self-determination.

MARX AND ENGELS: NATIONALITY AND INTERNATIONALISM

Marx offered neither a systematic theory of the national question, a precise definition of the concept of a "nation," nor a general political strategy for the proletariat in this domain. His articles on the subject were, for the most part, concrete political statements relating to specific cases. As far as the "theoretical" texts proper are concerned, the best-known and most influential are undoubtedly the rather cryptic passages in the *Manifesto* concerning communities and the nation. These passages have the historical value of proclaiming in a bold and uncompromising way the internationalist nature of the proletarian movement, but they are not always free from a certain economism and a surprising amount of free tradist optimism. This can be seen particularly in the suggestion that the victorious proletariat will merely carry on the task of abolishing national antagonisms that was begun by "the development of the bourgeoisie, Free Trade, the world market," etc. This idea, however, is contradicted in other texts from the same period in which Marx stressed that "while the bourgeoisie of each nation still retained separate national interests, big industry created a class, which in all nations has the same interest and with which nationality is already dead."[1] In his later writings (particularly those on the question of Ireland), Marx showed that not only does the bourgeoisie tend to foster national antagonisms, but it actually tends to increase them, since: a) the struggle to control markets creates conflicts between the capitalist powers; b) exploitation of one nation by another produces national hostility; c) chauvinism is one of the ideological tools that enable the bourgeoisie to maintain its domination over the proletariat.

Marx was on firm ground in stressing the internationalization of the economy by the capitalist mode of production: the emergence of the world market that "has destroyed industry's national base" by creating "the universal interdependence of nations." However, there was a tendency towards economism in his idea that the "standardization of industrial production and corresponding living conditions" helps to dissolve national barriers (*Absonderungen*) and antagonisms, as though national differences could be equated simply with differences in the production process.

As for Marx's famous ironical and provocative statement that "the proletariat has no country," this must be interpreted first and foremost in the sense that the proletariat of all nations have the *same interests*, a fact that Marx considered as being tendentially equivalent to the abolition of nationality (see the passage from *The German Ideology* quoted above): for the proletariat, the nation is merely the immediate political framework for the seizure of power. But Marx's antipatriotism had a deeper significance: a) for proletarian humanism, the whole of humanity is the meaningful totality, the supreme value, the final goal; b) for historical materialism, communism can only be established on a world scale, because of the immense development of productive forces that surpass the narrow framework of nation-states.

While the *Communist Manifesto* did lay the basis for proletarian internationalism, it gave hardly any indication of a concrete political strategy in relation to the national question. Such a strategy was only developed later, particularly in Marx's writings on Poland and Ireland (as well as in the struggle he waged in the International against the liberal-democratic nationalism of Mazzini and the national nihilism of the Proudhonists). Support for Poland's struggle for national emancipation was a tradition in the democratic workers' movement of the nineteenth century. Although they belonged to this tradition, Marx and Engels supported Poland less in the name of the general democratic principle of self-determination of nations than because of the struggle of the Poles against tsarist Russia, the main bastion of reaction in Europe and the bête noire of the founding fathers of scientific socialism. This approach contained a certain ambiguity: if Poland was only to be supported because her national struggle was also an antitsarist struggle, did this mean that pro-Russian Slavs (like the Czechs) did not have the right to self-determination? This was precisely the problem with which Engels was grappling in 1848–49.

The writings on Ireland, on the other hand, have a far wider application and state, implicitly, some general principles on the question of oppressed nations. In an early phase, Marx was in favor of Ireland having autonomy within a union with Britain and believed that the solution of the oppression of the Irish (by the big English landlords) would come through a working-class (Chartist) victory in England. In the sixties, on the other hand, he saw the liberation of Ireland as the condition for the liberation of the English proletariat. His writings on Ireland in this period elaborated three themes that were to be important for the future development of the Marxist theory of national self-determination, in its dialectical relationship with proletarian internationalism: a) only the national liberation of the oppressed nation enables national divisions and antagonisms to be overcome and permits the working class of both nations to unite against their common enemy, the capitalists; b) the oppression of another nation helps to reinforce the ideological hegemony of the bourgeoisie over workers in the oppressing nation: "Any nation that oppresses another forges its own chains"; c) the emancipation of the oppressed nation weakens the economic, political, military, and ideological bases of the dominating classes in the oppressor nation, and this contributes to the revolutionary struggle of the working class of that nation.

ENGELS

Engels's positions on Poland and Ireland were broadly similar to those of Marx. However, in his writings one finds a curious theoretical concept, the doctrine of "non-historic nations," which—although in my view fundamentally foreign to Marxism[2]—is well worth examining as an extreme example of the mistakes that can be made on the national question, even when one bases oneself on a revolutionary socialist, democratic position.

In 1848–49, analyzing the failure of the democratic revolution in Central Europe, Engels attributed it to the counterrevolutionary role played by the South Slav nations (Czechs, Slovaks, Croats, Serbs, Romanians, Slovenes, Dalmatians, Moravians, Ruthenians, etc.), who enlisted en masse in the Imperial Austrian and Russian armies and were used by the forces of reaction to crush the liberal revolutions in Hungary, Poland, Austria, and Italy.

In fact, the Imperial Austrian army consisted of peasants, both Slavs and German/Austrians. The victory of the counterrevolution was made possible by one important factor: the bourgeois-liberal leadership of the revolution was too hesitant, too "moderate," too fearful, to spark off a national agrarian revolution. Consequently, it was unable to win the mass of the peasants and national minorities to its side and prevent them from becoming the blind instrument of reaction. The 1848 revolution is the classic example of a revolution that failed because it did not provide a radical solution to the agrarian question and the national question (precisely what made the 1917 October Revolution successful!). This failure resulted from the narrow social base of its leadership: the central European liberal bourgeoisie was, by the nineteenth century, no longer a significant revolutionary class.

Because he failed to grasp the true *class* reasons for the failure of 1848–49, Engels tried to explain it with a metaphysical ideology: the theory of inherently counterrevolutionary "non-historic nations"—a category in which he includes, pell-mell, Southern Slavs, Bretons, Scots, and Basques. According to Engels, these "remnants of a nation, mercilessly crushed, as Hegel said, by the course of history, this *national refuse*, is always the fanatical representative of counter-revolution and remains so until it is completely exterminated or de-nationalized, as its whole existence is in itself a protest against a great historical revolution."[3] Hegel, the originator of that theory, had argued that nations that have not succeeded in creating a state, or whose state has long since been destroyed, are "non-historic" and condemned to disappear. As example, he mentioned precisely the Southern Slavs—the Bulgarians, Serbs, etc. Engels developed this pseudohistorical metaphysical argument in an article in 1855, which stated that "Pan-Slavism is a movement which is attempting to wipe out what a thousand years of history have created, a movement which cannot achieve its aims without sweeping Turkey, Hungary and half of Germany off the map of Europe. . . ."[4] There is no need to add that such an argument owed more to the conservative principles of the historical school of law (Savigny, etc.) than to the revolutionary ideas of historical materialism! Paradoxically, the same Engels, in an article from the same period (1853), had stressed that the Turkish Empire was destined to disintegrate as a result of the liberation of the Balkan nations, a fact that in no way surprised him since, as a good dialectician, he admired in history, "the eternal changes in human destiny . . . where nothing is stable except instability, nothing is immovable, except movement."[5]

An 1866 series of articles on Poland[6] demonstrated the ideological consistency of Engels, who persisted in contrasting the "great historical nations of Europe" (Italy, Poland, Hungary, Germany), whose right to national unity and independence was accepted, and the "many traces of nations" of no "European importance" and with no "national vitality" (Romania, Serbia, Croatia, Czechoslovakia, Slovenia, etc.), which were instruments in the hands of the tsar and Napoleon III. However, we might claim in Engels's defense that these were newspaper articles, lacking the rigorous character of a scientific work, and thus having a different status from his theoretical writings proper. Moreover, the basis of Engels's position was democratic and revolutionary: how to defeat tsarism and the Austrian Empire. He was in no way motivated by any kind of Slavophobia. In an article written before the 1848 revolution, he had called for the defeat of the

Austrian Empire in order to "clear all obstacles from the road to the liberation of the Italians and Slavs."[7] Neither was Engels prey to German chauvinism, as is proved by his attacks on the German minority in Hungary (*Siebenburger Sachsen*), who "persist in retaining an absurd nationality in the middle of a foreign country."[8]

The Radical Left against National Separatism

The "radical left" current (*Linksradikale*) represented by Luxemburg, Pannekoek, Trotsky (before 1917), and Strasser was characterized, to varying degrees and sometimes in very different forms, by its opposition to national separatism, in the name of the principle of proletarian internationalism. Moreover, its stance on the national question was one of the principal differences between this current and Lenin, to whom it was close in its Marxist and revolutionary approach.

ROSA LUXEMBURG

In 1893 Rosa Luxemburg founded the Social Democratic party of the Kingdom of Poland (SDKP), with a Marxist and internationalist program, as a counter to the Polish Socialist party (PPS), whose aim was to fight for the independence of Poland. Denouncing the PPS (with some justification) as a social patriotic party, Rosa and her comrades of the SDKP were resolutely opposed to the slogan of independence for Poland and stressed, on the contrary, the close link between the Russian and Polish proletariats and their common destiny. The "Kingdom of Poland" (part of Poland annexed to the tsarist Empire), they said, should proceed towards territorial *autonomy*, not towards independence, within the framework of a future Russian democratic republic.

In 1896 Luxemburg represented the SDKP at the Congress of the Second International. The positions for which she argued in her intervention were set out in a subsequent article:[9] the liberation of Poland is as utopian as the liberation of Czechoslovakia, Ireland, or Alsace-Lorraine. . . . The unifying political struggle of the proletariat should not be supplanted by a "series of sterile national struggles." The theoretical bases for this position were to be provided by the research she did for her doctoral thesis, "The Industrial Development of Poland" (1898).[10] The central theme of this work was that, from the economic point of view, Poland was already integrated into Russia. The industrial growth of Poland was being achieved thanks to Russian markets and, consequently, the Polish economy could no longer exist in isolation from the Russian economy. Polish independence was the aspiration of the feudal Polish nobility; now industrial development had undermined the basis of this aspiration. Neither the Polish bourgeoisie, whose economic future depended on the Russian economy, nor the Polish proletariat, whose historic interests lay in a revolutionary alliance with the Russian proletariat, was nationalist. Only the petty bourgeoisie and the precapitalist layers still cherished the utopian dream of a united, independent Poland. In this respect, Luxemburg considered her book to be the Polish equivalent of Lenin's "The Development of Capitalism in Russia,"[11] which was directed against the utopian and retrogressive aspirations of the Russian populists.

Her most controversial statement on the national question (which Lenin, in particular, attacked) was the 1908 series of articles published under the title "The National Question and Autonomy" in the journal of the Polish Social Democratic party (which had become the SDKPIL, after a Lithuanian Marxist group had joined). The main—and most debatable—ideas put forward in these articles were the following: a) the right of self-determination is an *abstract* and *metaphysical* right such as the so-called "right to work" advocated by the nineteenth-century utopians, or the laughable "right of every man to eat from gold plates" proclaimed by the writer Chernichevsky; b) support for the right of secession of each nation implies in reality support for *bourgeois* nationalism: the nation as a uniform and homogenous entity does not exist—each class in the nation has conflicting interests and "rights"; c) the independence of small nations in general, and Poland in particular, is utopian from the economic point of view and condemned by the laws of history. For Luxemburg, there was only one exception to this rule: the Balkan nations of the Turkish Empire (Greece, Serbia, Bulgaria, Armenia). These nations had reached a degree of economic, social, and cultural development superior to Turkey, a decadent empire whose deadweight oppressed them. From 1896 (following a Greek national uprising on the island of Crete) Luxemburg considered—in contrast to the position defended by Marx at the time of the Crimean War—that the Turkish Empire was not viable, and that its decomposition into nation-states was necessary for historical progress.

To back up her views on the lack of future for small nations, Luxemburg used Engels's articles on "non-historic nations" (though she attributed them to Marx: their true authorship was in fact only established in 1913, with the discovery of unpublished Marx/Engels letters). In particular, she used the article of January 1849 on the Hungarian struggle, quoting the passage we have already mentioned on "remnants of a nation mercilessly crushed by the course of history." She recognized that Engels's views on the Southern Slavs were mistaken, but she believed his method was correct and praised his "sober realism, free from all sentimentality" as well as his contempt for the metaphysical ideology of the rights of nations.[12]

As is well known, in 1914 Luxemburg was one of the few leaders of the

Second International who did not succumb to the great wave of social-patriotism that engulfed Europe with the advent of war. Imprisoned by the German authorities for her internationalist and antimilitarist propaganda, in 1915 she wrote and smuggled out of prison her famous "Junius Pamphlet." In this text Luxemburg to some extent adopted the principle of self-determination: "socialism gives to every people the right of independence and the freedom of independent control of its own destinies."[13] However, for her this self-determination could not be exercised within existing capitalist states, particularly colonialist states. How could one speak of "free choice" in relation to imperialist states like France, Turkey, or tsarist Russia? In the age of imperialism the struggle for the "national interest" is a mystification, not only in relation to the large colonial powers, but also for the small nations that are "only the pawns on the imperialist chessboard of the great powers."[14]

Luxemburg's theories on the national question, developed between 1893 and 1917, are based on four fundamental theoretical, methodological, and political errors.

1. Particularly before 1914, she adopted an economist approach to the problem: Poland is economically dependent on Russia, therefore cannot be politically independent—an argument that tends to ignore the specificity and the relative individuality of each political situation. This determinist-economist method is particularly striking in her doctoral thesis and her early writings on the Polish question: the industrial development of Poland, linked to the Russian market, determines "with the iron strength of historical necessity" (an expression which Luxemburg frequently used at this time, together with another of the same type: "with the inevitability of natural law") on one hand, the utopian nature of Polish independence and, on the other hand, the unity between the Russian and Polish proletariats. A characteristic example of this unmediated assimilation of politics to economics occurs in an article she wrote in 1902 on social-patriotism, which stressed that the economic tendency—"and therefore" the political tendency—in Poland was for union with Russia; the phrase "and therefore" was an expression of this lack of mediation, which was not demonstrated but simply assumed to be self-evident.[15] However, this type of argument began to disappear as Luxemburg increasingly succeeded in avoiding the economist trap, that is, particularly after 1914, when she coined the phrase "socialism or barbarism" ("Junius Pamphlet"), which represented a fundamental methodological break with fatalistic, Kautsky-type economism. Her arguments on the national question in the "Junius Pamphlet" were essentially political and not based on any mechanistic preconception.

2. For Luxemburg the nation was essentially a cultural phenomenon. Again, this tends to play down its political dimension, which cannot be

equated simply with economy or ideology and whose concrete form is the independent nation-state (or the struggle to establish it). This is why Luxemburg was in favor of abolishing national oppression and allowing "free cultural development" but refused to countenance separatism or the right to political independence. She did not understand that the denial of the right to form an independent nation-state is precisely one of the main forms of national oppression.

3. Luxemburg saw only the anachronistic, petty-bourgeois, and reactionary aspects of national liberation movements and did not grasp their revolutionary potential against tsarism (and later, in another context, against imperialism and colonialism). In other words, she did not understand the complex and contradictory dialectic of the *dual nature* of these nationalist movements. With regard to Russia, in general she underestimated the revolutionary role of the nonproletarian allies of the working class: the peasantry, the oppressed nations. She saw the Russian Revolution as *purely* working class, and not—like Lenin—as *led* by the proletariat.[16]

4. She failed to understand that the national liberation of oppressed nations is not only a demand of the "utopian," "reactionary" and "pre-capitalist" petty bourgeoisie but also of *the masses as a whole*, including the proletariat; and that, therefore, the recognition by the Russian proletariat of the right of nations to self-determination was an *indispensable condition* of its solidarity with the proletariat of oppressed nations.

What was the source of these mistakes, inconsistencies, and shortcomings? It would be wrong to think that they were logically linked to Luxemburg's method (apart from pre-1914 economism) or to her political positions as a whole (e.g., on the party, democracy, etc.). In fact, these theories on the national question were not peculiar to Luxemburg but were shared by the other leaders of the SDKPIL, even those who, like Dzerzhinsky, supported Bolshevism. It is most likely that Luxemburg's one-sided position was, in the last analysis, an ideological by-product of the continual, intense, and bitter ideological struggle of the SDKPIL against the PPS.[17]

The difference between Lenin and Luxemburg was, therefore, to a certain extent (at least as regards Poland), a result of the different standpoints of the Russian internationalists (struggling to defeat Great Russian chauvinism) and the Polish internationalists (combating Polish social-patriotism). Lenin at one time seemed to recognize a certain "division of labor" between Russian and Polish Marxists on this question. Having said this, his major criticism of Luxemburg was that she tried to generalize from a certain specific situation (Poland at a particular point in history) and therefore to deny not just Polish independence, but that of all other small oppressed nations.

However, in one article Luxemburg stated the problem in terms very similar to Lenin's: the 1905 introduction to the collection *The Polish Question and the Socialist Movement.*[18] In this essay, Luxemburg made a careful distinction between the undeniable *right* of every nation to independence ("which stems from the elementary principles of Socialism"), which she recognized, and the *desirability* of this independence for Poland, which she denied. This is also one of the few texts in which she recognized the importance, depth, and even justification of national feelings (though treating them as merely a "cultural" phenomenon) and stressed that national oppression is the "most intolerable oppression in its barbarity" and can only arouse "hostility and rebellion." This work, together with certain passages in the "Junius Pamphlet," shows that Luxemburg's thought was too realistic, in the revolutionary sense of the word, simply to present a linear coherence of a metaphysical and rigid kind.

TROTSKY

Trotsky's writings on the national question prior to 1917 can be defined as "eclectic" (the word Lenin used to criticize them), occupying a halfway position between Luxemburg and Lenin. It was in particular after 1914 that Trotsky became interested in the national question. He took it up in his pamphlet *The War and the International* (1914)—a polemical work directed against social-patriotism—from two different—if not contradictory—standpoints.

1. *A historical/economic approach.* The world war was a product of the contradiction between the productive forces, which tend towards a world economy, and the restrictive framework of the nation-state. Trotsky therefore heralded "the destruction of the nation state *as an independent economic entity*"—which, from the strictly economic point of view, was a totally justifiable proposition. However, he concluded from this premise the "collapse" (*Zusammenbruch*) and the "destruction" (*Zertrummerung*) of the nation-state *altogether*; the nation-state as such, the very concept of the nation, would only be able to exist in the future as a "cultural, ideological and psychological phenomenon." Of course, this was an evident non sequitur. The ending of the economic independence of a nation-state is in no way synonymous with the disappearance of the nation-state as a political entity. Like Luxemburg, Trotsky tended to reduce the nation either to economics or to culture, and thus lost sight of the specifically political aspect of the problem: the nation-state as a political phenomenon, distinct from the economic or ideological spheres (though, of course, having mediated relations with both).

2. *A concrete political approach.* Unlike Luxemburg, Trotsky explicitly proclaimed the right of nations to self-determination as one of the conditions for "peace between nations," which he contrasted with "the peace of

the diplomats." Moreover, he supported the perspective of an independent and united Poland (i.e., free from tsarist, Austrian, and German domination) as well as the independence of Hungary, Romania, Bulgaria, Serbia, Bohemia, etc. It was in the liberation of these nations and their association in a Balkan federation that he saw the best barrier to tsarism in Europe. Furthermore, with remarkable perception Trotsky demonstrated the dialectical relationship between proletarian internationalism and national rights: the destruction of the International by the social-patriots was a crime not just against socialism, but against the "national interest, in its widest and correct sense." since it dissolved the only force capable of reconstructing Europe on the basis of democratic principles and the right of nations to self-determination.[19]

In a series of articles in 1915 ("Nation and Economy"[20]), Trotsky tried to define the national question in a more precise way, but not without a certain ambiguity. The contradictory lines of his argument were indicative of a thought that had not yet crystallized. He began with a polemic against the social-imperialists, who justified their political position by the need to expand markets and productive forces. This polemic, from the methodological point of view, seemed to reject economism: yes, Marxists are in favor of the greatest possible expansion in the economic sphere, but not at the expense of dividing, disorganizing, and weakening the workers' movement. Trotsky's argument was somewhat confused, in that he wrote of the workers' movement as "the most important productive force in modern society"; nevertheless, what he did was to affirm the overriding importance of a *political* criterion. However, throughout both articles he returned to the "centralizing needs of economic development," which call for the destruction of the nation-state as a hindrance to the expansion of productive forces. How could these "needs" be reconciled with the right of nations to self-determination, which Trotsky also recognized? He escaped this dilemma by means of a theoretical somersault that led him back into economism: "the state is essentially an economic organization, it will be forced to adapt to the needs of economic development." Therefore, the nation-state would be dissolved into the "Republican United States of Europe," while the nation, divorced from the economy and freed from the old framework of the state, would have the right to self-determination . . . in the sphere of "cultural development."

In 1917 Trotsky abandoned these "eclectic" positions and adopted the Leninist conception of the national question, which he brilliantly defended at Brest-Litovsk in his capacity as people's commissar for foreign affairs.[21]

PANNEKOEK AND STRASSER

Pannekoek's *Class Struggle and Nation* and Strasser's *Worker and Nation* were both published in 1912 in Reichenberg (Bohemia) as an internationalist response to the theses of Otto Bauer.[22] The common central idea of both writers was the superiority of class interest over national interest; the practical conclusion was the unity of the Austrian Social Democratic party and the refusal to divide it into separate or autonomous national sections. Both compared the nation with religion, as an ideology destined to disappear with the advent of socialism, and rejected Bauer's doctrine on the national question as ahistorical, idealist, and national-opportunist.

For Pannekoek, the "national phenomenon is a bourgeois ideological phenomenon." Bauer's belief that this ideology can be an independent force was characteristic of a Kantian and not a materialist method. However, the interesting thing is that both Pannekoek and Strasser accepted in its essentials the national program of Bauer and Austrian social democracy: national autonomy, within the framework of the multinational Austro-Hungarian state. Pannekoek further stressed that this was an autonomy founded on the personal principle and not the territorial principle, which was consistent with his conception of the national phenomenon as purely ideological and cultural. It is true that Pannekoek and Strasser, in contrast to Bauer, did not consider the program could be realized within the framework of capitalism, but attributed to it a purely propagandist and educative value.

Economism was indirectly present in the common basic premise of the two writers: the priority of class interest over national interest was due to the economic origins of the former. In a very amusing passage of his pamphlet, Strasser explained that the good German-Austrian patriot would still do his shopping in Czech-owned shops if they were cheaper than their German equivalents. But is this really sufficient to allow one to say, as Strasser did, that when national and economic interests come into conflict, economic interests will triumph? Pannekoek's and Strasser's polemic against Bauer was inserted in a revolutionary perspective, but it was incomplete, to the extent that it confined itself to contrasting internationalism with Austro-Marxist national reformism, without laying down an alternative concrete political approach in the actual sphere of the national problem and particularly the struggle of oppressed nations.

The Austro-Marxist Center and Cultural Autonomy

The main idea of the Austro-Marxists was cultural autonomy within the framework of a multinational state, by means of the arrangement of nationalities into public juridical corporations, with a whole series of cultural, administrative, and legal powers. With regard to the national question, as all political questions, their doctrine was marked by "centrism," halfway between reform and revolution, between nationalism and internationalism. They wished both to recognize the rights of national minorities and at the same time to maintain the unity of the Austro-Hungarian state. Although, like the radical left, they tended to reject separatism as a solution to the national question, the Austro-Marxists did so not just for different reasons, but from an almost diametrically opposite standpoint.

KARL RENNER

Prior to 1917, the future chancellor of Austria (1918–20) published several studies on the national question, of which the first and best known is *The State and the Nation* (1899). His method was basically legal/constitutionalist, and his conception of the state had more in common with Lassalle than with Marx (as was correctly pointed out by Mehring, Kautsky, and the bourgeois lawyer, Hans Kelsen). The influence of Lassalle's statism was implicit even in his early writings but became much more obvious after 1914, for example in his work *Marxism, the War and the International* (1917), which contained the following ideas (their relationship to Marxism is somewhat problematical): a) "The economy serves the capitalist class more and more exclusively; on the other hand the state increasingly serves the proletariat." b) "The germ of socialism is to be found today in all the institutions of the capitalist state."[23]

It is in the light of this "social-statism" that Renner's positions on the national question must be understood; his essential aim was to stop the "disintegration of the Empire" and the "dissolution of Austria," that is, to save the "historic Austrian state." The Austro-Hungarian Imperial state therefore appeared as the basic framework of Renner's political thought, a framework that had to be preserved, through a certain number of democratic reforms and concessions (cultural, legal, etc.) to national minorities. Paradoxically, it was because of this statism that Renner tried to depoliticize the national question, to reduce it to an administrative and constitutional question,[24] to transform it into a legal problem. He sought to neutralize the danger of political separatism and the breakup of the multinational state by means of a subtle and complex juridical-institutional apparatus: national corporations based on the principle of personality, a "national register" listing all people having chosen a nationality, separate electoral rolls for each national minority, territorial and/or national bodies with administrative autonomy, etc. In reality, Renner's positions, which lacked any class perspective or revolutionary direction, despite their author's claims, lay largely outside the political and theoretical sphere of Marxism.

OTTO BAUER

Bauer's great work *The National Question and Social Democracy* (1907) had considerably more theoretical weight and influence than Renner's writings. However, Bauer shared with Renner the fundamental premise of Austro-

Marxism: the preservation of the multinational state. Bauer saw the solution to the national question in reformist terms ("national evolution" was the phrase he used to describe his strategy), as the progressive manipulation of the institutions of the Austro-Hungarian state: "It is hardly likely that national autonomy could be the result of a momentous decision, or a bold action. In a long process of evolution, in difficult struggles . . . Austria will journey step by step towards national autonomy. The new Constitution will not be created by a great legislative act, but by a series of provincial and local laws."[25]

What was peculiar to Bauer's analysis was the psycho-cultural nature of his theory of the national question, which was constructed on the basis of the vague and mysterious concept of "national characteristics," defined in psychological terms: "diversity of purpose, the fact that the same stimulus can provoke different movements and that the same external situations can lead to different decisions." In fact, this concept was purely metaphysical, of neo-Kantian origin. It was hardly surprising that it was severely criticized by Bauer's Marxist opponents (Kautsky, Pannekoek, Strasser, etc.).

The second key concept in Bauer's theoretical edifice was, of course, national culture, the basis for his entire strategy of national autonomy. Placing the analysis on the level of culture naturally leads one to ignore the political problem: self-determination through the creation of nation-states. In this sense, Bauer's "culturalism" played the same methodological role as Renner's "juridicism": it depoliticized the national question.

What is more, Bauer almost completely excluded classes and the class struggle from the sphere of national culture. His program aimed to give the working class access to "cultural advantages" and to "the national cultural community" from which they were excluded by capitalism. He therefore seemed to consider "cultural values" to be absolutely *neutral* and devoid of class content. He thus made the reverse mistake to the devotees of "Prolet-kult," who ignored the relative autonomy of the cultural world and wished to reduce it directly to its social base ("proletarian culture" versus "bourgeois culture"). It was thus easy for Pannekoek to stress in his polemic against Bauer that the proletariat reads very different things into Goethe and Schiller (or Freiligrath and Heine) than the bourgeoisie. The complex relationship of the proletariat to the bourgeois cultural heritage, a dialectical relationship of *Aufhebung* (conservation/negation/transcendence), was reduced by Bauer to a simple act of appropriation, or rather passive acceptance. Obviously Bauer was correct to stress the decisive importance of culture in defining the national question, but his theory resulted in a real fetishization of national culture, the most striking expression of which was the idea that socialism leads to a *growth in cultural differentiation* between nations.[26]

Because of his tendency to "nationalize" socialism and the workers' movement, his rejection of what he called the "naive cosmopolitanism" of the proletariat in its infancy, and his inability to conceive of an international socialist culture, Bauer's theory was to some degree contaminated by the nationalist ideology it was seeking to defeat. It is thus not surprising that it became the doctrine of "nationalist/cultural" currents in the workers' movement, not just in Austria-Hungary but also in the Russian Empire (Bund, Caucasian social democrats, etc.) and elsewhere. However, despite these limitations, Bauer's work had an undeniable theoretical value, particularly with regard to the *historicist* nature of its method. In defining the nation as the product of a common historical destiny (the material basis of which is man's struggle against nature), as the "never-finished outcome of a constant process," as a crystallization of past events, a "frozen piece of history," Bauer stood firmly on the ground of historical materialism and in outright opposition to bourgeois national conservatism, the reactionary myths of the "eternal nation" and racist ideology. This historical approach gave Bauer's book a real methodological superiority, not just over Renner, but over most Marxist writers of the period, whose writings on the national question often had an abstract and rigid character. In so far as Bauer's method entailed not only a historical explanation for existing national structure, but a conception of the nation as a process, a movement in perpetual transformation, he was able to avoid Engels's mistake in 1848–49: the fact that a nation (like the Czechs) "has had no history" does not necessarily mean that it will have no future. The development of capitalism in Central Europe and the Balkans leads not to the assimilation but to the *awakening* of "non-historic" nations.[27]

Lenin and the Right of Self-Determination

The national question is one of the fields in which Lenin greatly developed Marxist theory, by spelling out (on the basis of Marx's writings, but going far beyond them) a coherent, revolutionary strategy for the workers' movement, based on the fundamental slogan of national self-determination. In its coherence and realism, the Leninist doctrine was far in advance of the positions of other Marxists of the period, even those closest to Lenin on this question: Kautsky and Stalin.

Kautsky's position prior to 1914 was similar to Lenin's, but was distinguished by its unilateral and almost exclusive concentration on language as the basis of the nation, and by a lack of clarity and boldness in the formulation of the right of nations to secession. After 1914, the ambiguous and contradictory positions of Kautsky on the rights of nations in the context of the war were violently denounced by Lenin as "hypocritical" and "opportunist."

STALIN

As for the famous article by Stalin "Marxism and the National Question,"[28] it is true that it was Lenin who sent Stalin to Vienna to write this and that in a letter to Gorky in February 1913 he spoke of the "marvellous Georgian who has sat down to write a big article."[29] But once the article was finished, it does not appear (contrary to a popular myth) that Lenin was particularly enthusiastic about it, as he does not mention it in any of his numerous writings on the national question, apart from a brief, parenthetical reference in passing in an article dated December 28, 1913. It is obvious that the main ideas in Stalin's work were those of the Bolshevik party and Lenin. Having said this, Trotsky's suggestion that the article was inspired, supervised, and corrected "line by line" by Lenin seems questionable.[30] On the contrary, on a certain number of fairly important points Stalin's work implicitly and explicitly differs from, and even contradicts, Lenin's writings.

1. The concept of "national character," of "common psychological make-up" or "psychological particularity" of nations, *is not at all Leninist.* This problematic is a legacy from Bauer, whom Lenin explicitly criticized for his "psychological theory."[31] In fact, the idea of a national psychology has more in common with a certain superficial and prescientific folklore than with a Marxist analysis of the national question.

2. By baldly stating that "it is only when all these characteristics [common language, territory, economic life, and "psychic formation"] are present together that we have a nation," Stalin gave his theory a dogmatic, restrictive, and rigid character that one never finds in Lenin. The Stalinist conception of a nation was a real ideological Procrustean bed. According to Stalin, Georgia before the second half of the nineteenth century was not a nation, because it had no "common economic life," being divided into economically independent principalities. There is no need to add that on this criterion Germany, prior to the Customs Union, would not have been a nation either. . . . Nowhere in Lenin's writings do we find such an ultimatist, rigid, and arbitrary "definition" of a nation.

3. Stalin explicitly refused to allow the possibility of the unity or association of national groups scattered within a multinational state: "The question arises: is it possible to unite into a single national union groups that have grown so distinct? . . . Is it conceivable, that, for instance, the Germans of the Baltic Provinces and the Germans of Transcaucasia can be 'united into a single nation'?" The answer given, of course, was that all this was "not conceivable," "not possible," and "utopian."[32] Lenin, by contrast,

vigorously defended the "*freedom* of association, including the association of any communities no matter what their nationality, in any given State," citing as an example precisely the Germans of the Caucasus, the Baltic, and the Petrograd area. He added that freedom of association of every kind between members of the nation, scattered in different parts of the country or even the globe, was "indisputable, and can be argued against only from the hidebound, bureaucratic point of view."[33]

4. Stalin made no distinction between Great Russian tsarist oppressive nationalism and the nationalism of oppressed nations. In a very revealing paragraph in his article, he rejected in one breath the "warlike and repressive" nationalism of the tsars "from above" and the "wave of nationalism from below which sometimes turns into crass chauvinism" of the Poles, Jews, Tatars, Georgians, Ukrainians, etc. Not only did he fail to make any distinction between nationalism "from above" and "from below," but he aimed his most severe criticisms at social democrats in oppressed countries who had not "stood firm" in the face of the nationalist movement. Lenin, on the other hand, not only considered the difference between the nationalism of the oppressor and the oppressed nation to be absolutely decisive, but always attacked most bitterly those who capitulated, consciously or unconsciously, to Great Russian national chauvinism. It is no accident that one of the main targets of his polemic were the Marxist social democrats of an oppressed nation, Poland, who by their "firm" stand against Polish nationalism ended up by denying Poland's right to secede from the Russian Empire. This difference between Lenin and Stalin was highly significant, and already contained the germ of the later violent conflict between them on the national question in Georgia (December 1922)—Lenin's famous "last fight."

LENIN

Lenin's starting point in working out a strategy on the national question was the same as for Luxemburg, Trotsky, and Pannekoek: proletarian internationalism. However, Lenin understood better than his comrades of the revolutionary left the dialectical relationship between internationalism and the right of national self-determination. He understood, firstly, that only the *freedom* to secede makes possible *free* and voluntary union, association, cooperation and, in the long term, fusion between nations; secondly, that only the recognition by the workers' movement in the oppressor nation of the right of the oppressed nation to self-determination can help to eliminate the hostility and suspicion of the oppressed and unite the proletariat of both nations in the international struggle against the bourgeoisie.

Similarly, Lenin grasped the dialectical relationship between national-democratic struggles and the socialist revolution and showed that the popular masses (not just the proletariat, but also the peasantry and petty bourgeoisie) of the oppressed nation were the allies of the conscious proletariat: a proletariat whose task it would be to *lead* the struggle of this "disparate, discordant and heterogenous mass," containing elements of the petty bourgeoisie and backward workers with their "preconceptions, reactionary fantasies, weaknesses and errors," against capitalism and the bourgeois state.[34] It is true, however, that in relation to Russia it was only really after April 1917, when Lenin adopted the strategy of permanent revolution, that he began to see the national liberation struggle of oppressed nations within the Russian Empire not only as a *democratic* movement, but as an ally of the proletariat in the Soviet *socialist* revolution.

From the methodological point of view, Lenin's principal superiority over most of his contemporaries was his capacity to "put politics in command," that is, his obstinate, inflexible, constant, and unflinching tendency to grasp and highlight the *political* aspect of every problem and every contradiction. This tendency stood out in his polemic against the economists on the question of the Party in 1902–1903; in his discussion with the Mensheviks on the question of the democratic revolution in 1905; in the originality of his writings on imperialism in 1916; in the inspired turn which the "April Theses" represented in 1917; in the whole of his most important work, *State and Revolution*; and, of course, in his writings on the national question. It is this methodological aspect that explains (amongst other things) the striking *actuality* of Lenin's ideas in the twentieth century, an age of imperialism, which has seen the political level become increasingly *dominant* (even though, in the last analysis, it is of course *determined* by the economic).

On the national question, while most other Marxist writers saw only the economic, cultural, or "psychological" dimension of the problem, Lenin stated clearly that the question of self-determination "belongs wholly and exclusively to the sphere of political democracy,"[35] that is, to the realm of the right of *political* secession and the establishment of an independent nation-state. What is more, Lenin was perfectly conscious of the methodological foundation of the differences: "An 'autonomous' nation does not enjoy rights equal to those of a 'sovereign' nation; our Polish comrades could not have failed to notice this had they not (like our old Economists) obstinately avoided making an analysis of *political* concepts and categories."[36] Thanks to Lenin's understanding of the relative autonomy of the political process, he was able to avoid both subjectivism and economism in his analysis of the national question.[37]

Needless to say, the political aspect of the national question for Lenin was not at all that with which chancelleries, diplomats, and armies concern themselves. He was totally indifferent to whether this or that nation had an independent state or what the frontiers were between two states. His aim was *democracy* and the *internationalist unity* of the proletariat, which both require the recognition of the right of nations to self-determination. What is more, precisely because it concentrates on the political aspect, his theory of self-determination makes absolutely no concession to nationalism. It is situated solely in the sphere of the democratic struggle and the proletarian revolution.

It is true that these two aims did not have equal importance in Lenin's eyes; democratic demands must always be subordinated to the overriding interests of the revolutionary class struggle of the world proletariat. For example, according to Lenin, if the republican movement turns out, in a particular case, to be an instrument of reaction (Cambodia 1971!), Marxists will not support it. This does not mean that the working-class movement must strike out republicanism from its program. The same goes, mutatis mutandis, for self-determination. Even though there are some exceptions, the general rule is the right of secession for each nation. In fact, Lenin's analysis that the recognition of the right to self-determination is of primary importance in creating the conditions for internationalist unity among workers tends implicitly to exclude even the possibility of "exceptions," that is, of a contradiction between the interests of the proletariat and the democratic rights of nations.

CONCLUSION: THE LESSON OF HISTORY

Some of the specific debates among Marxists on aspects of the national question have been settled by history. The multinational state of Austria-Hungary broke up into several nation-states after the First World War. The Basques, "an essentially reactionary nation" according to Engels, are today at the peak of revolutionary struggle in Spain. The reunification of Poland, which Luxemburg referred to as petty-bourgeois utopianism, became a reality in 1918. The "non-historic" Czech nation, which was destined to disappear because of its lack of "national vitality" (Engels), did set up a state, through voluntary federation with the Slovak nation.

The experience of post-1917 history also shows us that the nation is not simply a collection of abstract, external criteria. The subjective element, that is, the consciousness of a national identity, a national political movement, are no less important. Obviously these "subjective factors" do not come out of the blue; they are the result of certain historical conditions—persecution, oppression, etc. But this means that self-determination must have a wider application; it must relate not just to secession, but to the "national entity" itself. It is not a doctrinaire "expert" armed with a list of "objective criteria" (of the Stalin type) who will determine whether a community constitutes a nation or not, but *the community itself.*[38]

On the other hand, ever since Woodrow Wilson the nationalism of the great powers has restocked its ideological arsenal by appropriating the slogans of democracy, equality of nations, and the right of self-determination. These principles are now proclaimed by bourgeois statesmen everywhere. Lyndon Johnson, when president of the United States, declared solemnly in 1966: "We are fighting to uphold the principle of self-determination, so that the people of South Vietnam may be free to choose their own future."[39] Since the nineteenth century—when Treitschke wrote, on the occasion of an uprising in Africa: "It is pure mockery to apply normal principles of war in wars with savages. A negro tribe must be chastised by setting its villages on fire, because this is the only kind of remedy that is effective"[40]—how the policy of the great powers in relation to small nations has changed out of all recognition!

The real threat today to the political health of the workers' movement is not the infantile disorder that Luxemburg's generous errors represented but pathological phenomena of a far more dangerous kind: the viruses of great-power chauvinism and opportunist capitulation to bourgeois nationalism that are spread abroad by the Russian and Chinese bureaucracies and their disciples internationally. Indeed, "ultra-leftism" on the national question hardly survives today. Only in certain sectors of the revolutionary left does one still sometimes find a distant echo of Luxemburg's theses, in the form of an abstract opposition to national liberation movements, in the name of "working-class unity" and internationalism. The same is true with respect to Engels's notion of "reactionary nations." Thus, if one looks at certain of the national questions of today, complex questions where national, colonial, religious, and ethnic aspects combine and interlace—for example, the Arab-Israeli conflict or the struggle between Catholics and Protestants in Northern Ireland—one can see that there are two contrary temptations that haunt the revolutionary left. The first temptation is to deny the legitimacy of the national movement of Palestinians or of Catholics in Ulster: to condemn these movements as "petty-bourgeois" and divisive of the working class, and to proclaim abstractly against them the principle of the necessary unity between proletarians of all nationalities, races, or religions. The second temptation is to espouse uncritically the nationalist ideology of these movements and condemn the dominant nations (Israeli Jews or Northern Irish Protestants) en bloc, without distinction of class, as "reactionary nations"—nations to which the right of self-determination is denied.

The task facing revolutionary Marxists is to avoid these twin reefs and discover—through a concrete analysis of each concrete situation—an authentically internationalist course, which draws its inspiration from the nationalities policy of the Comintern when it was led by Lenin and Trotsky (1919–23) and from the famous resolution of the Second International's 1896 Congress whose rare privilege it was to be approved by both Lenin and Luxemburg: "The Congress proclaims the füll right to self-determination of all nations; and it expresses its sympathy to the workers of all countries at present suffering beneath the yoke of military, national or any other kind of absolutism; the Congress calls on the workers of these countries to join the ranks of the conscious workers of the whole world, in order to struggle beside them to defeat international capitalism and attain the goals of international social democracy."

Notes

1. Karl Marx, *The German Ideology* (Moscow, 1964), p. 76. Cf. Friedrich Engels, "Das Fest der Nationen in London," 1846, in Karl Marx, Friedrich Engels, and Ferdinand Lassalle, *Aus dem literarische Nachlass*, vol. 2 (Stuttgart, 1902), p. 408: "The dreams of European Republic, of a lasting peace under political organization, have become as grotesque as phrases about the unity of nations under the aegis of universal freedom of commerce. . . . In each country the bourgeoisie has its own particular interests and cannot transcend nationality. . . . But in every country the proletariat has a sole and common interest, a sole and common enemy, a sole and common struggle. Only the proletariat can abolish nationality, only the vigilant proletariat can make the brotherhood of nations possible. . . ."
2. See on this question the remarkable essay by the Ukrainian Marxist, Roman Rosdolsky, "Friedrich Engels und das Problem der 'geschichtlosen Völker,'" *Archiv für Sozialgeschichte* 4 (1964). This exists in English as *Engels and the "Nonhistoric Peoples": The National Question in the Revolution of 1848*, translated, edited with an introduction by John-Paul Hinka—a special issue of the Glasgow-based magazine *Critique*, 18–19 (1987).
3. Friedrich Engels, "The Magyar Struggle," in Karl Marx, *The Revolutions of 1848* (London, 1973), pp. 221–22.
4. Friedrich Engels, "Deutschland und der Panslawismus," (*Neue Oder-Zeitung*, 1855), in Marx and Engels, *Werke*, vol. II (Berlin), cited in Rosdolsky, "Friedrich Engels," p. 174.
5. Friedrich Engels, "What is to Become of Turkey in Europe?" (*New York Daily Tribune*, 1853), in Marx and Engels, *Werke*, vol. 9, cited in Rosdolsky, "Friedrich Engels," p. 174.
6. Friedrich Engels, "What Have the Working Classes to Do with Poland?," in Karl Marx, *The First International and After* (London, 1974), pp. 378–88.
7. Friedrich Engels, "Anfang des Endes in Österreich" (1847), in Marx and Engels, *Werke*, vol. 4, p. 510.
8. Friedrich Engels, "The Magyar Struggle," p. 219.

9. Rosa Luxemburg, "La questione polacca al congresso internazionale di Londra," *Critica Sociale* 14 (July 16, 1896), pp. 217–20.
10. Rosa Luxemburg, *Die industrielle Entwicklung Polens* (Leipzig, 1898).
11. V. I. Lenin, *Collected Works*, vol. 3 (Moscow, 1972).
12. Rosa Luxemburg, "Nationalität und Autonomie," 1908, in *Internationalismus und Klassenkampf* (Neuwied, 1971), pp. 236, 239.
13. Rosa Luxemburg, "The Junius Pamphlet," in *Rosa Luxemburg Speaks*, ed. Mary-Alice Waters (New York, 1970), p. 304.
14. Rosa Luxemburg, "Theses on the Tasks of International Social Democracy," in Waters, *Rosa Luxemburg Speaks*, p. 329.
15. Rosa Luxemburg, "Sozial-patriotische Programakrobatik," in *Internationalismus and Klassenkampf*.
16. Cf. Georg Lukács, "Critical Observations on Rosa Luxemburg's 'Critique of the Russian Revolution,'" in *History and Class Consciousness* (London, 1971), pp. 272–95.
17. Cf. Lenin, "On the Right of Nations to Self-Determination," in *Collected Works*, vol. 20, p. 430: "It is quite understandable that in their zeal (sometimes a little excessive, perhaps) to combat the nationalistically blinded petty bourgeoisie of Poland the Polish Social Democrats should overdo things."
18. Rosa Luxemburg, "Vorwort zu dem Sammelband 'Die polnische Frage und die sozialistische Bewegung,'" in *Internationalismus und Klassenkampf*.
19. Leon Trotsky, *The Bolsheviki and World Peace* (New York, 1918), pp. 21, 230–31, etc.
20. *Nashe Slovo* 130, 135 (July 3 and 9, 1915), reprinted in Russian in Trotsky's *Collected Works*, vol. 9, 1927.
21. Cf. Leon Trotsky, *History of the Russian Revolution*, vol. 3 (London, 1967), p. 62: "Whatever may be the further destiny of the Soviet Union . . . the national policy of Lenin will find its place among the eternal treasures of mankind."
22. Anton Pannekoek, *Klassenkampf und Nation* (Reichenberg, 1912); Josef Strasser, *Der Arbeiter und die Nation* (Reichenberg, 1912).
23. Karl Renner, *Marxismus, Krieg, und Internationale* (Stuttgart, 1917), p. 26.
24. Cf. Arduino Agnelli, *Questione nazionale e socialismo: K. Renner e O. Bauer* (Bologna, 1969), p. 109.
25. Otto Bauer, *Die Nationalitätenfrage und die Sozialdemokratie* (Vienna, 1924), p. 404.
26. Ibid., pp. 105–8.
27. Ibid., pp. 239–72. It should be added that Bauer's program of cultural autonomy had some value as a *complement*—not an alternative—to a policy based on recognition of the right to self-determination. Indeed, the first constitution of the Soviet Union in a sense incorporated the principle of cultural autonomy of national minorities.
28. Joseph Stalin, "Marxism and the National Question," in *Works*, vol. 2 (Moscow, 1953), pp. 300–381.
29. Lenin, *Collected Works*, vol. 35, p. 84.
30. Cf. Leon Trotsky, *Stalin*, vol. 1 (London, 1969), p. 233.
31. V. I. Lenin, "The Right of Nations to Self-Determination," in *Collected Works*, vol. 20, p. 398.
32. Stalin, *Works*, vol. 2, pp. 305, 306–7, 339.
33. V. I. Lenin, "The National Programme of the RSDLP," in *Collected Works*,

vol. 19, p. 543, and "Critical Remarks on the National Question," in *Collected Works*, vol. 20, pp. 39, 50.

34. On this question, Lenin's analysis of the 1916 Rising in Ireland is a model of revolutionary realism: see "The Discussion of Self-Determination Summed Up," in *Collected Works*, vol. 22, pp. 353–58.
35. V. I. Lenin, "The Socialist Revolution and the Right of Nations to Self-Determination," in *Collected Works*, vol. 22, p. 145.
36. V. I. Lenin, "The Discussion on Self-Determination Summed Up," p. 344. (Translation modified.)
37. As A. S. Naïr and C. Scalabrino stressed in their excellent article, "La question nationale dans la théorie marxiste révolutionnaire," *Partisans* 59–60 (May–August 1971).
38. Cf. Trotsky on the blacks in the United States: "An abstract criterion is not decisive in this case: much more decisive are historical consciousness, feelings and emotions" (*Trotsky on Black Nationalism and Self-Determination* [New York, 1967], p. 16).
39. Quoted in A. Schlesinger, Jr., *The Bitter Heritage* (Boston, 1967), p. 108.
40. Heinrich von Treitschke, *Politics*, vol. 2 (London, 1916), p. 614.

6

From the "Logic" of Hegel to the Finland Station in Petrograd

A man who talks that kind of stupidity is not dangerous.
—Stankevich, a Socialist; April 1917

That is raving, the ravings of a lunatic!
—Bogdanov, a Menshevik; April 1917

They're mad dreams . . .
—Plekhanov, a Menshevik; April 1917.

For many years the place of Bakunin in the Russian Revolution has remained vacant; now it is occupied by Lenin.
—Goldenberg, an ex-Bolshevik; April 1917

On that day (April 4) Comrade Lenin could not find open sympathizers even in our own ranks.
—Zalezshki, a Bolshevik; April 1917

As for the general scheme of Lenin, it seems to us unacceptable in that it starts from the assumption that the bourgeois democratic revolution is ended and counts upon an immediate transformation of this revolution into a socialist revolution.
—Kamenev, in an editorial in *Pravda*, organ of the Bolshevik party, April 8, 1917

Such was the unanimous reception accorded by the official representatives of Russian Marxism to the heretical theses that Lenin had presented first to the crowd massed in the forecourt of the Finland Station in Petrograd from the top of an armored car and then, on the morrow, to the Bolshevik and Menshevik delegates of the Soviet: the "April Theses." In his celebrated memoirs, Sukhanov (a Menshevik, later to become a Soviet functionary) testifies that Lenin's central political formula—All power to the Soviets—

"echoed like a thunderclap from a clear blue sky" and "stunned and confused even the most faithful of his disciples." According to Sukhanov, one leading Bolshevik had even declared that "the speech (of Lenin) had not sharpened the differences within the social democracy but had, on the contrary, suppressed them because there could be only agreement between the Bolsheviks and Mensheviks in face of Lenin's position!"[1] The *Pravda* editorial of April 8 confirmed at the time that impression of anti-Lenin unanimity; according to Sukhanov, "it seemed that the Marxist rank and file of the Bolshevik party stood firm and unshakable, that the mass of the party was in revolt against Lenin to defend the elementary principles of the scientific socialism of the past; alas, we were mistaken!"[2]

How are we to explain the extraordinary storm that Lenin's words raised, and this chorus of general condemnation that came down on them? Sukhanov's simple but revealing description suggests the reply: Lenin had done just that—he had *broken with* the "scientific socialism of the past," with a particular way of understanding the "elementary principles" of Marxism, a way which was, to some extent, common to all currents of Marxist social democracy in Russia. The perplexity, the confusion, the indignation, or the scorn with which the "April Theses" were received at one and the same time by Menshevik and Bolshevik leaders are only the symptoms of the radical break they imply with the Second International's tradition of "orthodox Marxism" (we refer to that of the ruling current and not to that of the radical left: Rosa Luxemburg, etc.), a tradition for which materialism (mechanical, deterministic, evolutionary) was crystallized into a rigid and paralyzing political syllogism:

> Russia is a backward barbarous, semi-feudal country.
> It is not ripe for socialism.
> The Russian Revolution is a bourgeois revolution.—Q.E.D.

Rarely has a turn in theory been richer in historic consequences than that inaugurated by Lenin in his speech at the Finland Station in Petrograd. What were the *methodological sources* of that turn? What were the *differentia specifica* in method compared with the canons of the Marxist orthodoxy of the past?

Here is Lenin's own reply, written in a polemic directed *precisely against Sukhanov*, in January 1923: "Everyone calls himself a Marxist understanding Marxism in the most pedantic way possible. They haven't at all understood the essential of Marxism, namely, its revolutionary dialectic."[3] *Its revolutionary dialectic*: here, in a nutshell, is the precise point of Lenin's *break* with the Marxism of the Second International and to some extent with *his own "past" philosophical consciousness*. Beginning on the morrow of the First World War, the break was nourished by a return to the Hegelian sources of

Marxist dialectics, coming to a head in the monumental, "mad," "raving" challenge of the night of April 3, 1917.

I. "Old Bolshevism" or "Past Marxism": Lenin Pre-1914

One of the chief sources of Lenin's political thinking pre-1914 had been Marx's *The Holy Family* (1844), which he had read and summarized in a notebook in 1895. He had been particularly interested by the chapter headed "Critical Battle against French Materialism," which he described as "one of the most valuable in the book."[4] Now, this chapter constitutes the *only* writing of Marx in which he "clings," in *noncritical* fashion, to the French materialism of the eighteenth century, which he presents as the "logical basis" for communism. The quotations drawn from this chapter of *The Holy Family* provide one of those shibboleths that make possible the identification of "metaphysical" materialism in a Marxist current.

On the other hand, it is a clear and well-known fact that Lenin was, at that time, greatly influenced *in philosophical outlook* by Plekhanov. While being *politically* more flexible and radical than his master who, after the 1903 break, became the principal theoretician of Menshevism, Lenin accepted certain fundamental ideological premises of Plekhanov's "pre-dialectical" Marxism and his strategic corollary: the *bourgeois* nature of the Russian Revolution. With this "common basis" it is not difficult to understand how, despite his severe and intransigent criticism of the "tailism" of the Mensheviks in regard to the liberal bourgeoisie, he had been able to accept, from 1905 to 1910, several attempts at reunification of the two fractions of the Russian social democracy. Moreover, it was at the moment of his closest political rapprochement with Plekhanov (against liquidationism, 1908–1909) that he wrote *Materialism and Empirio-Criticism*, a work in which the philosophical influence of the "father of Russian Marxism" can be seen and read.

What is remarkable and altogether characteristic of Lenin pre-1914 is that the Marxist authority he often referred to in his polemic against Plekhanov was none other than . . . Karl Kautsky. For example: he finds in an article by Kautsky on the Russian Revolution (1906) "a direct blow aimed at Plekhanov," and he underlines enthusiastically the coincidence of the Kautskyist and Bolshevik analyses: "The bourgeois revolution, carried through by the proletariat and the peasantry despite the instability of the bourgeoisie, is an essential thesis of Bolshevik tactics entirely confirmed by Kautsky."[5]

A close analysis of Lenin's main political text of this period, *Two Tactics of the Social Democracy in the Democratic Revolution* (1905), reveals with extraordinary clarity the *tension* in Lenin's mind between his rich, revolutionary realism and the limitations imposed on him by the straitjacket of what was called "orthodox" Marxism. On the one hand, we find in it illuminating and penetrating analyses of the incapacity of the Russian bourgeoisie to lead successfully a democratic revolution, which can be carried out only by a worker-peasant alliance exercising its revolutionary dictatorship; he even speaks of the *leading role* of the proletariat in this alliance and, at times, seems to put his finger on the idea of an uninterrupted transition towards socialism: this dictatorship "will be unable (without a series of intermediary stages of revolutionary development) to affect the foundations of capitalism."[6] With this little parenthesis, Lenin opens a window on the unknown country of the socialist revolution, only to close it immediately to return to the closed area circumscribed by the limits of orthodoxy. These limits we find in numerous formulae in *Two Tactics*, where Lenin categorically reaffirms the bourgeois nature of the Russian Revolution and condemns "the idea of seeking salvation for the working class in anything save the further development of capitalism is *reactionary*."[7]

The main argument he offers to develop this thesis is the "classic" theme of "pre-dialectical" Marxism: Russia is not ripe for socialist revolution: "The degree of Russia's economic development (an objective condition) and the degree of class-consciousness and organization of the broad masses of the proletariat (a subjective condition, inseparably bound up with the objective condition) make immediate and complete emancipation of the working class impossible. Only the most ignorant people can close their eyes to the bourgeois nature of the democratic revolution which is now taking place."[8] The objective determines the subjective; the economy is the condition of consciousness; here, in two phrases are the Moses and the Ten Commandments of the materialist gospel of the Second International which weighed upon Lenin's rich, political intuition.

The formula that was the quintessence of prewar Bolshevism—"old Bolshevism"—reflects within itself all the ambiguities of the first Leninism: "the revolutionary dictatorship of the proletariat and the peasantry." Lenin's profoundly revolutionary innovation (which marks it off radically from the Menshevik strategy) is expressed in the flexible and realistic formula of *worker and peasant power*, a formula of "algebraic" character (as Trotsky put it) where the specific weight of each class is not determined a priori. On the other hand, the apparently paradoxical term "*democratic dictatorship*" is the shibboleth of orthodoxy, the visible presence of the limitations imposed by "past" Marxism: the revolution is only democratic, that is, *bourgeois*, a premise which, as Lenin wrote in a revealing passage, "flows necessarily from the whole of Marxist philosophy"—that is to say, Marxist philosophy as conceived by Kautsky, Plekhanov, and the other ideologists of what it was agreed to call at the time "revolutionary social democracy."[9]

Another theme in *Two Tactics* which testifies to the methodological obstacle created by the *analytical* nature of that Marxism is the explicit and formal rejection of the Paris Commune as a model for the Russian Revolution. According to Lenin, the Commune went wrong because it was "unable [to] distinguish between the elements of a democratic revolution and a socialist revolution," because it "confused the tasks of fighting for a republic with those of fighting for socialism. . . . Consequently, it was a government such as *ours* (the future provisional revolutionary government—M.L.) should not be."[10] We shall see later that this is precisely one of the nodal points around which Lenin was to undertake, in April 1917, the heartbreaking revision of "old Bolshevism."

II. The 1914 "Break"

"It's a fabrication of the German High Command," declared Lenin when they showed him the copy of *Vorwaerts* (the organ of the German social democracy) with the news of the socialist vote for the war credits, on August 4, 1914. This famous story (like his stubborn refusal to believe that Plekhanov had supported the "national defence" of tsarist Russia) illustrates at one and the same time the illusions Lenin held about "Marxist" social democracy, his astonishment when confronted with the failure of the Second International, and the abyss that was opening between himself and the "ex-orthodox" who had become social-patriots.

The catastrophe of August 4 was, for Lenin, striking evidence that something was rotten in the state of Denmark of official "orthodox" Marxism. The political bankruptcy of that orthodoxy led him, therefore, to a profound revision of the philosophical premises of the Kautsky-Plekhanov Marxism. "The failure of the Second International in the first days of the war incited Lenin to reflect on the theoretical foundations of so great a betrayal."[11] It will be necessary one day to retrace the precise track that led Lenin from the trauma of August 1914 to the *Logic* of Hegel, scarcely a month after. The simple desire to return to the sources of Marxist thought? Or a clear intuition that the methodological Achilles' heel of the Marxism of the Second International was the noncomprehension of the dialectic?

Whatever the reason, there is no doubt that his vision of the Marxist dialectic was profoundly changed by it. Evidence of this is the text itself of the *Philosophical Notebooks*, and also the letter he sent on January 4, 1915, shortly after having finished reading *The Science of Logic* (December 17, 1914), to the editorial secretary of Granat Publishers to ask if "there was still time to make some corrections (to his *Karl Marx*) in the section of dialectics."[12] And it was by no means a "passing enthusiasm" as, seven years later, in one of his last writings, *On the Significance of Militant Marxism* (1922), he called on "the editors and contributors" of the party's theoretical journal (*Under the Banner of Marxism*) to "be a kind of Society of Materialist Friends of Hegelian Dialectics." He insists on the need for a "systematic study of Hegelian Dialectics from a materialist standpoint," and proposes even to "print in the journal excerpts from Hegel's principal works, interpret them materialistically and comment on them with the help of examples of the way Marx applied dialectics."[13]

What were the tendencies (or at least, the attempts) in the Marxism of the Second International which gave it its predialectic character?

1. Primarily, the tendency to efface the distinction between Marx's dialectical materialism and the "ancient," "vulgar," "metaphysical" materialism of Helvetius, Feuerbach, etc. Plekhanov, for example, could write these astonishing lines: "In Marx's *Theses on Feuerbach* . . . none of the fundamental ideas of Feuerbach's philosophy are refuted; they merely amend them . . . the materialist views of Marx and Engels have been elaborated in the direction indicated by the inner logic of Feuerbach's philosophy!" What is more, Plekhanov criticized Feuerbach and the French materialists of the eighteenth century for having too . . . *idealist* an outlook in the domain of history.[14]

2. The tendency that flows from the first, to reduce historical materialism to mechanical economic determinism in which the "objective" is always the cause of the "subjective." For example, Kautsky untiringly insists on the idea that "the domination of the proletariat and the social revolution cannot come about before the preliminary conditions, as much economic as psychological, of a socialist society are sufficiently realised." What are these "psychological conditions"? According to Kautsky, "intelligence, discipline and an organisational talent." How will these conditions be created? "It is the historical task of capitalism" to realize them. The moral of history: "It is only where the capitalist system of production has attained a high degree of development that economic conditions permit the transformation, by the power of the people, of capitalist property in the means of production into social ownership."[15]

3. The attempt to reduce the dialectic to Darwinian evolution, where the different stages of human history (slavery, feudalism, capitalism, socialism) follow a sequence rigorously determined by the "laws of history." Kautsky, for example, defines Marxism as "the scientific study of the evolution of the social organism."[16] Kautsky had, in fact, been a Darwinian before becoming a Marxist, and it is not without reason that his disciple Brill defined his method as "bio-historico-materialism. . . ."

4. An abstract and naturalistic conception of the "laws of history," strikingly illustrated by the marvelous pronouncement of Plekhanov when he heard the news of the October Revolution: "But it's a violation of all the laws of history!"

5. A tendency to relapse into the *analytical* method, grasping only "distinct and separate" objects, fixed in their differences: Russia—Germany; bourgeois revolution—socialist revolution; party—masses; minimum program—maximum program, etc.

It is clearly understood that Kautsky and Plekhanov had carefully read and studied Hegel; but they had not, so to speak, "absorbed" and "digested" him into their preceding systems of evolutionism and historical determinism.

How far did Lenin's notes on (or about) Hegel's *Logic* constitute a challenge to predialectical Marxism?

1. Primarily, Lenin insists on the philosophical abyss separating "stupid," that is, "metaphysical, undeveloped, dead, crude," materialism from Marxist materialism, which, on the contrary, is nearer to "intelligent," that is, dialectical, idealism. Consequently, he criticizes Plekhanov severely for having written nothing on Hegel's great *Logic*, "that is to say, *basically* on the dialectic as philosophical knowledge," and for having criticized Kant from the standpoint of vulgar materialism rather than in the manner of Hegel.[17]

2. He acquires for himself a dialectical understanding of causality: "Cause and effect, *ergo*, are merely moments of universal reciprocal dependence, of (universal) connection, of the reciprocal connection of events. . . ." At the same time, he approves the dialectical process by which Hegel dissolves the "opposition of solid and abstract" of subjective and objective and destroys their one-sidedness.[18]

3. He underlines the major difference between the vulgar evolutionist conception and the dialectical conception of development: "the first, [development as decrease and increase, as repetition] is lifeless, pale and dry; the second [development as a unity of opposites] alone furnishes the key to the 'leaps,' to the 'break in continuity,' to the 'transformation into the opposite,' to the destruction of the old and emergence of the new."[19]

4. With Hegel, he struggles "against making the concept of *law* absolute, against simplifying it, against making a fetish of it" (and adds: "NB for modern physics!!!"). He writes likewise that "laws, all laws, are narrow, incomplete, approximate."[20]

5. He sees in the category of sum total, in the development of the entire ensemble of the moments of reality, the essence of dialectical cognition.[21] We can see the use Lenin made immediately of this methodological principle in the pamphlet he wrote at the time, *The Collapse of the Second*

International; he submits to severe criticism the apologists of "national defence"—who attempt to deny the imperialist character of the Great War because of the "national factor" of the war of the Serbs against Austria—by underlining that Marx's dialectic "correctly excludes any isolated examination of an object, i.e., one that is one-sided and monstrously distorted."[22] This is of capital importance since, as Lukács says, the reign of the dialectical category of sum total brings the revolutionary principle into science.

The isolation, fixation, separation, and abstract opposition of different moments of reality are dissolved in part through the category of sum total, in part by the statement of Lenin's that "the dialectic is the theory which shows . . . why human understanding should not take contraries as dead and petrified but as living, conditioned, mobile, interpenetrating each other."[23]

Obviously, what interests us here is less the study of the philosophical content of the *Notebooks* "in themselves" than their *political consequences*. It is not difficult to find the red thread leading from the category of sum total to the theory of the weakest link in the imperialist chain; from the interpenetration of opposites to the transformation of the democratic revolution into the socialist revolution; from the dialectical conception of causality to the refusal to define the character of the Russian Revolution solely by Russia's "economically backward base"; from the critique of vulgar evolutionism to the "break in continuity" in 1917; and so on, and so on. But what is most important is quite simply that the critical reading, the materialist reading of Hegel had *freed* Lenin from the straitjacket of the pseudo-orthodox Marxism of the Second International, from the *theoretical limitation* it imposed on his thinking. The study of Hegelian logic was the instrument by means of which Lenin cleared the theoretical road leading to the Finland Station in Petrograd. In March–April 1917, freed from the obstacle represented by predialectical Marxism, Lenin could, *under the pressure of events*, rid himself in good time of its *political corollary*: the abstract and rigid principle according to which "The Russian revolution could only be bourgeois—that Russia was not economically ripe for a socialist revolution." Once he crossed the Rubicon, he applied himself to studying the problem from a *practical, concrete, and realistic* angle: what are the measures, constituting *in fact* the transition towards socialism, that could be made acceptable to the majority of the people, that is, the masses of the workers and *peasants*?

III. THE APRIL THESES OF 1917

The truth is, the "April Theses" were born in March, more exactly, between March 11 and 26, that is, between the third and fifth "Letters from Afar." Close analysis of these two documents (which, by the way, were not published in 1917) allows us to grasp the very movement of Lenin's thought. To the main question: Can the Russian Revolution take transitional measures towards socialism? Lenin replies in two ways: in the first (Letter 3) he questions the traditional answer; in the second letter (Letter 5) he gives a new reply.

Letter 3 in itself contains two juxtaposed moments in unresolved contradiction. Lenin describes certain concrete measures in the sphere of control of production and distribution that he considers indispensable for the advance of the revolution. He first underlines that these measures *are not yet* socialism, or the dictatorship of the proletariat; they do not go beyond the limits of the "revolutionary democratic dictatorship of the proletariat and the peasantry." But he immediately adds this paradoxical short passage that clearly suggests a doubt about what he has just said, that is, an explicit questioning to the "classical" theses: "It is not a matter of finding a theoretical classification. We would be committing a great mistake if we attempted to force the complex, urgent, rapidly developing practical tasks of the revolution into the Procrustean bed of cut and dried theory. . . ."[24]

Fifteen days later, in the fifth letter, the abyss has been crossed, the political break consummated: "In their entirety and in their development, these steps [control of production and distribution, etc.] will mark the transition to socialism, which cannot be achieved in Russia directly, at one stroke, without transitional measures, but is quite achievable and urgently necessary as a result of such transitional measures."[25] Lenin no longer refuses to make a "theoretical classification" of these measures and defines them not as "democratic" but as transitional to *socialism*.

Meanwhile, the Bolsheviks in Petrograd remained loyal to the old schema (they were trying to lay the Russian Revolution, that unmanageable, unconquered, and liberated maid, in the Procrustean bed of a petrified theory . . .) and were sitting tight in prudent silence. *Pravda* of March 15 even gave conditional support to the Provisional (Cadet!) Government "to the extent that it fights the reaction and counter-revolution"; according to the frank statement of the Bolshevik leader Shliapnikov, in March 1917, "we agreed with the Mensheviks that we were passing through the period of the breakdown of feudal relations, and that in their place would appear all kinds of 'freedoms' proper to bourgeois regimes."[26]

One can understand, then, their surprise when the first words Lenin addressed at the Finland Station in Petrograd to the crowds of workers, soldiers, and sailors, were a call to *struggle for the socialist revolution*.[27]

On the evening of April 3, and the next day, he revealed the "April Theses," which produced, according to the Bolshevik Zalezshky, a member of the Petrograd Committee, *the effect of an exploding bomb*. Moreover, on April 8, this same Petrograd Committee *rejected Lenin's theses by thirteen votes to two, with one abstention.*[28] And it must be said that the "April Theses" were to some extent a *retreat* from the conclusions already reached in the fifth of the "Letters from Afar"; they do not speak explicitly of the transition to socialism. It seems that Lenin, in the face of the astonishment and perplexity of his comrades, was forced to moderate his words somewhat. In fact, the "April Theses" do speak of the *transition* between the first stage of the revolution and the second "which must give the power to the proletariat and the layers of the poor peasants," but that is not necessarily in contradiction with the traditional formula of the old Bolshevism (except for the mention of the "layers of the poor peasants" instead of the peasantry as a whole, which is clearly very significant) since the *content* of the tasks of this power (democratic only or already socialist?) is not defined. Lenin even underlines that "It is not our immediate task to introduce socialism, but only to bring social production and the distribution of products at once under the *control* of the Soviets of Workers Deputies"—a flexible formula where the character of the content of this "control" is not defined.[29] The only theme which, at least implicitly, is a revision of the former Bolshevik conception is that of the *State-Commune* as a model for the Republic of Soviets, and for two reasons:

1. Traditionally, the Commune had been defined, in Marxist literature, as the first attempt at *the dictatorship of the proletariat.*

2. Lenin himself had characterized the Commune as a workers' government that had wished to carry through *simultaneously a democratic and a socialist revolution.* That was why Lenin, prisoner of "past Marxism," had criticized it in 1905. For the same reason, Lenin, the revolutionary dialectician, *took it as a model* in 1917. The historian E. H. Carr is, therefore, correct in underlining that Lenin's first articles after his arrival in Petrograd "implied the transition to socialism, though it stopped short of explicitly proclaiming it."[30] Explication was to be made during the month of April, in proportion as Lenin won the rank and file of the Bolshevik party to his political line. It was made especially around two axes: the revision of "old Bolshevism" and the perspective of the transition to socialism. The major text on this subject is a small pamphlet—not well known—*Letters on Tactics,* composed between April 8 and 13, probably under the pressure of the anti-Lenin *Pravda* editorial of April 8. There we find the key phrase that summarizes the historic turn Lenin made and his definitive, explicit, and radical break with what had become outlived in the "past Bolshevism": "Whoever, *to-day,* speaks only of the revolutionary democratic dictatorship of the proletariat and the peasantry is behind the times, has, by this fact, *gone over,* in practice, to the petty bourgeoisie, and deserves to be relegated to the museum of pre-revolutionary 'Bolshevik' curiosities—to the museum of the 'old Bolsheviks,' one could say."[31] In this same pamphlet, while

defending himself against wishing to introduce socialism "immediately," Lenin declares that the Soviet power would take steps "to march towards socialism." For example, "control of the banks, the fusion of all banks into one is *not yet* socialism, but is a *step* towards socialism."[32]

In an article published on April 23, Lenin defined in the following terms what distinguished the Bolsheviks from the Mensheviks: while the latter "are for socialism, but think it would be premature to think about it and to take as of now practical measures to bring it about," the former think the "Soviets should take immediately all the measures realisable in practice to bring about the triumph of socialism."[33]

What does "measures realisable in practice" mean? For Lenin, it means especially *the measures that can receive the support of the majority* of the population. That is, not only of the workers but also of the peasant masses. Lenin, freed from the theoretical limitation imposed by the predialectical schema—"the going-over to socialism is objectively unrealisable"—is now occupied with real, political-social conditions to ensure "steps towards socialism." So, in his speech to the Eighth Congress of the Bolshevik Party (April 24–29), he poses the problem in a realistic and concrete way: "We must speak of actions and practical steps. . . . We cannot be partisans of the 'introduction' of socialism. The majority of the population in Russia consists of peasants, small-landowners who can in no way want socialism. But what objection could they make to the establishment in each village of a bank which would allow them to improve their holdings? They can say nothing against that. We must recommend these measures throughout the country and strengthen in them the consciousness of that need."[34] The "introduction" of socialism, in this context, means the immediate imposition of socialism "from above," against the will of the majority of the population. Lenin, on the contrary, proposes getting the support of the peasant masses for certain concrete measures, of an objectively socialist character, taken by the Soviet power (with workers' leadership). To within a few degrees, this conception is astonishingly like that defended by Trotsky since 1905: "the dictatorship of the proletariat supported by the peasantry" that effects the *uninterrupted* going over from the democratic revolution to the socialist. So, it is not by chance that Lenin was regarded as a "Trotskyist" by the "old Bolshevik" Kamenev in April 1917. . . .[35]

Conclusion

There is no doubt that the "April Theses" represent a "break" in theory and policy with the prewar tradition of Bolshevism. That said, it is none the less true that, to the extent that Lenin had, since 1905, preached the revolutionary alliance of the proletariat and the peasantry (and the radical deepening of the revolution *without* or even *against* the liberal bourgeoisie), the "new Bolshevism," born in April 1917, is the true heir and legitimate child of the "old Bolshevism."

On the other hand, if it is undeniable that the *Notebooks* constitute a philosophical break with the "first Leninism," it must be recognized that the methods *in action* in the political writings of pre-1914 Lenin were much more "dialectical" than those of Plekhanov or Kautsky.

Finally, and to avoid any possible misunderstandings, we in no way wish to suggest that Lenin "deduced" the "April Theses" from Hegel's *Logic*. . . . The theses are the product of revolutionary, realistic thinking in the face of a new situation: the world war, the objectively revolutionary situation it created in Europe, the February revolution, the rapid defeat of tsarism, the massive appearance of the Soviets. They are the result of what constitutes the very essence of the Leninist method: *concrete analysis of a concrete situation*. The critical reading of Hegel helped Lenin to free himself from an abstract, cut-and-dried theory that was *an obstacle to this concrete analysis*: the predialectical pseudo-orthodoxy of the Second International. It is in this sense and in this sense only that we can speak of the theoretical journey that led Lenin from the study of the *Great Logic* in the library at Berne, in September 1914, to the challenging speech that "shook the world," launched for the first time on the night of April 3, 1917, in the Finland Station in Petrograd.

Notes

1. Nikolai N. Sukhanov, *The Russian Revolution of 1917* (Paris: Stock, 1965), chap. 1. (Fr. pp. 139, 140, 142.)
2. Ibid., p. 143.
3. V. I. Lenin, *On Our Revolution* (On the Memoirs of N. Sukhanov). (Fr. *Œuvres*, vol. 23, p. 489.)
4. V. I. Lenin, *Philosophical Notebooks*, in *Collected Works* (hereafter *CW*), vol. 38, p. 41.
5. V. I. Lenin, *Selected Works*, vol. 2 (Moscow, 1970). (Fr. *Œuvres*, vol. 11, pp. 432, 433.)
6. V. I. Lenin, *Two Tactics of the Social Democracy*, in *CW*, vol. 9, p. 56.
7. Ibid., p. 49. Cf. also p. 48: "Marxists are absolutely convinced of the bourgeois character of the Russian revolution. What does that mean? It means that the democratic reforms in the political system, and the social and economic reforms that have become a necessity for Russia, do not in themselves imply the undermining of capitalism, the undermining of bourgeois rule; on the contrary, they will, for the first time, really clear the ground for a wide and rapid, European, and not Asiatic, development of capitalism; they will, for the first time, make it possible for the bourgeoisie to rule as a class."

8. Ibid., p. 28.
9. The only (or almost the only) exception to this iron rule was Trotsky, who was the first in *Results and Prospects* (1906) to go beyond the dogma of the bourgeois-democratic nature of the future Russian Revolution; he was, however, politically neutralized by his organizational conciliationism.
10. Lenin, *Two Tactics of the Social Democracy*, pp. 80–81.
11. R. Garaudy, *Lénine* (Paris: Presses Universitaires de France, 1969), p. 39.
12. Ibid., p. 40.
13. Lenin, *Selected Works*, vol. 3 (1970) pp. 672; (1967) pp. 667–68. This is very contemporary today when attempts are being made once more to write off old Hegel on Lenin's authority.
14. George V. Plekhanov, *Fundamental Problems of Marxism* (London: Martin Lawrence, n.d.), pp. 21–22: "Marx's theory of cognition is directly derived from Feuerbach's. If you like, we can even say that, strictly speaking, it is Feuerbach's theory . . . given a profounder meaning in a general way by Marx."
15. Karl Kautsky, *The Social Revolution* (Chicago: Charles H. Kerr, 1903), pp. 185–87. [The English translation is slightly different here.—Ed.]
16. *The Agrarian Question*. Plekhanov, on the other hand, had, at least in principle, criticized vulgar evolutionism, basing himself on Hegel's *Science of Logic*. Cf. *The Agrarian Question*, p. 27.
17. V. I. Lenin, *Philosophical Notebooks*, pp. 179, 276, 277.
18. Ibid., pp. 159, 187, 260.
19. Ibid., p. 360.
20. Ibid., p. 151.
21. Ibid., pp. 157–58. Cf. also pp. 171, 196, 218.
22. V. I. Lenin, *The Collapse of the Second International*, in *CW*, vol. 21, p. 235.
23. V. I. Lenin, *Karl Marx*, in *CW*, vol. 21, p. 23.
24. V. I. Lenin, "Letters from Afar," in *CW*, vol. 21, p. 33.
25. Ibid., p. 341.
26. Leon Trotsky, *The History of the Russian Revolution*, vol. 1 (New York: Simon and Schuster, 1936), chap. 15.
27. See F. Somilov, "Memoirs of Lenin," in *Lénine tel qu'il fut* (Moscow: Ed. Livre Etranger, 1958), p. 673. Cf. also the stenographic notes of Lenin's first speech taken by the Bolshevik Bonch-Bruevich at the railway station: "You must struggle for the socialist revolution, struggle to the end, till the complete victory of the proletariat. Long live the socialist revolution!" in G. Golikov, *La révolution d'Octobre* (Moscow: Ed. du Progres, 1966).
28. Leon Trotsky, *The History of the Russian Revolution*, vol. 1, chap. 14. Cf. E. H. Carr, *The Bolshevik Revolution*, vol. 1 (London: Macmillan), p. 77: "Nobody had yet contested the view that the Russian revolution was not, and could not be, other than a bourgeois revolution. This was the solid and accepted framework of doctrine into which policy had to fit. Yet it was difficult to discover within this framework any cogent reason to reject out of hand the Provisional Government, which was indubitably bourgeois, or at least a transfer of power to the Soviets, which were essentially proletarian, or—least of all—to denounce the quest for a "democratic" peace and preach civil war and national defeat. It was left to Lenin, before the eyes of his astonished followers, to smash the framework." Cf. also the testimony of the Bolshevik Olminsky, quoted by Trotsky in *The History of the Russian Revolution*, p. 335: "The coming revolution was to be only a bourgeois revolution. . . . That was an obligatory premise for

every member of the party, the official opinion of the party, its continual and unchanging slogan right up to the February revolution of 1917, and even some time after."

29. Lenin, *Selected Works*, vol. 2, p. 45.
30. E. H. Carr, *The Bolshevik Revolution*, p. 82.
31. Lenin, *Letters on Tactics*, in *CW*, vol. 24. (Fr. *Œuvres*, vol. 24, p. 35. Cf. also p. 41.) "Comrade Kamenev's formula, inspired with *old Bolshevism*: The democratic revolution is not yet completed, does it take into account this reality? No, this formula has grown old. It's no longer good for anything. It is dead. It is useless to try to revive it."
32. Ibid., (Fr. p. 44).
33. V. I. Lenin, *The Political Parties in Russia and the Tasks of the Proletariat* (Fr. *Œuvres*, vol. 24, p. 89).
34. Lenin, *The Political Parties in Russia*, p. 241.
35. Leon Trotsky, *The Permanent Revolution* (New York: Merit, 1969), chaps. 3, 4. It should not be forgotten, on the other hand, that for Lenin as much as for Trotsky, there was an "objective limit" for socialism in Russia, to the extent that a *completely socialist society*—abolition of classes, etc.—could not be established in an *isolated and backward* country.

7

Rosa Luxemburg's Conception of "Socialism or Barbarism"

Is socialism the inevitable and necessary product of economically determined historical development, or is it only a moral choice, an ideal of Justice and Liberty? This "dilemma of impotence" between the fatalism of pure laws and the ethic of pure intentions[1] arose within the German Social Democracy before 1914. It was transcended—in the dialectical sense: *Aufheben*—by Rosa Luxemburg, precisely through the expression, in the "Junius Pamphlet" of 1915, of the famous formulation "socialism or barbarism." In this sense, Paul Frölich was correct in writing that this brochure (whatever the errors and deficiencies criticized by Lenin) "is more than a historic document: it is the thread of Ariadne in the labyrinth of our times."[2] We will attempt to trace the *methodological* meaning of this phrase, a meaning which seems to us of *essential* importance for Marxist thought, but which has not always been sufficiently understood and evaluated.

For Bernstein, after his "revision" of Marxism in *The Premises of Socialism and the Tasks of Social Democracy* (1899), socialism no longer had an objective, material base in the contradictions of capitalism and in the class struggle. (In fact, the negation of these phenomena is exactly the central theme of his book.) He therefore sought another basis, which could only be *ethical*: the eternal moral principles, Right, Justice. It is in this sense that the concluding chapter of his book ("Kant without Cant") can be understood, where he opposes Kant to "materialism" and to the "scorn for the ideal" of official Social Democratic thought. These morals are quite evidently historical and above social classes. For Bernstein, in effect, "the sublime ethics of Kant" is "at the base of actions eternally and universally human"; to seek there the expression of something so coarse and vulgar as the class interests of the exalted bourgeoisie was in his opinion simply "folly."[3]

In *Reform or Revolution* (1899) Rosa Luxemburg replied to the "father of revisionism" with a passionate and rigorous demonstration of the profoundly contradictory character of capitalist development. Socialism proceeded from economic necessity and by no means from the "principle of justice, . . . the old war horse on which the reformers of the earth have rocked for ages."[4]

Yet, in the heat of the argument, Rosa didn't fully escape the temptation of "revolutionary fatalism": for example, insisting in the first section of the anti-Bernstein pamphlet that the anarchy of the capitalist system "leads *inevitably* to its ruin," that the collapse of the capitalist system is the *inevitable* result of its insurmountable contradictions, and that the class consciousness of the proletariat is only "the simple intellectual reflection of the growing contradictions of capitalism and of its *approaching* decline."[5] Most certainly, even in this document, which is her most "determinist" work, Rosa insists on the fact that the tactic of the Social Democracy in no way consisted of *waiting* for the development of the antagonisms, but of being "guided by the direction of this development, once it is ascertained, and inferring from this direction what consequences are necessary for the political struggle."[6] Yet the conscious intervention of the Social Democracy remains, in a certain sense, an "auxiliary" element, a "stimulant" to a process which is, in any case, objectively necessary and inevitable.

If "optimistic fatalism" is to Rosa Luxemburg in 1899 a temptation, for Karl Kautsky, on the contrary, it constitutes *the central axis of his entire worldview*. The thought of Kautsky is the product of a marvelously successful fusion between the illuminist metaphysic of progress, social-Darwinist evolutionism,[7] and pseudo "orthodox Marxist" determinism. This amalgam exercised a profound influence on German Social Democracy, making Kautsky the doctrinaire "Pope" of the party and of the Second International. This was not only due to the undeniable talent of its author, but also and especially to a certain historic conjuncture, at the end of the nineteenth and beginning of the twentieth centuries, a period in which the Social Democracy saw, with extraordinary regularity, an expansion of its adherents and its voting base.

Kautsky: Proletarian Revolution Is "Inevitable"

To Kautsky the problematic of revolutionary initiative tends to disappear, to the profit of the "bronze laws which determine the necessary transformation of society." In his most important book, *The Road to Power* (1909), he insists several times on the idea that the proletarian revolution is "irresistible" and "inevitable" and "as irresistible and inevitable as the unceasing development of capitalism," which leads to this amazing conclusion, in that remarkable and transparent phrase which sums up admirably his whole passive vision of history: "The socialist party is a revolutionary party, but not a revolution-making party. We know that it is just as little in our power to create this revolution as it is in the power of our opponents to prevent it. It is no part of our work to instigate a revolution or to prepare the way for it."[8]

It is especially beginning with the Russian Revolution of 1905 that Rosa Luxemburg began to differ politically with Kautsky and to criticize more and more the "rigid and fatalist" conception of Marxism which consists of "waiting with folded arms for the dialectic of history to bear us its ripe fruits."[9] From 1909 to 1913, her polemic with Kautsky on the mass strike crystallized the theoretical divergences latent within the orthodox Marxist current of the German Social Democracy. The principal object of Rosa's critique seemed to be the purely parliamentary character of the "strategy of attrition" extolled by Kautsky. But at a more profound level, it is the whole "passive radicalism" of Kautsky (in the words of Pannekoek), his pseudo-revolutionary fatalism, which is put into question by Rosa. Faced with this waiting-theory, of which the obstinate belief in the "inevitable" electoral-parliamentary victory was one of the political manifestations, Rosa developed her strategy of the mass strike founded on the principle of conscious intervention: "The task of Social Democracy and of its leaders is not to be dragged by events, but to be consciously ahead of them, to have an overall view of the trend of events and to shorten the period of development by conscious action, and to accelerate its progress."[10]

The Role of the Proletariat

Still, before 1914 the break with Kautsky and with "socialist fatalism" isn't complete. As the passage that we've cited shows, there was for Rosa *a* "course of evolution"; the only question is of "shortening" and "hastening" it. It was necessary for there to be the catastrophe of August 4, 1914, the shameful capitulation of the German Social Democracy to the Kaiser's war policy, the dislocation of the International, and the enrollment of the proletarian masses in that immense fractricidal massacre called "the First World War" in order to shake Rosa's deep-rooted conviction in the necessary and "irresistible" coming of socialism. It was to overcome this trauma that Rosa Luxemburg wrote, in 1915, in the "Junius Pamphlet," that remarkably *revolutionary* formula (in both the theoretical and political sense): "socialism or barbarism." That is to say: there is not *one* single "direction of development," one single "course of evolution," but several. And the role of the proletariat, led by its party, is not simply to "support" or to "shorten" or to "accelerate" the historical process, but to *decide* it:

> Man does not make history arbitrarily, but he makes history nevertheless. . . . The final victory of the socialist proletariat . . . will never be accomplished if the material conditions that have been built up by past development don't flash with the sparkling animation of the conscious will of the great popular masses. . . . Friedrich Engels once said: Capitalist society faces a dilemma, either an advance to socialism or a reversion to barbarism. . . . We stand today, as Friedrich Engels prophesied more than a generation ago, before the awful proposition: either the triumph of imperialism and the destruction of all culture, and, as in ancient Rome, depopulation, desolation, degeneration, a vast cemetery or, the victory of socialism, that is, the conscious struggle of the international proletariat against imperialism, against its methods, against war. This is the dilemma of world history, its inevitable choice, whose scales are trembling in the balance awaiting the decision of the proletariat.[11]

What is the origin in Marxist thought of the formula "socialism or barbarism"?

Marx, in the first sentence of the *Manifesto*, emphasizes that the class struggle has ended each time "either in a revolutionary reconstitution of society at large, or in the common ruin of the contending classes." It is probably this sentence that inspired Rosa Luxemburg when she spoke of the downfall of civilization in ancient Rome as preceding the return to barbarism. But there is not, to our knowledge, any indication in all the works of Marx that this alternative, which he presented in the *Manifesto* as the record of a past occurrence, might be for him valid also as a possibility for the future.

The Socialist Alternative

As for the phrase from Engels to which Rosa Luxemburg makes reference: it is evidently a passage from *Anti-Dühring* (published in 1877, which was almost forty years before Rosa was writing) that she attempted to reconstruct from memory (not having access in prison to her Marxist library). Here then is the text of Engels where for the first time the idea of socialism appears as an *alternative* in a great historic dilemma:

> . . . it is because both the productive forces created by the modern capitalist mode of production and also the system of distribution of goods established by it have come into burning contradiction with that mode of production itself, and in fact to such a degree that, *if the whole of modern society is not to perish*, a revolution of the mode of production and distribution must take place, a revolution which will put an end to all class divisions.[12]

The difference between the text of Rosa Luxemburg and that of Engels is evident: a) Engels poses the problem above all in economic terms, Rosa in political terms. b) Engels doesn't raise the question of the *social forces* that will be able to decide one solution or another: the whole text only sets the stage for forces and relations of production. Rosa on the other hand emphasizes that it is *the conscious intervention of the proletariat* which will be "tilting the balance" to one side or the other. c) One frankly has the impression that the choice posed by Engels is rather *rhetorical*, that it is more a question of demonstrating *ad absurdum* the necessity of socialism rather than a real choice between socialism and the "perishing of modern society."

It seems therefore that, in the last analysis, it was *Rosa Luxemburg herself* who (while inspired by Engels) had, for the first time, explicitly posed socialism as being not the "inevitable" product of historical necessity, but as an objective historical *possibility*. In this sense, the phrase "socialism or barbarism" means that, in history, *the dice aren't cast*: the "final victory" or the defeat of the proletariat is not decided in advance, by the "bronze laws" of economic determinism, but depends also on the conscious action, on the revolutionary will of the proletariat.

What is the meaning of "barbarism" in the Luxemburgian phrase? For Rosa, the world war itself was a sporadic form of the relapse into barbarism, the destruction of civilization. It is, to be sure, undeniable that for an entire generation, in Germany and in Europe, the forecast of Rosa revealed itself to be tragically correct: the failure of the *socialist* revolution in 1919 led in the final analysis to the triumph of Nazi *barbarism* and the Second World War.

Socialism: One Possibility

However, in our view, the methodologically essential element in the phrase of the "Junius Pamphlet" is not that barbarism is offered as the only alternative to socialism, but *the very principle of a historical choice*, the very principle of "open" history, in which socialism is one *possibility among others*. The important, theoretically *decisive* element in the formula is not the "barbarism" but the "*socialism or. . . .*"

Is it the case that Rosa Luxemburg reverted to Bernstein's position, to the abstract moralist conception of socialism as simply an ethical option, as a "pure" ideal whose sole foundation was the "will-o'-the-wisp" called "the Eternal Principles of Justice"? In reality, the position of Rosa in 1915 is distinguished from, or rather diametrically opposed to, that of neo-Kantian revisionism by two crucial aspects:

1. Socialism is not for Rosa the ideal of "absolute" humanism and above the classes, but that of a *class* morality, of a proletarian humanism, of an ethic situated *in the point of view of the revolutionary proletariat.*
2. Above all, socialism is for Rosa an *objective* possibility, that is to say,

founded on reality itself, on the internal contradictions of capitalism, on the crises, and on the antagonism of class interests. There are socio-economic conditions which determine, in the last instance, and in the long run, socialism as an objective possibility. It is these which mark *the limits of the scope of what is possible*: socialism is a real possibility at the end of the nineteenth century, but it was not in the sixteenth century, in the epoch of Thomas Münzer. Men make their own history, but they make it within the framework of the given conditions.

This category of objective possibility is eminently *dialectical*. Hegel employs it to criticize Kant (real possibility as opposed to formal possibility) and Marx utilizes it in his doctoral thesis in order to distinguish between the philosophy of nature of Democritus and Epicurus: "*Abstract possibility* . . . is the direct *antipode of real possibility*. The latter is restricted within sharp boundaries, as is the intellect; the former is unbounded, as is the imagination." Real possibility seeks to prove the reality of its object; for abstract possibility it is necessary simply that the object is conceivable.[13]

It is therefore because there are *objective* contradictions in the capitalist system and because it corresponds to the *objective* interests of the proletariat that socialism is a real possibility. It is the infrastructure, the concrete historical conditions, that determine which possibilities are real; but the choice between diverse objective possibilities depends on the consciousness, on the will, and on the action of human beings.

The Conscious Intervention of the Masses

Revolutionary practice, the subjective factor, the conscious intervention of the masses guided by their vanguard now gain a whole other status in the theoretical system of Rosa: it is no longer a question of a secondary element that is able to "support" or "accelerate" the "irresistible" march of society. It is no longer a question of the *rhythm* but of the *direction* of the historical process. The "sparkling animation of the conscious will" is no longer a simple "auxiliary" factor but that which has the final word, that which is *decisive.*[14]

It is only now, in 1915, that the thought of Rosa becomes truly *coherent.* If one accepts the Kautskyan premise of the inevitability of socialism, it is difficult to escape a "waiting" and passive political logic. To the extent that Rosa only justified her theses on revolutionary intervention by the need for "acceleration" of that which was in any case inevitable, it was easy for Kautsky to denounce her strategy as "rebellious impatience." The definitive methodological rupture between Rosa Luxemburg and Kautsky only produces itself in 1915, through the phrase "socialism or barbarism."[15]

WAR OR PROLETARIAN REVOLUTION

A similar theoretical evolution can be found in Lenin and Trotsky: under the traumatic impact of the failure of the Second International, Lenin broke not only on the political level but also on the methodological level with Kautsky (of whom he had until then considered himself a disciple). He discovered in 1914–15 the Hegelian dialectic (the *Philosophical Notebooks*) and transcended the vulgarly evolutionist materialism of Kautsky and Plekhanov—a transcendence which constitutes *the methodological premise of the April Theses of 1917.*[16] As for Trotsky: in his early writings such as *Our Political Tasks* (1904), he proclaimed himself convinced not only of "the *inevitable* growth of the political party of the proletariat, but also of the *inevitable* victory of the ideas of *revolutionary* socialism within the Party"[17] (our emphasis). This naive fatalist hope was to be cruelly disappointed in August 1914. . . . Several months after the beginning of the world war, in a pamphlet published in Germany, *The War and the International* (1914)—and which was perhaps read by Rosa Luxemburg—Trotsky already posed the problem in entirely different terms: "the capitalist world is confronted with the following choice: either *permanent war* . . . or the *proletarian revolution.*"[18] The methodological principle is the same as the Luxemburgian phrase, but the alternative is different, and no less realistic, in the light of the historical experience of the past fifty years (two world wars, two U.S. wars in Asia, etc.).

In attributing to conscious will and to action the determining role in the decision of the historical process, Rosa Luxemburg in no way denied that this will and this action are conditioned by the entire previous historical development, by "the material conditions that have been built up by the past." It is a question though of recognizing in the subjective factor, in the sphere of consciousness, at the level of political intervention, their *partial* autonomy, their specificity, their "internal logic," and their *proper efficacy.*

Now, it appears to us that this understanding of the subjective factor, will and consciousness, is precisely one of the basic methodological principles of Lenin's *theory of the party*, the foundation of his polemic with the Economists and the Mensheviks. Thus, in spite of all the undeniable differences that existed even after 1915 between Rosa Luxemburg and Lenin, on the subject of the party/masses problematic there was a real rapprochement, as much in practice (constitution of the Spartacus League) as in theory: the "Junius Pamphlet" explicitly proclaims that the revolutionary intervention of the proletariat "seizes the helm of society" to take it "in the direction of Social Democracy." And, of course, it is not a question of the old Social Democratic International that had failed miserably in 1914, but of a "new workers' International, which will take into its own hands the leadership and coordination of the revolutionary class struggle against imperialism."[19] The significant evolution of the ideas of Rosa Luxemburg on this subject are revealed by a symptomatic fact: in a letter to Rosa in 1916, Karl Liebknecht criticized her concept of the International as "too mechanically centralist," with "too much 'discipline', too little spontaneity"—a distant and paradoxical echo of the criticisms that Rosa herself had made in another context, addressed to Lenin.[20]

—Trans. by Paul Le Blanc

Notes

1. Cf. Georg Lukács, *History and Class Consciousness* (Cambridge: MIT Press, 1971), p. 39.
2. Paul Frölich, *Rosa Luxemburg* (New York: Monthly Review Press, 1972), p. 222. [According to Greek mythology, Ariadne was a woman who gave a ball of thread to the Athenian hero Theseus; with this thread he would be able to find his way out of the labyrinth which contained the murderous, cannibalistic monster, the Minotaur.—Trans.]
3. Cf. article of Bernstein in defense of the neo-Kantian Vorlander and against the "folly" of the leftist Pannekoek, in *Dokumente des Sozialismus* 3, p. 487.
4. Rosa Luxemburg, "Reform or Revolution," *Rosa Luxemburg Speaks*, ed. Mary-Alice Waters (New York: Pathfinder Press, 1970), p. 73.
5. Ibid., pp. 39, 41.
6. Ibid., p. 60.
7. Kautsky had in his youth been an ardent disciple of Darwin, and still in his last work, *The Materialist Conception of History* (1927), he proclaims that his goal is to find the laws which are common "to the evolution of humans, animals and plants." Cf. Erich Mathias, "Kautsky und der Kautskyanismus," *Marxismus-studien* 2 (1957): p. 153.
8. Karl Kautsky, *The Road to Power* (Chicago: Samuel A. Bloch, 1909), p. 50. Cf. also the Erfurt Program of the German Social Democratic party (1891), drafted by Kautsky and presenting socialism as a "naturnotwendiges Ziel," a goal resulting from "natural necessity."
9. Discussion at the 1907 Congress of the International at Stuttgart, in Lelio Basso, "Introduzione," in Rosa Luxemburg, *Scritti politici* (Rome: Riuniti, 1967), p. 85.
10. Article of 1913 by Rosa Luxemburg against Kautsky's "strategy of attrition," in Frölich, *Rosa Luxemburg*, p. 143.
11. Rosa Luxemburg, "The Junius Pamphlet: The Crisis in the German Social Democracy," *Rosa Luxemburg Speaks*, p. 269. [This translation has been modified somewhat on the basis of Löwy's own translation.—Trans.]
12. Friedrich Engels, *Anti-Dühring* (New York: International Publishers, 1966), p. 174, our emphasis. Cf. also p. 183: "its own productive powers have grown beyond its control, and, as with the force of a law of Nature, are driving the whole of bourgeois society forward to ruin or revolution."

13. Karl Marx, "Difference between the Democritean and Epicurean Philosophy of Nature," in Karl Marx and Friedrich Engels, *Collected Works*, vol. 1 (New York: International Publishers, 1975), p. 55. According to Lukács in *History and Class Consciousness* (p. 79), the revolutionary consciousness of the proletariat appears precisely under the conceptual form of an *objective possibility*.
14. Cf. Lelio Basso, "Introduzione," p. 48.
15. In 1915, Rosa's faith in the future of humanity consequently appeared somewhat like the Pascalian *wager*: risk, possibility of failure, hope of success, in a "game" in which one engages one's life for a transcendent value. The difference with Pascal, of course, being: a) the content of that value, and b) its objective foundation for Rosa Luxemburg. On this subject see Lucien Goldmann, *The Hidden God* (London: Routledge and Kegan Paul, 1964), pp. 300–302, which compares the Pascalian wager with the Marxist wager.
16. On this subject see Michael Löwy, "From the Great Logic of Hegel to the Finland Station of Petrograd," *Critique* 6 (Spring 1976).
17. Leon Trotsky, *Our Political Tasks* (London: New Park, 1980), p. 123.
18. In *The Age of Permanent Revolution: A Trotsky Anthology* (New York: Dell, 1964), p. 79.
19. Luxemburg, "The Junius Pamphlet," in *Rosa Luxemburg Speaks*, p. 330.
20. Karl Liebknecht, "A Rosa Luxemburg—Remarques à propre de son projet de thèses pour le groupe 'Internationale,'" *Partisans* 45 (January 1969): p. 113.

8

Gramsci and Lukács

Gramsci and Lukács are frequently represented as the founders of "Western Marxism." This geographically defined concept is too vague to convey the convergence and similarity of their thought. More interesting, even if hostile, is Althusser's characterization: both are responsible for a *historical humanist* interpretation of Marxism. Supporters and adversaries alike of the two Marxists agree on the deep affinity of their theoretical and political orientation. The attempt to *go beyond the positivist version of Marxism*—the dominant interpretation as much in the Second as in the Third International (especially after 1924)—is one of the principal traits common to their dialectical and revolutionary, humanist and historicist philosophy.

The affinity between Gramsci and Lukács is in no way due to some "influence" of one over the other. It is unlikely that Gramsci ever read *History and Class Consciousness (HCC)*. The only passage in *Prison Notebooks (PN)* where Lukács is mentioned is formulated in conditional terms:

> Professor Lukács's [*sic*, M. L.] position on the philosophy of praxis must be studied. Lukács seems to state that one can only talk about dialectics in terms of the history of men and not in terms of nature. He may be wrong and he may be right. If his statement presupposes a dualism between nature and man, he is wrong because he falls into a conception of nature peculiar to religion and Greco-Christian philosophy; and also to idealism which in reality only succeeds in unifying and relating man and nature in words. But if human history must conceive of itself also as the history of nature (also through history of science), how can the dialectic be separated from nature? Perhaps in reaction to the baroque theories of Bukharin's *Popular Manual* Lukács fell into the opposite error, into a sort of idealism.[1]

Judging by the content of this passage, it is likely that Gramsci's source was one of the "orthodox" critics of Lukács, who saw only "heresy" in *HCC* on the dialectic of nature. Lukács was practically unknown in Italy during the 1920s and 1930s. His only translated work was the article "Rosa Luxemburg Marxist," published in *Rassegna communista* in 1921. *Ordine*

Nuovo published a few lines by Lukács on workers councils, on June 12, 1920: "The workers' councils, as organisations of the whole class, its unconscious as well as conscious part, by their very existence set into motion the overtaking of bourgeois society."[2]

As Robert Paris remarks, this is a loosely reworked version of a phrase in the conclusion of the essay on class consciousness in *HCC*. Paris raises the hypothesis that Gramsci could have been indirectly influenced by Lukács's ideas through the mediation of the 1926 articles by his Hungarian disciple, Laszlo Rudas, directed against the Italian Communist Party (PCI) economist, Antonio Graziadei.[3] This supposition does not seem credible to me. Not only was Rudas not Lukács's disciple in 1926 (had he ever been?) but, on the contrary, since his political rupture with Lukács around 1923, he became his most vociferous (vulgar) "materialist" critic.

A Similarity of Conceptions

This absence of direct or indirect rapport makes the similarity of their conceptions even more significant. If Gramsci knew almost nothing of Lukács, Lukács did not "discover" the Italian Marxist until well after the Second World War, with the publication of *Prison Notebooks*. He mentioned Gramsci in the 1960s, recognizing his closeness to the worldview expressed in *HCC*:

> This book [*HCC*, M. L.] must be considered a product of the 1920s, as a theoretical echo of the series of events unleashed by the 1917 revolution and the activity of Lenin and, by the same token, the writings of Gramsci and Korsch which have the same character despite sometimes essential differences.[4]

In an interview in *New Left Review*, Lukács stressed that Korsch, Gramsci, and he had fought during the 1930s against the mechanistic heritage of the Second International. He even adds, in passing, that Gramsci was "the best among us."[5] Gramsci's path towards Marxism resembles Lukács's in significant respects, to the extent that it went through antipositivist Hegelianism (Croce and Labriola) and romanto-ethical voluntarism (Sorel and Bergson).

The point of departure of his political evolution is a sort of "Sardinian socialism" made up of southern regionalism, peasant revolt, and struggle against the "rich." Influenced by Gaetano Salvemini, Gramsci tended to set Sardinia and the Mezzogiorno against industrial Italy as a whole,[6] within an ideological framework that is not without certain analogies to the anticapitalist romanticism of Central Europe. On the other hand, Gramsci's "ethical communism" of 1917–19 has a surprising resemblance to that of Lukács's essays of the same period. It is enough to mention the April 1917 article where he sees revealed in the February Russian Revolution "a new moral order" and the realization of Man "whom Immanuel Kant, the theoretician of absolute ethical conduct, had called for—the sort of man who says: the immensity of the heavens above me, the imperative of my conscience within me."[7]

In 1918 Lukács wrote that the proletariat is the heir of "the ethical idealism of Kant and Fichte which suppresses all terrestrial attachments and must—metaphysically—tear the old world off its hinges."[8] The same idea is found in the famous provocative and "heretical" essay *The Revolution against Capital* (1917), which salutes the October Revolution fervently and develops a radically voluntarist interpretation of the politics of the Bolsheviks:

> They live Marxist thought—that thought which is eternal, which represents the continuation of German and Italian idealism. (. . .) This thought sees as the dominant factor in history, not raw economics, facts, but man, men in societies (. . .) men coming to understand economic facts, judging them and adapting them to their will until this becomes the driving force of the economy and moulds objective reality.[9]

Lukács's 1919 brochure *Tactics and Ethics* strikes the same chord. He hails the Bolsheviks as authentic revolutionary Marxists, who dare to proclaim "with the words of Fichte, one of the greatest classical German philosophers: 'So much the worse for the facts.'"[10]

The reference to "idealist" thought—notably Bergson and Croce—is Gramsci's way in 1917–18 of setting himself against the positivist scientism and economico-determinist orthodoxy of Claudio Treves and Filippo Turati, official representatives of the Marxism of the Second International at the head of Italian socialism. An attempt that finds its precise equivalent in the sui generis revolutionary ideology of Lukács in the same period, made up of a combination of a Hegel-Ady-Dostoyevski-Sorel radically opposed to Kautskyism. Gramsci's "Bergsonism," an ambiguous term employed particularly by his positivist adversaries,[11] was gradually superseded (*aufgehoben*) during the course of his ideological evolution, just as Lukács went beyond his "Fichtism" after the Hungarian revolution of the workers' councils.

In this first attempt to formulate a nonpositivist revolutionary Marxism, Gramsci as well as Lukács made much use of Sorel, that paradigmatic representative of romantic anticapitalist socialism. In a letter written in 1968, Lukács describes retrospectively his political evolution during 1917–18:

> I tried to read the contemporary social-democratic theoreticians, but Kautsky made such a loathsome impression upon me (. . .) It was precisely Sorel who exercised the strongest influence on my spiritual evolution. Positive, in that he reinforced my rejection of any revisionist

and opportunist interpretation of Marxist theory; negative, in that a conception of the party mythologising pure and direct class struggle became dominant in my theoretical views.[12]

The references to the philosopher of French revolutionary syndicalism are numerous in Gramsci's early writings. The October 11, 1919, article in *Ordine Nuovo* is particularly significant even if it is "far from accepting everything" in Sorel's work. Gramsci warmly salutes "this unbiased friend of the proletariat" who "has not locked himself into any formula and, having preserved what was vital and new in his doctrine, that is, this highly proclaimed necessity that the proletarian movement express itself through its own forms and give life to its own institutions, he can today follow (. . .) with a spirit full of understanding, the effort of realisation undertaken by the Russian workers and peasants. . . ."[13] What the two young revolutionaries owe to Sorel is, before any precise political orientation, a certain spiritual climate formed from antiliberal romanticism and moral idealism.

Revolutionary Realism

Gramsci, like Lukács, lived through the experience of participation in a real revolutionary movement in 1919–20, the workers' council in Turin. If the reference to Rosa Luxemburg and to her conception of the mass movement is common to both, the writings of Gramsci during this period, in the weekly *Ordine Nuovo,* are much more concrete and "political" than Lukács's own essays. He moves quicker than Lukács from "ethical Bolshevism" towards a more realistic conception of the revolutionary struggle of the proletariat.

Unlike Lukács, Gramsci did not go through a "leftist" stage in 1919–20. While the Hungarian Marxist defended abstract antiparliamentary concepts in the pages of *Kommunismus,* Gramsci refused both the "abstentionist" theses of Bordiga and the reformist parliamentarism of the leadership of the Italian Socialist party (then the section of the Third International). Lenin hailed his strategic orientation in *Theses on the Fundamental Tasks of the Second Congress of the Communist International* (1920), saying "they fully correspond to all the basic principles of the Third International."[14]

It is true that at the Second Congress of the PCI in 1922 Gramsci lined up with Bordiga's "sectarian" theses, opposed to the Comintern's orientation for the united workers' front (June–July 1921). But, as he wrote in 1926, this was a tactical concession to Bordiga, made to maintain party unity and to prevent a new internal crisis.[15]

In the final analysis, all of Gramsci's political conceptions, from 1919 to his arrest in 1926, developed on the terrain of "revolutionary realism," in which the first four congresses of the Communist International formed the global political framework. Gramsci's political work during this period could thus be considered the "political equivalent" of *HCC* founded, like Lukács's book, on simultaneous superseding of "sectarianism" (Bordiga) and of "opportunism" (Serrati) in the Communist movement. If Gramsci did not produce any philosophical or theoretical text comparable to Lukács's *HCC* during these years, it is very probably because the political activity in the leadership of the PCI absorbed his intellectual energy.

Among the texts most characteristic of Gramscian revolutionary realism are *The Southern Question* and *Lyons Theses* both in 1926. Gramsci's main theme is the necessity of workers and peasants unity within the framework of a revolutionary anticapitalist strategy (completely analogous to Lukács's analysis in his 1924 pamphlet *Lenin*).

> The proletariat can become the leading and ruling class to the extent to which it succeeds in creating a system of class alliances which enables it to mobilize the majority of the working population against capitalism and the bourgeois state; this means in Italy, in the actual relations existing in Italy, to the extent to which it succeeds in obtaining the support of the large peasant masses.[16]

Nevertheless after 1926, with his article on Moses Hess, Lukács begins to distance himself from this common perspective in favor of "realism"—the Hegelian "reconciliation with reality"—at the expense of the utopian-voluntarist dimension. During the 1930s he even went along with the Soviet *diamat* (up to a certain point), submitting his 1923 book to a severe self-criticism and denouncing "the idealist front" as identical to "the front of the fascist counter-revolution."[17]

From the political point of view a comparison between the *Lyons Theses* (1926) edited by Gramsci (in collaboration with Togliatti) and Lukács's *Blum Theses* (1929) shows how, starting from the same concern—breaking the isolation of the Communist party, searching for allies for the proletariat—the two thinkers arrived at relatively distinct political conclusions. Lukács's theses proclaimed that the Hungarian Communist party "is the only party that fights seriously for the democracy of the proletariat and the peasantry" and proposed as a slogan "the democratic dictatorship of the proletariat and the peasantry," conceived as a regime where the bourgeoisie "while maintaining economic exploitation abandons at least part of its power to the broad mass of workers."[18]

In the *Lyons Theses* Gramsci proposes a seemingly similar slogan, the "workers' and peasants' government," but he takes care to specify that it is "an agitational slogan" which does not "correspond to a real phase of historical development"; it is impossible "for the problem of the state to be resolved in the interests of the working class in any other form than the dictatorship of the proletariat."[19]

PRISON NOTEBOOKS

In 1926 Gramsci was arrested by the fascist police. His major political and theoretical work does not date from 1923, like Lukács's and Korsch's, but was written in prison between 1929 and 1935. Despite the difference of the period, the analogy between *Prison Notebooks* and the 1922–25 writings of Lukács is undeniable.

This problematic is hinged around a certain number of narrowly linked theoretical and political axes. There is no need to dwell on the most well-known aspects found in both *HCC* and *PN*: importance of the Hegel-Marx rapport (what Althusser called, imprecisely, "a radical return to Hegel"); the dialectic of subject-object and the importance of the "subjective factor" (class consciousness, ideological hegemony); the rejection of metaphysical materialism and of the economism of certain "orthodox" Marxist currents, etc. I want to draw attention to three particularly important questions where the antipositivist "convergence" between Gramsci and Lukács manifests itself:

1. *Radical historicism* implying the application of historical materialism to itself and the definition of its historical limits. Lukács wrote in *HCC* that the truths of Marxism are determined truths within a social order of production: this does not exclude the appearance of societies which, "following the essence of their social structure, need other categories, other ensembles of truth."[20] The same reasoning is found in Gramsci: understanding the historicity of Marxism means recognizing that it can—or rather must—be overtaken by historical development, with the passage from the rule of necessity to the rule of liberty, from a class society to a classless society. Obviously one cannot say what the content of this new form of post-Marxist thought will be without falling into utopianism.[21]

It is the resolutely historicist approach of Gramsci and Lukács, their confirmation of the necessary historicity of all social phenomena, that separates them decisively from all the variations of scientifico-naturalist materialism, from all semipositivist doctrines of the natural law (*Natur Gesetzlichkeit*) of social life.

2. *The comprehension of Marxism as a radically new and specific worldview*, situated from the point of view of the working class: "Graziadei (. . .) considers Marx as a unity of a series of great men of science. Fundamental error: none of the others has ever produced an original and integral conception of the world."[22] This coherent worldview (*Weltanschauung*) cannot be split up into a positive science on the one hand and an ethic on the other

hand; it goes beyond, in a dialectical synthesis and traditional opposition between "facts" and "values," what "is" and what "should be," consciousness and action.[23] As a philosophy of praxis, as an indissoluble unity between theory and practice, Marxism can break what Lukács called "the dilemma of impotence": the duality between the fatalism of pure laws and the ethics of pure intentions. From which comes the Lukácsian criticism of Austro-Marxism (Hilferding), which preaches an impossible separation between the "pure" science of Marxism and socialism.[24]

3. *The proletarian revolution as the keystone of all theoretical reflection*, as unifying element (implicit or explicit) of the entirety of philosophical, historical, cultural, or political questions broached: "The theoretical elevation of *Notebooks* must never make us forget that the watermark of the most subtle pages of philosophy and praxis is revolutionary action."[25]

This remark also applies to *HCC*. The link between dialectical method and revolutionary strategy is found at the very heart of Gramsci's approach, as with Lukács. In a significant passage in *PN*, Gramsci stresses the decisive relationship between theoretical method and political orientation: within the framework of a Marxist critique of Croce, he shows that the work of the Italian philosopher "essentially represents a reaction towards economism and fatalistic mechanism." He adds:

> That this is not without interest is demonstrated by the fact that, of the same time as Croce, the greatest modern theoretician of the philosophy of praxis (Lenin, M. L.), on the terrain of political struggle and organisation, using a political terminology in opposition to various "economistic" forms, revalorized the front of cultural struggle and constructed the doctrine of hegemony as a complement to the theory of State-force and as the present form of the doctrine of the "permanent revolution" of 1848.[26]

The theoretical similarities between Gramsci and Lukács are particularly striking if one compares their respective analyses of the principal philosophical work of Bukharin, *Theory of Historical Materialism: Popular Manual of Sociology* (1922). Both severely criticize his "materialism," bourgeois and contemplative for Lukács, metaphysical and vulgar for Gramsci. Lukács also rejects what he calls the scientism of Bukharin, his "ill-considered, uncritical, ahistoric, and non-dialectical" utilization of the scientifico-natural method for understanding of society—which constitutes one of the most essential characteristics of positivism. Gramsci states that the author of the *Popular Manual* is "totally a prisoner of natural sciences, as if they were the only sciences . . . according to the conception of positivism"; which results in his comprehension of history not as dialectical but as "flat and vulgar evolutionism." For Gramsci as for Lukács, it is following this semipositivist method that one can understand a series of erroneous theses in the *Popular Manual*, which they both show up: the substitution of "technical instruments" for the concept of productive forces; the claim to produce, in history, "scientific forecasts," similar to those of the "exact sciences," etc.[27]

The philological question as to whether Gramsci did or did not read Lukács's critical review of Bukharin—which appeared in 1925 in the German magazine *Archiv für die Geschichte des Sozialismus und der Arbeiterbewegung*, which may have had some readers in Italy—seems to me to be secondary. The essential aspect is the profound convergence of the polemic of both Marxists against one who appeared at the time as the principal theoretician of the Comintern. This coincidence is only a "concentrated" aspect of a more general phenomenon: from the point of view of Marxist method, Gramsci's *Notebooks* as a whole are fundamentally on the same positions as Lukács's writings of 1922–25. Moreover, while Lukács's works correspond to a period of revolutionary rise, and appear as a manifestation of an entire theoretical current (Korsch in Germany, Revai and Fogorasi in Hungary, Mariátegui in Peru, etc.), this is not really the case for *PN*.

Paradoxically, it is perhaps Gramsci's isolation in prison from 1926 to 1935 that contributed to making his *PN* an oasis of authentic Marxism in a period of political and intellectual regression within the workers' movement. His thinking retained the high theoretical and revolutionary level reached in 1919–26, without experiencing any crisis similar to Lukács's after 1926. Gramsci's imprisonment spared him the dilemma that broke Lukács's revolutionary resilience: to capitulate to Stalinism or to be banished from the Communist movement, like Korsch. The bars of the fascist jail were brutal, but purely external, limitations that were not an obstacle to Gramsci's thinking. Lukács however was a prisoner of subtle and insidious chains of self-censorship and "reconciliation with reality."

Studying Gramsci's writings from prison, one cannot help but recognize that, as Jean-Marie Vincent observed, "the revolutionary perspective does not disappear from his horizon. Despite the trials of captivity, he refuses to adapt to the progressive Stalinization of his party by abandoning the practical and theoretical acquisitions of the *Ordine Nuovo* group (of the battle of the workers' councils at the anti-fascist struggle)."[28]

This does not mean to say that Gramsci's texts of 1929–35 were all on the same line as the writings of his youth (the articles in *Ordine Nuovo*). The impact of Stalinism made itself felt despite everything, for example in a more "authoritarian" conception of the Communist party. In his 1920 article, Gramsci insisted that the Communist party should not be a gathering of "little Machiavellis" ("*Piccoli Machiavelli*"), not "a party which uses the masses to attempt a heroic imitation of the French Jacobins," but the party of the masses who want to liberate themselves by their own means, in an autonomous fashion, the instrument of the "process of deep-seated liberation by which the worker, from the *executor*, becomes the *initiator*, from *a mass*, becomes *head* and *leader*, from arm, becomes brain and will."[29] By contrast, in *PN*, the party must exercise the role of a "modern prince," legitimate heir of the tradition of Machiavelli and the Jacobins. As such, it "takes the place, in the conscience, of the divinity or of the categorical imperative"; its base is made up of "common, average men, whose participation is provided by discipline and faith, not by a creative and organizational spirit."[30]

Nevertheless, Gramsci shows his critical lucidity in analyzing the bureaucratic phenomenon in the political parties:

> The bureaucracy is the most dangerously habitual and conservative force; if it ends up by constituting a solid body, standing by itself and feeling independent from the masses, the party ends by becoming anachronistic, and in moments of acute crisis, becomes emptied of all its social content, like an empty shell.[31]

Criticisms as penetrating against the bureaucracy also appear in Lukács's writings . . . of 1922—notably the remarkable polemical text against the leadership of the Hungarian Communist party called "Noch einmal Illusionspolitik" ("The Politics of Illusion—Yet Again").[32] These criticisms disappeared during the Stalin era (except for a few scattered remarks written in coded language, in a literary context) and only reappeared after the Twentieth Congress of the Communist Party of the Soviet Union (CPSU).

It is also in his later works of 1956 that Lukács begins to refer to Gramsci. In his last major work, *The Ontology of Social Being*, he compares Gramsci's writings with *HCC*. In both cases, there were analogous attempts, inspired by the revolutionary wave following October 1917, to put forward Marxist thoughts that were "new, fresh, not deformed by bourgeoisified traditions of social democracy"—attempts reduced to silence by the "schematizing and homogenizing" pressure of Stalinism.[33] But one does not have the impression that Gramsci's thought played a central role in his ontological reflection.

The comparison outlined here does not aim to deny the existence of differences, even opposite views, between the prison writings of Gramsci and the works of the young Lukács (1922–25). But beyond differences of style and content (philosophical as well as political), of the contrasts between two very distinct historical periods, and despite the (probable) absence of any relationship or direct influence, one cannot deny the profound affinity of their approach and the "objective convergence" that makes *History and Class Consciousness* and *Prison Notebooks* the two philosophical high points of the revolutionary dialectic of the twentieth century and the necessary point of departure of any attempt at a Marxism free from positivist shackles.

Notes

1. Antonio Gramsci, *Il materialismo storico e la filosofia di Benedetto Croce* (Torino: Einaudi, 1955), p. 145. (Translation *International Marxist Review* [hereafter *IMR*].)
2. Quoted by Robert Paris in "Gramsci e la crisi teorica del 1923," *Nuovo Rivista Storica*, Anno LIII, Fas. I–II (1969), pp. 167–68. (Tr. *IMR*.)
3. Paris, "Gramsci e la crisi teorica," p. 168. (Tr. *IMR*.)
4. Georg Lukács, "Mon chemin vers Marx," 1969, *Nouvelles etudes hongroises*, vol. 8 (1974): p. 85. (Tr. *IMR*.)
5. "Lukács on His Life and Work," *New Left Review* 68 (July, 1971): p. 51.
6. See Guiseppe Fiori, *Antonio Gramsci: Life of a Revolutionary* (London: New Left Books, 1970), pp. 57–81.
7. Antonio Gramsci, "Notes on the Russian Revolution," in *Antonio Gramsci, Selections from Political Writings*, vol. 1, ed. Q. Hoare (London: Lawrence and Wishart, 1977), p. 30.
8. Georg Lukács, "Le Bolchévisme comme problème moral," 1918, translated into French as an appendix to M. Löwy, *Pour une sociologie des intellectuels révolutionnaires: L'évolution politique de György Lukács 1909–1929* (Paris: Presses Universitaires de France, 1976), p. 310. (Tr. *IMR*.)
9. Antonio Gramsci, "The Revolution against *Capital*," in Hoare, *Antonio Gramsci*, vol. 2, p. 34. In other 1918 writings Gramsci stressed: "Critical communism has nothing in common with philosophical positivism, the metaphysics and mysticism of evolution and nature. . . . Marxism is founded on philosophical idealism. . . . For *natural law*, the fatal movement of things of pseudo-scientists, is substituted *tenacious will of men*." Quoted by E. Garin, "La formazione di Gramsci e Croce," in *Prassi rivoluzionaria e storicismo in Gramsci* (Roma: *Quaderni Critica Marxista*, 1967), p. 127. (Tr. *IMR*.)
10. Georg Lukács, "Tactics and Ethics," in *Political Writings 1919–1929—The Questions of Parliamentarians and Other Essays* (London: New Left Books, 1972), p. 27.
11. Robert Paris, "Introduction à Gramsci," in Antonio Gramsci, *Ecrits politiques, I, 1914–1920* (Paris: Gallimard, 1974), p. 29–30. Gramsci mocks the use of the term by his reformist and positivist adversaries in the Italian Socialist party: "Do you not know what to answer your contradictor? Say to him that he is a voluntarist or a pragmatist or—while making the sign of the cross—a Bergsonian." From Gramsci, *Socialismo e fascismo, ordine nuovo 1921–1922* (Torino: Einaudi, 1972), p. 13. (Tr. *IMR*.)
12. Georg Lukács, "Lettre au directeur de la Bibliothèque Erwin-Szabo de Budapest," in Eva Fekete and Eva Karadi, *Georg Lukács: Sein Leben in Bildern, Selbstzeugnissen und Dokumente* (Budapest: Corvina Kiado, 1981), p. 72. (Tr. *IMR*.) On Lukács's relation to Sorel during the course of his life, see M. Löwy, "Sorel et George Lukács: Sous l'étoile du romantisme," in *Georges Sorel* (Paris: Cahiers de l'Herme, 1986).
13. Gramsci, *Ecrits politiques, I*, p. 277. Enzo Santarelli, Nicola Badaloni, and Paolo Spriano have already provided sufficient evidence of Sorel's influence over

Gramsci. For a recent balance sheet on the question, see Michel Charzat, "A la source du 'marxisme' de Gramsci," in *Georges Sorel.*

14. Quoted by Fiori, *Antonio Gramsci,* p. 134.
15. Ibid., p. 153.
16. Antonio Gramsci, "The Southern Question," in *The Modern Prince and Other Writings* (New York: International Publishers, 1957), p. 30.
17. Georg Lukács, "Die Bedeutung von *Materialismus und Empirio-kritizismus* für die Bolshevisierung der kommunistischen Parteien—Selbst-kritik zu *Geschichte und Klassenbewusstsein,*" 1934, in *Geschichte und Klassenbewusstsein heute* (Amsterdam, 1971), p. 261.
18. Georg Lukács, "Blum Theses," 1929, extracts in *Political Writings,* pp. 227–53.
19. Antonio Gramsci, "The Italian Situation and the Tasks of the PCI" ("Lyons Theses"), in Hoare, *Antonio Gramsci,* vol. 2, p. 375.
20. As Robert Paris correctly states, the reading of *Prison Notebooks* shows how "the essence of the great philosophical discussion of 1923 is found in Gramsci" ("Gramsci e la crisi teorica," p. 177). (*Tr. IMR.*)
21. Georg Lukács, *Histoire et conscience de classe,* p. 263. Also see M. Löwy, "Le marxisme historiciste de Lukács," in *Littérature, philosophie, marxisme* (Paris: Presses Universitaires de France, 1978). The work of Gramsci's which is mentioned is found in *Il materialismo storico,* pp. 84, 98–101.
22. Gramsci, *Il materialismo storico,* p. 83. Faced with Althusser's position: "To understand Marx, we must treat him like a scientist among others. . . . Marx appears as a founder of science comparable to Galileo and Lavoisier" (*Lire le capital,* part II [Paris: Maspero, 1965], p. 119). (Tr. *IMR.*)
23. See Paris, "Gramsci e la crisi teorica," p. 170: "In reality, Gramsci finds—say after Vico and Croce—precisely the problem of *HCC*: to try to resolve the dilemma that bourgeois thought poses between judgements of fact and value judgements, between the 'indicative premises' and the 'imperative' conclusions (Poincaré), in the final analysis, to establish Marxism as knowledge of the present." (Tr. *IMR.*)
24. Lukács, *Histoire et conscience de class,* pp. 41, 61.
25. E. Garin, "La formazione di Gramsci," p. 122.
26. Gramsci, *Il materialismo storico,* p. 203. The reference to Lenin, whom it was impossible to name because of prison censorship—is transparent. (Tr. *IMR.*)
27. See Georg Lukács, "N. Bukharin, Historical Materialism," in *Political Writings 1919–1929,* pp. 134–42.
28. Jean-Marie Vincent, *Fétischisme et société* (Paris: Anthropos, 1973), p. 294. (Tr. *IMR.*)
29. Antonio Gramsci, *Ordine Nuovo, 1919–1929* (Torino: Einaudi, 1954), pp. 139, 140, 157. (Tr. *IMR.*)
30. Antonio Gramsci, "The Modern Prince," in *The Modern Prince and Other Writings* (London: Lawrence and Wishart, 1957), pp. 140, 150.
31. Ibid., p. 175.
32. Georg Lukács, "The Politics of Illusion—Yet Again," in *Political Writings 1919–1929,* p. 121: "There can be no doubt that such artificial and illegitimate cultivation of authority serves only to make the party bureaucracy even more hollow and soulless; it turns it into an *office,* with bosses and subalterns, not a communist organization which is centralized by and based on comradely cooperation."
33. Georg Lukács, *Zu Ontologie des Geselschaftlichen Seins: Die Ontologische Grundprinzipien von Marx* (Neuwied: Luchterhand, 1972), p. 30.

9

"The Poetry of the Past": Marx and the French Revolution

Like so many German intellectuals of his generation, Marx was literally *fascinated* by the French Revolution: in his eyes it was quite simply the Revolution par excellence or, more precisely, "the most colossal revolution that history has ever known."[1] We know that in 1844 he was intending to write a book on the French Revolution, beginning with the history of the Convention. From 1843 onwards, he had begun to consult works on the subject, to take notes and to research periodicals and document collections. He began with German works (Carl Friedrich Ernst Ludwig, Wilhelm Wachsmuth) but, as time went on, French works came to predominate in his reading—particularly the *Mémoires* of Levasseur, a member of the Convention, extracts from which fill several pages of Marx's Paris notebooks of 1844. Apart from these notebooks (which Maximilien Rubel reproduces in Volume 3 of the Pléiade French edition of Marx's works), the references cited in his articles and books (particularly during the years 1844–48) provide evidence of the vast bibliography consulted: Buchez and Roux's *L'Histoire parlementaire de la Révolution française*, Louis Blanc's *Histoire de la Révolution française*, the histories of Carlyle, Mignet, Thiers, and Cabet, and texts by Camille Desmoulins, Robespierre, Saint-Just, Marat, etc. A partial list of this bibliography can be found in Jean Bruhat's article "Marx et la Révolution française," published in the *Annales Historiques de la Révolution française*, April–June 1966.

The planned book on the Convention was never written, but we find scattered about Marx's writings throughout his whole lifetime, a number of remarks, analyses, historiographical excursions, and interpretative outlines on the French Revolution. These various writings are not all of a piece: we can see changes, reorientations, hesitations, and sometimes even contradictions in his reading of the events. But we can also identify certain lines of force which make it possible to define the essence of the phenomenon—lines of force that have inspired socialist historiography for a century and a half.

This definition starts out, as we know, from a critical analysis of the *results* of the revolutionary process: from this point of view, what Marx was dealing with was, without a shadow of a doubt in his view, a *bourgeois* revolution. This was not, in itself, a new idea; the new step introduced by Marx was the fusing of the Communist critique of the limits of the French Revolution (from Babeuf and Buonarotti to Moses Hess) with the class analysis of the revolution made by the historians of the Restoration period (Mignet, Thiers, Thierry, et al.) and the situating of the whole within the framework of world history thanks to his materialist historical method. The result was a vast and coherent *overall vision* of the French revolutionary landscape, which brought out the *underlying logic* of events, beyond the myriad details, the—heroic or sordid—episodes, and the various retreats and advances. It is a *critical and demystificatory* vision, which reveals, behind the smoke of battle and the heady language of the speeches, the victory of a class interest, the interest of the bourgeoisie. As Marx emphasizes in a brilliant and ironic passage in *The Holy Family* (1845), which captures the thread running through this period of history at a single stroke: "That *interest* was so powerful that it was victorious over the pen of Marat, the guillotine of the Terror and the sword of Napoleon as well as the crucifix and the blue blood of the Bourbons."[2]

In actual fact, the victory of this class marked, at the same time, the coming of a new civilization, new relations of production, and new values (and not just economic values but social and cultural ones as well). In short, it saw the coming of a new way of life. Gathering the historical significance of the revolutions of 1648 and 1789 into one paragraph (though his remarks relate more directly to the latter than to the former), Marx observes, in an article in the *Neue Rheinische Zeitung* in 1848: "In these revolutions the bourgeoisie gained the victory; but the *victory of the bourgeoisie* was at that time the *victory of a new social order*, the victory of bourgeois property over feudal property, of nationality over provincialism, of competition over the guild, of the partition of estates over primogeniture, of the owner's mastery of the land over the land's mastery of its owner, of enlightenment over superstition, of the family over the family name, of industry over heroic laziness, of civil law over privileges of medieval origin."[3]

Naturally, this analysis of the—ultimately—bourgeois character of the French Revolution was not an exercise in academic historiography: it had a precise political objective. In demystifying 1789, its aim was to show the necessity of a *new revolution*, the social revolution—the one Marx spoke of in 1844 as "human emancipation" (by contrast with merely political emancipation) and in 1846 as the Communist revolution.

One of the main characteristics which would, in Marx's view, distinguish this new revolution from the French Revolution of 1789–94 would be its "anti-statism," its break with the alienated bureaucratic apparatus of the state. Up to this point, "All political upheavals perfected this machine instead of smashing it. The parties that strove in turn for mastery regarded possession of this immense state edifice as the main booty for the victor." Presenting this analysis in the *Eighteenth Brumaire*, he observed—in a manner reminiscent of Tocqueville—that the French Revolution had merely "had to carry further the centralization that the absolute monarchy had begun, but at the same time it had to develop the extent, the attributes and the number of underlings of the governmental power. Napoleon perfected this state machinery." However, under the absolute monarchy, the Revolution, and the First Empire, that apparatus had merely been a means for preparing the domination of the bourgeois class that would be exerted more directly under Louis-Philippe and the Republic of 1848, only to make way, once again, for the autonomy of the political under the Second Empire—when the state *seemed* to have made itself "completely independent." In other words, the state apparatus served the class interests of the bourgeoisie without necessarily being under its direct control. The fact that it did not engage with the basis of this parasitic, alienated "machine" was, in Marx's view, one of the most crucial *bourgeois limitations* of the French Revolution. As we know, this idea, which Marx sketched out in 1852, would be developed in 1871 in his writings on the Commune, the first example of a proletarian revolution that smashed the state apparatus and put an end to that "boa constrictor" which "grips the social body in the inescapable meshes of its bureaucracy, its police and its standing army." By its bourgeois character, the French Revolution could not emancipate society from that "parasitic excrescence," that "swarm of State vermin," that "enormous governmental parasite."[4]

The "Breadth of Soul" of the Bourgeoisie

The recent attempts by revisionist historians to "go beyond" the Marxian analysis have generally ended in a regression to older liberal or speculative interpretations, thus confirming Sartre's profound observation that Marxism is the ultimate possible horizon of our age and that attempts to go beyond Marx frequently end up *falling short* of him. We may illustrate this paradox by examining the procedure adopted by the most talented and intelligent member of this school, François Furet, who can find no other way to pass beyond Marx than to return to Hegel. According to Furet,

"Hegelian idealism is infinitely more concerned than Marx's materialism with the concrete facts of the history of France in the eighteenth century." What then are these "concrete facts" that are infinitely more important than relations of production and the class struggle? The answer is "the long labour of Spirit in history." Thanks to this—Spirit with a capital *S*—we are at last able to understand the true nature of the French Revolution: rather than the triumph of a social class, the bourgeoisie, it is the "affirmation of self-consciousness as free will, which is co-extensive with the universal, transparent to itself and reconciled with being." This Hegelian reading of the events leads Furet to the curious conclusion that the French Revolution ended in a "failure," the cause of which is to be found in an "error," the desire "to deduce the political from the social." The man responsible for that "failure," in the last analysis, is said to be Jean-Jacques Rousseau. Rousseau's error and that of the French Revolution lay in the attempt to affirm the "precedence of the social over the State." Hegel, by contrast, fully understood that "it is only through the State—that superior historical form—that society can be organized according to reason." The French Revolution failed and the fault was Rousseau's: this is one possible interpretation of the events, but is it really "infinitely more concrete" than the one outlined by Marx?[5]

We still have to ask, however, to what extent this bourgeois revolution was actually led, impelled forward, and directed by the bourgeoisie. In certain of Marx's texts, he positively sings the praises of the revolutionary French bourgeoisie of 1789; in almost every case, he does so in writings in which he is comparing it with its social counterpart across the Rhine, the nineteenth-century German bourgeoisie.

From 1844 onwards, Marx begins to lament the nonexistence in Germany of a bourgeois class which possesses "the breadth of soul which identifies it, if only for a moment, with the soul of the people; that genius which animates material force into political power, that revolutionary boldness which flings at its adversary the defiant phrase: I am nothing and I should be everything."[6] In the articles he published during the revolution of 1848, he continually denounced the "weakness" and "treachery" of the German bourgeoisie, contrasting it with the glorious French paradigm: "The Prussian bourgeoisie was not, like the French bourgeoisie of 1789, the class which represented the *whole* of modern society in face of the representatives of the old society, the monarchy and the nobility. It had sunk to the level of a type of *estate* . . . inclined from the outset to treachery against the people and compromise with the crowned representative of the old society."[7] In another article in the *Neue Rheinische Zeitung* (July 1848), he examined this contrast in more detail.

> The French bourgeoisie of 1789 did not leave its allies the peasants in the lurch for one moment. It knew that the basis of its rule was the destruction of feudalism on the land and the establishment of a class of free peasant landowners.
>
> The German bourgeoisie of 1848 does not hesitate to betray the peasants who are its *natural allies*, its own flesh and blood, and without the peasants this bourgeoisie is powerless against the nobility.[8]

This celebration of the revolutionary virtues of the French bourgeoisie would later inspire linear and mechanistic visions of historical progress in certain currents within Marxism (especially in the twentieth century). We shall return to this below.

Reading these texts, one often gets the impression that Marx only extolled the virtues of the revolutionary bourgeoisie of 1789 the more effectively to stigmatize the "misbegotten" German version of 1848. This impression is confirmed by writings from the years preceding 1848, in which the role of the French bourgeoisie appears much more heroic. In *The German Ideology*, for example, commenting on the decision of the Estates General to proclaim itself a sovereign assembly, he observed: "The National Assembly had to take this step because it was being urged forward by the immense mass of the people that stood behind it."[9] And in an article of 1847, writing of the abolition of the vestiges of feudalism in 1789–94, he stated: "The timidly considerate bourgeoisie would not have accomplished this task in decades. The bloody action of the people thus only prepared the way for it."[10]

Understanding the Terror

If Marx's analysis of the bourgeois character of the revolution is remarkably clear and coherent, the same cannot be said of his attempts to interpret Jacobinism and the Terror of 1793. Confronted with the mystery of Jacobinism, Marx hesitates. This hesitation is visible in the variations from one period to another, from one text to another, and sometimes within the same document. Not all the hypotheses he advances are of the same interest. Some of them, which are quite extreme—and, moreover, mutually contradictory—are not particularly convincing. For example, in a passage in *The German Ideology*, he presents the Terror as the implementation of the "vigorous liberalism of the bourgeoisie"! A few pages earlier, however, Robespierre and Saint-Just are defined as the "real representatives of revolutionary power, i.e. of the class which *alone* was truly revolutionary, the 'innumerable' mass."[11]

This last hypothesis is suggested once again in a passage in the 1847 article against Karl Heinzen: if, "as in 1794" "the proletariat overthrows the political domination of the bourgeoisie" before the material conditions for its power are present, its victory "will only be transient" and will, in the end, only assist the bourgeois revolution itself.[12] The formulation is indirect and the reference to the French Revolution is only made in passing, in relation to a contemporary political debate, but it is nonetheless surprising to find that Marx was able to see the events of 1794 as representing a "victory of the proletariat."

Other interpretations in these writings are more pertinent and may be regarded as mutually complementary.

1. The Terror is a moment in which the political becomes autonomous and then comes into violent conflict with bourgeois society. The locus classicus of this hypothesis is a passage in *On the Jewish Question* (1844).

> Of course, in periods when the political state as such is born violently out of civil society . . . the state can and must go as far as the *abolition of religion*. . . . But it can do so only in the same way that it proceeds to the abolition of private property, to the maximum, to confiscation, to progressive taxation, just as it goes as far as the abolition of life, the *guillotine*. . . . [P]olitical life seeks to suppress its prerequisite, civil society and the elements composing this society, and to constitute itself as the real species-life of man devoid of contradictions. But it can achieve this only by coming into *violent* contradiction with its own conditions of life, only by declaring the revolution to be *permanent*, and therefore the political drama necessarily ends with the re-establishment of religion, private property, and all elements of civil society. . . .[13]

Seen in this light, Jacobinism seems to be a vain and necessarily abortive attempt to confront bourgeois society in a strictly political manner *by the use of the state*.

2. The men of the Terror—"Robespierre, Saint-Just and their party"—were victims of an illusion: they confused the ancient Roman Republic with the modern representative state. Caught up in an insoluble contradiction, they sought to sacrifice bourgeois society "to an ancient mode of political life." This idea, which is developed in *The Holy Family* (1845), implies, as does the previous hypothesis, both an exacerbation and an autonomization of the political sphere in this period of history. It leads to the somewhat surprising conclusion that Napoleon was the heir to Jacobinism; he represented "the last battle of *revolutionary terror* against the bourgeois society, which had been proclaimed by this same Revolution, and against its policy." Admittedly, he was "no terrorist with his head in the clouds"; nonetheless, "he still regarded the *state* as an *end in itself* and civil life only as a treasurer and his *subordinate* which must have no *will of its own*. He *perfected* the *Terror* by substituting permanent war for permanent revolution."[14]

We find the same thesis again in the *Eighteenth Brumaire* (1852), but this time Marx stressed the "ruse of reason" that made the Jacobins (and Bonaparte) the midwives of that same bourgeois society which they scorned.

> Camille Desmoulins, Danton, Robespierre, Saint-Just and Napoleon, the heroes of the old French Revolution, as well as its parties and masses, accomplished the task of their epoch, which was the emancipation and establishment of modern *bourgeois* society, in Roman costume and with Roman slogans. . . . Once the new social formation had been established, the antediluvian colossi disappeared along with the resurrected imitations of Rome—imitations of Brutus, Gracchus, Publicola, the tribunes, the senators and Caesar himself. Bourgeois society in its sober reality had created its true interpreters and spokesmen in such people as Say, Cousin, Royer-Collard, Benjamin Constant and Guizot.[15]

Robespierre and Napoleon fighting the same battle? The formula is a questionable one. It had already been seen from liberals like Mme. de Staël, who described Bonaparte as "a Robespierre on horseback." At least from Marx's pen, this formula shows a rejection of any idea that there was a direct line of descent leading from Jacobinism to socialism. One gets the impression, however, that this derives less from a critique of Jacobinism (as in the work of Daniel Guérin a century later) than from a certain "idealization" of the man of the Eighteenth Brumaire, considered by Marx—in keeping with a tradition of the Rhenish Left (for example, Heinrich Heine)—as having continued the work of the French Revolution.

3. The Terror was a plebian method of doing away with the last vestiges of feudalism in a radical way and, in this sense, it played a functional role in the emergence of bourgeois society. This hypothesis is suggested in several texts, particularly in the article, "The Bourgeoisie and the Counter-Revolution" of 1848. Analyzing the behavior of the urban popular strata ("the proletariat, and the other sections of the town population which did not form a part of the bourgeoisie"), Marx states: ". . . where they stood in opposition to the bourgeoisie, as for example in 1793 and 1794 in France, they were in fact fighting for the implementation of the interests of the bourgeoisie, although not *in the manner* of the bourgeoisie. The *whole of the French terror* was nothing other than a *plebian manner* of dealing with the *enemies of the bourgeoisie*, with absolutism, feudalism and parochialism."[16]

The clear advantage of this analysis was that it integrated the events of 1793–4 into the overall logic of the French Revolution—the emergence of bourgeois society. Using the dialectical method, Marx showed that the "anti-bourgeois" aspects of the Terror only served, in the last analysis, the better to ensure the social and political triumph of the bourgeoisie.

The three aspects brought out here by these three lines of interpretation of Jacobinism—the hypertrophy of the political sphere in conflict with bourgeois society, the illusion of returning to the Republic of antiquity, and the role of plebian instrument serving the objective interests of the bourgeoisie—are entirely compatible and allow us to grasp different facets of the historical reality.

Two aspects of this are, however, striking: on the one hand, there is the rather excessive importance Marx attributes to the "Roman illusion" as a key to the explanation of the Jacobins' behavior. And this is all the more surprising in that it is one of the exigencies of historical materialism that ideologies and illusions be explained in terms of the position and interests of social classes. Yet there is in the work of Marx (and Engels) no even approximate attempt to define the *class nature* of Jacobinism. There is no shortage of class analysis in Marx's writings on the French Revolution: the roles of the aristocracy, the clergy, the bourgeoisie, the peasants, the urban plebs, and even the "proletariat" (a somewhat anachronistic term in eighteenth-century France) all come under review. But Jacobinism remains hanging in the air, consigned to the celestial realm of the politics of "antiquity"—or else associated, somewhat hastily, with the whole set of nonbourgeois, plebian strata.

Though in his works on the revolution of 1848–52 Marx did not hesitate to characterize the modern heirs of the *Montagne* as *petty-bourgeois democrats*, only very seldom did he extend that social definition to the Jacobins of 1793. One of the only passages in which that is even hinted at is to be found in the "Address to the Central Committee to the Communist League (March 1850)": "As in the first French Revolution, the petty bourgeoisie will want to give the feudal lands to the peasants as free property; that is, they will try to perpetuate the existence of the rural proletariat, and to form a petty-bourgeois peasant class which will be subject to the same cycle of impoverishment and debt which still afflicts the French peasant."[17] But this once again is a remark made "in passing," in which the Jacobins are not even referred to by name. It is a curious fact, but there are very few elements in Marx's work (or that of Engels) for a class analysis of the contradictions of Jacobinism—like, for example, that of Daniel Guérin, for whom the Jacobin party was "at once petty-bourgeois at its head and popular at its base."[18]

In any case, one thing is clear: for Marx, 1793 *was by no means a paradigm for the future proletarian revolution*. Whatever his admiration for the historical greatness and revolutionary energy of a Robespierre or a Saint-Just, Jacobinism is explicitly rejected as a model or source of inspiration for socialist revolutionary praxis. This is clear from the first communist texts of 1844 that distinguish the goals of social emancipation from the impasse and illusions of the political voluntarism of the men of the Terror. But it was during the years 1848–52, in his writings on France, that Marx most emphatically denounced the "traditional superstition in 1793," the "pedants of the old tradition of 1793," the "illusions of the republicans of the tradition of 1793," and all those who "are intoxicated by the opium of the sentiments and the 'patriotic' formulas of 1793." Such reasoning had led him to the celebrated conclusion formulated in the *Eighteenth Brumaire*: "The social revolution of the nineteenth century can only create its poetry from the future, not from the past. It cannot begin its own work until it has sloughed off all its superstitious regard for the past."[19] This is a highly questionable affirmation—the Commune of 1793 inspired that of 1871, and that, in its turn, fed into October 1917—but it bears witness to the hostility Marx showed against any resurgence of Jacobinism within the proletariat movement.

This in no way means that Marx did not see personalities, groups, and movements in the French Revolution that were forerunners of socialism. In a very well-known passage from *The Holy Family* (1845) he rapidly runs through the chief representatives of that tendency: "The revolutionary movement which began in 1789 in the *Cercle social*, which in the middle of its course had as its chief representatives *Leclerc* and *Roux*, and which finally with *Babeuf's* conspiracy was temporarily defeated, gave rise to the *communist* idea which *Babeuf's* friend *Buonarotti* re-introduced in France after the Revolution of 1830. This idea, consistently developed, is the *idea* of the *new world order*."[20]

Curiously, Marx only seemed interested in the *idea* of communism and paid little attention to social developments, to the *class struggle* within the Third Estate. Moreover, in his later writings he continued to show scant interest in these "germs of communism" within the French Revolution (with the exception of Babeuf) and never attempted to study the class conflicts between bourgeois and *bras nus* in the course of the Revolution. In Engels's last writings (in 1889), we find a few hasty references to the conflict between the Commune (Hébert, Chaumette) and the Committee of Public Safety (Robespierre), but there is no mention of the *enragé* tendency represented by Jacques Roux.[21]

Amongst the figures who might be seen as precursors, *Babeuf* was thus the only one who seemed really important to Marx and Engels, who referred to him on several occasions. For example in the article against Heinzen (1847), Marx observed: "The first manifestation of a truly active communist party is contained within the bourgeois revolution, at the moment when the constitutional monarchy is eliminated. The most consistent *republicans*, in England, the *Levellers*, in France, *Babeuf*, *Buonarotti*, etc. were the first to proclaim these 'social questions'. *The Babeuf Conspiracy* by Babeuf's friend and party-comrade Buonarotti, shows how these republicans derived from the 'movement' of history the realization that the disposal of the social question of *rule by princes* and *republic* did not mean that even a single 'social question' has been solved in the interests of the proletariat."[22] Moreover, the sentence in the *Communist Manifesto* that describes "the first direct attempts of the proletariat to attain its own ends," which occurred during the period "when feudal society was being overthrown," also refers to Babeuf (explicitly mentioned in this context).[23] This interest is understandable insofar as several of the communist currents in France before 1848 were more or less directly inspired by Babouvism. But the question of the *antibourgeois* popular movements (*sans-culottes*) of the years 1793–94, which were more advanced than the Jacobins, is barely touched upon by Marx or Engels.

Beyond the Bourgeois Revolution

In these circumstances, may we then say that Marx perceived in the French Revolution not only the bourgeois revolution but also a *dynamic of permanent revolution*, an embryo of "proletarian" revolution bursting through the strictly bourgeois framework? The answer must be both that he did and he did not.

It is true, as we have seen above, that Marx used the term "permanent revolution" in 1843–44 to characterize the politics of the Terror. Daniel Guérin interprets this formula as being consonant with his own interpretation of the French Revolution: "Marx used the expression 'permanent revolution' in relation to the French Revolution. He showed that the revolutionary movement in 1793 attempted, for a moment, to go beyond the bounds of the bourgeois revolution."[24] However, the sense in which Marx used the expression (in *On the Jewish Question*) was not at all identical with the sense given to it by Guérin: "permanent revolution" did not at this point signify a semiproletarian *social movement* seeking to develop the class struggle against the bourgeoisie by outflanking the Jacobin government, but a vain attempt by "*political life*" (embodied in the Jacobins) to emancipate itself from civil/bourgeois society and to abolish the latter using the guillotine. The comparison Marx sketched out a year later (in *The Holy Family*) between Robespierre and Napoleon, in which the latter is seen as having perfected "the Terror by *substituting permanent war* for *permanent revolution*," well illustrates the distance between this formula and the idea of the seeds of proletarian revolution.

The other example Guérin cites is an article from January 1849 in which Engels refers to "permanent revolution" as one of the characteristic features of the "glorious year 1793." In that article, however, Engels mentions as a contemporary example of this "permanent revolution" the Hungarian national-popular rising of 1848 led by Lajos Kossuth "who for his nation is Danton and Carnot rolled into one." It is clear that for Engels this term was simply synonymous with the revolutionary mobilization of the people and in no way had the sense of the Revolution growing over into a socialist one.[25]

These remarks are not intended to be a criticism of Daniel Guérin, but, rather, to throw into relief the profound *originality* of his approach: he did not simply develop the indications already present in Marx and Engels, but, using the Marxist method, he formulated a new interpretation that brings out the "permanent" dynamic of the revolutionary movement of the *bras nus* of 1793–94.

Having said this, there is no doubt that the expression "permanent revolution" is closely associated in Marx (and in Engels) with memories of the French Revolution. This connection exists on three levels: a) The immediate origin of the formula probably goes back to the fact that the revolutionary clubs often declared that they were assembled "*en permanence.*" Moreover, this expression appeared in one of the German books on the Revolution that Marx had read in 1843–44.[26] b) The expression also implies the idea of an uninterrupted advance of the Revolution, from absolute to constitutional monarchy, from the Girondin to the Jacobin republic, etc. c) In the context of the articles of 1843–44, it suggests a tendency within political revolution (in its Jacobin form) to become an end in itself and to come into conflict with civil/bourgeois society.

By contrast, the *idea* of permanent revolution in its strong sense—that of revolutionary Marxism in the twentieth century—appeared in Marx for the first time in 1844, and it did so *in relation to Germany*. In the article, "A Contribution to the Critique of Hegel's 'Philosophy of Right,'" he registered the German bourgeoisie's inability to fulfil its revolutionary role: at the moment when it begins its struggle against the monarchy and the nobility, "the proletariat is already beginning its struggle against the bourgeoisie. The middle class hardly dares to conceive of the idea of emancipation from its own point of view, and already the development of social conditions and the progress of political theory show that this point of view itself is antiquated, or at least questionable." It follows that in Germany, "it is not *radical* revolution, *universally human* emancipation which is . . . a utopian dream; it is, rather, partial revolution, *purely political* revolution, the revolution which leaves the pillars of the old house standing." In other words, "In France, partial emancipation is the basis of universal emancipation. In Germany, universal emancipation is the *conditio sine qua non* for any partial emancipation."[27] It was therefore in opposition to the "purely political," "partial" model of the French Revolution that the idea emerged—in a language as yet philosophical—that, in certain countries, the socialist revolution would have to accomplish the historical tasks of the bourgeois-democratic revolution.

Only in March 1850, in the "Address of the Central Committee to the

Communist League," did Marx and Engels *fuse the French expression with the German idea, the formula inspired by the Revolution of 1789–94 with the perspectives of developing the (German) democratic revolution into a proletarian one*: "While the democratic petty-bourgeois want to bring the revolution to an end as quickly as possible . . . it is our interest and our task to make the revolution permanent until all the more or less propertied classes have been driven from their ruling positions, until the proletariat has conquered state power" . . . in all the leading countries of the world and "the decisive forces of production" are concentrated in its hands.[28] Here "permanent revolution" first takes on the meaning it will have in the twentieth century (most notably in the writings of Trotsky). In its new sense, what the formula retains of its origins in the historical context of the French Revolution is chiefly the second aspect mentioned above: the idea of a progression, radicalization, and uninterrupted enriching of the revolution. We also find in it the aspect of confrontation with civil/bourgeois society, but contrary to the Jacobin model of 1793, this confrontation is no longer the terrorist action of the political sphere as such (which is necessarily doomed to failure)—trying in vain to attack private property through the guillotine—but *comes from within civil society itself* in the form of (proletarian) *social revolution*.

The Incomplete Revolution

What then is the heritage of the French Revolution for twentieth-century Marxism? As we have seen, Marx believed that the socialist proletariat should divest itself of the revolutionary tradition of the eighteenth century. It seems to me that Marx was both right and wrong at the same time. *He was right* insofar as Marxists, throughout the twentieth century, have often sought inspiration in the paradigm of the French Revolution, with relatively negative results. This was the case, first of all, with Russian Marxism in its two major branches:

1. Plekhanov and the Mensheviks—who thought the Russian democratic bourgeoisie was going to play the same role in the struggle against tsarism as the French bourgeoisie played (according to Marx) in the Revolution of 1789. From that point on, the concept of "revolutionary bourgeoisie" entered the vocabulary of Marxists and became a key element in elaboration of political strategies, ignoring Marx's warning—in relation to Germany (but with more general implications)—that those bourgeoisies which arrived too late (i.e., which were already threatened by the proletariat) would be incapable of a coherent revolutionary practice. Admittedly, thanks to Stalinism, the dogma of the democratic/revolutionary (or national) bourgeoisie and the idea of a repetition—in new conditions—of the para-

digm of 1789 have been an essential component of the ideology of the Communist movement in colonial, semi-colonial, and dependent countries since 1926—with baneful consequences for the dominated classes.

2. Lenin and the Bolsheviks, who, for their part, had no illusions about the Russian liberal bourgeoisie, but who, particularly before 1905, took *Jacobinism* as their political model. The result of this was an often authoritarian conception of the party, revolution, and revolutionary power. Rosa Luxemburg and Leon Trotsky criticized this Jacobin paradigm—especially during the years 1903–1905—by stressing the essential difference between the spirit, methods, practices, and organizational forms of Marxism and those of Robespierre and his friends. Lenin's *State and Revolution* may be considered as a move beyond this Jacobin model.

To speak of Stalin and his acolytes as the heirs of Jacobinism would be too unfair to the revolutionaries of 1793, and it would be an obvious historical absurdity to compare the Committee of Public Safety's Terror with that of the GPU (Stalin's secret police) in the 1930s. On the other hand, one can detect the presence of a Jacobin element in the work of a Marxist as subtle and innovative as Antonio Gramsci. Though in his articles for *Ordine Nuovo* in 1919 he proclaimed that the proletarian party must not be "a party which makes use of the masses for its own heroic attempts to imitate the French Jacobins," in his *Prison Notebooks* of the 1930s we find a relatively authoritarian vision of the vanguard party, which is presented as the legitimate heir to the tradition of Machiavelli and the Jacobins.

At another level, however, it seems to me that Marx *was wrong* to deny the revolutionary tradition of 1789–94 any value for the socialist struggle. His own thinking provides an excellent example here: the very idea of *revolution* in his writings (and those of Engels), as an insurrectional movement of the dominated classes overthrowing an oppressive state and an unjust social order, was in very large measure inspired by this tradition. More generally, the French Revolution is part of the *collective memory* of the working people—in France, Europe, and throughout the globe—and constitutes a vital source of socialist thinking in all its variants (communism and anarchism included). Contrary to what Marx wrote in the *Eighteenth Brumaire*, without "poetry from the past," there can be no dream of the future.

In a certain sense, the legacy of the French Revolution remains, even today, something living, contemporary, and *active*. It still has something incomplete about it. It contains a promise that is not yet fulfilled; it is the beginning of a process that is not yet ended. The best proof of this can be seen in the insistent attempts, beginning with Napoleon himself on Eighteenth Brumaire, to "put an end," officially and definitively, to the French Revolution. And yet who today would form the bizarre idea of declaring the English Revolution of 1648 ended? Or the American Revolution of

1776? Or the French Revolution of 1830? If such passionate efforts are still being devoted to the Revolution of 1789–94, it is precisely because that revolution is far from "ended." In other words, it continues to have effects in the political field and in cultural life, in the social imaginary and ideological struggles (in France and elsewhere).

What are the aspects of this struggle that are most worthy of interest? Who are the "spirits of the past" who deserve mention two hundred years after the event? What are the elements of the revolutionary tradition of 1789–94 that most profoundly bear witness to this *state of incompleteness*? I shall here mention four of the most important.

1. The French Revolution was a crucial moment in the constitution of the oppressed people—the "innumerable mass" (Marx) of the exploited—as *historical subject*, as actor in its own liberation. In this sense, it was a giant step in what Ernst Bloch called the "*upright carriage" of humanity*—a historical process that is still far from ended. Certainly, precedents can be found in earlier movements (the Peasant Wars of the sixteenth century, the English Revolution in the seventeenth), but none attained the lucidity, the political and moral force, the universal vocation and spiritual boldness of the Revolution of 1789–94, which was, up to that point, the most "colossal" of all.

2. In the course of the French Revolution, social movements appeared with aspirations that went beyond the bourgeois limits of the process initiated in 1789. The chief forces of that movement—the *bras nus*, the Republican women, the *enragés*, the *égaux* and their representatives (Jacques Roux, Leclerc, etc.)—were defeated, crushed, guillotined. Their memory, systematically repressed by official history, is part of the *tradition of the oppressed* of which Walter Benjamin used to speak, the tradition of the martyred ancestors that feeds the struggles of today. The works of Daniel Guérin and Maurice Dommanget—two "marginals" from outside academic historiography—have rescued the *bras nus* and the *enragés* from oblivion, while more recent research is gradually discovering what richness is to be found among the "hidden half" of the revolutionary people—the women.

3. The French Revolution gave birth to conceptions of a "new world order," the ideas of communism (the *"Cercle social,"* Babeuf, Sylvain, Maréchal, François Bossel, etc.), and feminism (Olympe de Gouges, Théroigne de Méricourt). The revolutionary explosion unleashed dreams, images of desire, and radical social demands. In this sense, too, it still carries within it a future that remains open and as yet unachieved.

4. The ideals of the French Revolution—Liberty, Equality, Fraternity, the Rights of Man (particularly in the 1793 version), the sovereignty of the people—contain a *utopian surplus* (Ernst Bloch) that exceeds the uses to

which they were put by the bourgeoisie. *Their effective realization demands the abolition of the bourgeois order.*

The conclusion and moral of the story (and of History with a capital *H*): the French Revolution of 1789–94 was just a beginning. The struggle continues . . .

Notes

1. Karl Marx, *The German Ideology*, in *Marx-Engels Collected Works* (hereafter *Marx-Engels*), vol. 5 (London, 1976), p. 193.
2. Karl Marx, *The Holy Family*, in *Marx-Engels*, vol. 4, p. 81.
3. Karl Marx, "The Bourgeoisie and the Counter-Revolution," in *The Revolutions of 1848*, ed. D. Fernbach (Harmondsworth, 1973), pp. 192–93.
4. Karl Marx, *The Eighteenth Brumaire*, in *Surveys from Exile*, ed. D. Fernbach (Harmondsworth, 1973), p. 237; Karl Marx, "The Civil War in France," first and second versions, quoted in Karl Marx and Friedrich Engels, *Sur la révolution française*, ed. Claude Mainfroy (Paris, 1985), pp. 187–92.
5. François Furet, *Marx et la révolution française* (Paris, 1896), pp. 81–84. Cf., p. 83: "However, in order to affirm the abstract universality of freedom, the Revolution had to proceed by splitting civil society from the State and by deducing, so to speak, the political from the social. That was its error and its failure, just as it was the failure of the theories of contract, particularly that of Rousseau."
6. Karl Marx, *Critique of Hegel's "Philosophy of Right"* (Cambridge, 1970), p. 140.
7. Marx, "The Bourgeoisie and the Counter-Revolution," pp. 193–94.
8. Karl Marx, "The Bill for the Abolition of Feudal Burdens," in Fernbach, *The Revolutions of 1848*, p. 143.
9. Marx, *The German Ideology*, p. 199.
10. Karl Marx, "Moralising Criticism and Critical Morality: A Contribution to German Cultural History. Contra Karl Heinzen," in *Marx-Engels*, vol. 6, p. 319.
11. Marx, *The German Ideology*, p. 178.
12. Marx, "Moralising Criticism," p. 319.
13. Karl Marx, *On the Jewish Question*, in *Marx-Engels*, vol. 3, pp. 155–56.
14. Marx, *The Holy Family*, p. 123.
15. Marx *The Eighteenth Brumaire*, p. 147.
16. Marx "The Bourgeoisie and the Counter-Revolution," p. 192. Cf. also the article of 1847 against Karl Heinzen: "The terror in France could thus by its mighty hammer-blows only serve to spirit away, as it were, the ruins of feudalism from French soil. The timidly considerate bourgeoisie would not have accomplished this task in decades" (Marx, "Moralising Criticism," p. 319).
17. Karl Marx and Friedrich Engels, "Address of the Central Committee to the Communist League (March 1850)," in Fernbach, *The Revolutions of 1848*, pp. 327–28.
18. Danìel Guérin, *La lutte de classes sous la Première République bourgeoise et "bras nus" 1793–1797* (Paris, 1946), p. 12.
19. Marx, *The Eighteenth Brumaire*, p. 149.
20. Marx, *The Holy Family*, p. 119.

21. Letter from Engels to Karl Kautsky, Dec. 20, 1889, quoted in Marx and Engels, *Sur la révolution française.*
22. Marx, "Moralising Criticism," p. 321.
23. Karl Marx and Friedrich Engels, "Manifesto of the Communist Party," in Fernbach, *The Revolutions of 1848*, p. 94.
24. Guérin, *La lutte de classes*, p. 7.
25. Ibid.; Friedrich Engels, "The Magyar Struggle," in Fernbach, *The Revolutions of 1848*, p. 213.
26. Cf. Wilhelm Wachsmuth, *Geschichte Frankreichs im Revolutionsalter*, vol. 2 (Hamburg, 1842), p. 341: "Von den Jakobinern ging die Nachricht ein, dass sie in Permanenz erklärt hatten."
27. Marx, *Critique of Hegel's*, p. 141.
28. Marx and Engels, "Address of the Central Committee," pp. 323–24.

10

The First Revolution of the Twentieth Century

Teodor Shanin's two-volume *Roots of Otherness: Russia's Turn of the Century* (New Haven: Yale University Press, 1986) is not only "a distinguished piece of scholarship" (Dennis Wrong), representing "historical sociology at its best" (William G. Rosenberg). It is all that and also something else: a radical change of paradigm in the historical and sociological understanding of the Russian Revolution. Real breakthroughs in social sciences are rare and should not be overlooked: Shanin's book is one of them.

From the late nineteenth century to 1917 most scholars, historians, political leaders, and social philosophers saw tsarist Russians as *either* totally unique *or* as a backward section of Europe. It was neither. As Shanin persuasively shows, Russia at the turn of the century was not unique, nor was it on the threshold of becoming another England; it was the first country in which the specific social syndrome of what we call today a "developing" society had materialized. The Russian Revolution of 1905–1907 marked the time and the place of the first fundamental challenge to the relevance of the Western experience for the rest of humanity. It was not the last of the European revolutions of the nineteenth century but the first of a new series of revolutionary movements in the dependent, peripheral, "developing" societies that unfolded during the twentieth century.

What is at issue is not just a historical debate, since up to now the conventional wisdom—the so-called Modernization Theory—has tried to interpret such "developing" societies simply as *backward*, that is, as societies proceeding toward modernity along a necessary scale of social and economic advances but for some reason not yet "there" or else moving "there" too slowly. What is needed is a different approach that considers the possibility of *different* models of development, not necessarily following the Western (European and North American) pattern.

Inspired by Paul Baran's pioneering work on imperialism and underdevelopment, as well as (with some reservations) by Gunder Frank's dependency theory, Shanin's first volume presents *dependent development* as Russia's major characteristic. The centerpiece of this demonstration is a remarkable analysis of the Russian countryside at the turn of the century, incorporating historical, sociological, economic, and anthropological elements, and focusing on the "rural triangle of (mutual) determination" between capitalism, the state, and the peasantry. Criticizing the linear conception of both liberals and Second International Marxists in their interpretation of tsarist Russia and its future—in particular their prediction that capitalism soon would "disintegrate" the peasantry—Shanin rescues the fruitful intuitions of the revolutionary populists and the late Marx. Drawing on his previous work (*Late Marx and the Russian Road*, [Monthly Review Press, 1983])—a brilliant piece of unorthodox Marxology—he shows that both Marx (in his later years) and his friends from the People's Will (*Narodnaya Volya*) considered the peasant commune (*obschchina*) as the source for the regeneration of Russian society; for them postcapitalist society would dialectically resemble the communalism of capitalism's predecessors.

In the 1905–1907 Revolution, the Russian peasant commune would dramatically reveal its characteristics as at once a unit of class organization, a generator of egalitarian ideology, and a school for collective action capable of turning overnight into well-organized revolt. A careful study of this fruitful historical event is the object of the second volume.

The Russian revolutionaries, considering that Russia was backward by half a century at least, hoped for a Russian version of 1789 or 1848. What happened was quite unexpected and "deviated" from this classic European norm. The Russian Revolution of 1905–1907 was the first of a distinctive set of revolutionary upheavals characteristic of the twentieth century. In quick succession it was followed by Turkey (1908), Iran (1909), Mexico (1910), and China (1911), and in Russia itself the revolution resumed in 1917. Revolutions in the periphery have proceeded apace ever since.

Shanin's analysis of the revolutionary process is not a piece of dry academia: it is full of the vitality of the real thing. One methodological remark deserves to be quoted at length, because it reveals the kind of empathic quality that distinguishes Shanin's work, and gives it such a superiority over most scholarly studies of the same kind:

> Social scientists often miss a centerpiece of any revolutionary struggle—the fervor and anger which drives revolutionaries and makes them into what they are. Academic training and bourgeois convention deaden its appreciation. The "phenomenon" cannot be easily "operationalized" into factors, tables and figures. . . . Yet, without this factor, any understanding of revolutions falls flat. That is why clerks, bankers, generals, and social scientists so often fail to see revolutionary upswing even when looking at it directly. At the very center of revolution lies an emotional

> upheaval of moral indignation, revulsion, and fury with the powers-that-be, such that one cannot demur or remain silent, whatever the cost. Within its glow, for a while, men surpass themselves, breaking the shackles of intuitive self-preservation, convention, day-to-day convenience, and routine. (pp . 30–31)

The main focus of Shanin's interpretation of the revolutionary events of 1905–1907 is the peasant struggle for land and liberty. After the defeat of Pugachev (eighteenth century), peasant revolts seemed to have disappeared from the Russian countryside—expect for a few local "agrarian disturbances." Peasant rebellions seemed a thing of the past for Russia and for the world at large. With hindsight, however, we now know that what happened in Russia in 1905–1907 was only the beginning of a new wave of peasant wars at the periphery of the global capitalist system: Mexico, Russia again, China, Algeria, Vietnam, etc.

The autonomous struggle of the Russian noncapitalist peasantry—a struggle for communal property, against private ownership of land—upset the evolutionist predictions of most Russian Marxists (particularly Plekhanov and his followers), which considered peasants conservative, backward, "petty-bourgeois," and unlikely to become a revolutionary force. Other unexpected surprises occurred in 1905–1907: the massive revolutionary mobilization of the ethnic minorities, the outstanding importance of alternative bases of authority (the workers' Soviets, the All-Russian Peasant Union), the major revolutionary role of the students and the left intelligentsia, etc.

Of course, one can try to treat these "deviations" from the expected as exceptions that require only partial revision and adjustments of an analysis that did not fit some particularly obnoxious facts—without putting the more general theoretical understanding in question. Shanin calls for a different approach to consider these deviations to be elements of a syndrome representing a social reality systematically different from the "orthodox" conceptual model. This implies that Russia at the turn of the century can be best understood neither as exceptional nor as yet another case of the "general" development of Western Europe—a delayed carriage rolling along a well-known track. The only way to a full grasp of the new realities of the 1905–1907 revolution is through an understanding that the Russian Empire displayed the characteristics of a "developing society" without yet recognizing itself as such.

As a matter fact, so radical a reconceptualization is not accepted even today—a tribute to the power of the Modernization Theory in the West and the combination of Russian evolutionism and nationalism in the East. It is therefore no surprise that most of the contemporary Russian political leaders (conservative, liberal, or revolutionary) were not able to draw any original or important lessons from 1905–1907. Only a minority were open to and willing to learn from the teachings of history. But for these few, even if what they learned amounted to no more than a partial and contradictory revision of the conventional wisdom, their new understanding gave them an immense political superiority.

Among the rulers it was Peter Stolypin who drew the most far-reaching conclusions. His policy has since become a standard model for authoritarian regimes in developing societies: a kind of "revolution from above," including an agrarian reform based on the privatization of communal lands and a modernization/reformation of the administrative apparatus, combined with brutal repressive measures against the popular "revolution from below." Shanin descries this as the "Second Amendment" to Smith and Ricardo's classical political economy—the First Amendment being Friedrich List's doctrine of state intervention and protectionism, implemented by Bismarck.

Among the revolutionaries the main exceptions were Trotsky and Lenin. Shanin also mentions the Georgian Menshevik leader Zhordania, but his innovations were limited to the willingness to fight for a social democratic government in Georgia. Although leading the world's first Marxist party outside Europe with a mass peasant membership, Zhordania was unable to overcome the traditional Menshevik distrust of the peasantry.

Trotsky's theory of permanent revolution was a major "unorthodox" rebellion against Second International evolutionism. While the political imagination of his friend Parvus (Alexander Helphand) stopped at the proposition of a workers' postrevolutionary government that would accomplish the most democratic version of capitalism (the first bourgeois "stage"), Trotsky made a decisive step forward by suggesting that once set in motion proletarian rule would necessarily transcend bourgeois democracy and directly attack capitalist property. Trotsky's main conclusion from 1905–1907 about the possibility of a "great leap" into immediate socialist-led and socialist-aimed transformation of Russia became crucial in 1917: "its essence was part of the political masterplan which the Bolsheviks adopted in April 1917" (p. 257).

However, this was, according to Shanin, a one-sided intellectual breakthrough: Trotsky was indifferent or hostile to both ethnicity and the peasantry. His shortsightedness concerning peasants was quite remarkable. Against Lenin, Trotsky insisted that peasants could under no circumstances play an independent political role nor form a party of their own. Rejecting Lenin's suggestion of a "democratic dictatorship of workers and peasants," Trotsky insisted that the only viable regime would be a workers' dictatorship "resting on" the peasant majority and its goodwill-cum-indifference, but in no way accepting peasants as partners in state power.

But for Lenin the most important lesson from the revolution of 1905–

1907 was a new strategy of a revolutionary alliance (and government) of workers and peasants. This decisive change from his own previous ideas (inherited from Plekhanov) about the "disintegration" of the peasantry was eventually to make Bolshevism into a new ideological creed of global appeal embedded in the Third International and the Soviet Union. This meant an immediate revolutionary alliance between the Bolsheviks and the Socialist Revolutionary party (SR); it also implied a new agrarian program, including the call for the nationalization of the land (until then considered a typically "populist" demand).

In April 1917 Lenin raised the call for a socialist revolution, for the establishment of a Republic of Soviets along the lines of the Paris Commune of 1871. The "democratic dictatorship of workers and peasants" as defined in 1905 was treated as "overtaken by the events"—the aim was a socialist revolution led by socialists. But as the civil war unfolded, the issues that had surfaced in 1905–1907 came back into focus. Adopting lock, stock, and barrel the SR agrarian program, Lenin was able to win massive support from the peasantry—an important element in the revolutionary victory. And in 1921 he decided for a full-scale conciliatory policy toward the peasants: the New Economic Policy (NEP).

One brief comment on Shanin's assessment of Trotsky and Lenin: it seems to me that his criticism of Trotsky's "shortsightedness" in relation to the decisive role of the peasantry in the revolution of 1905–1907 is quite justified. However, in view of what happened in 1917–22, there is at least one key aspect where Trotsky's predictions proved more realistic than Lenin's: the revolutionary peasantry had to follow the political leadership of the proletariat. Except for a short period (the coalition with the left SR), the proletarian party (i.e., the Bolsheviks) did not share power with a "peasant party," and the Soviet government looked much more like "a proletarian dictatorship supported by the peasantry" than a "democratic dictatorship of the workers and peasants." Peasant participation on the revolutionary side in the civil war was indeed decisive, but again the leadership of the process was firmly in the hands of the workers' party (and of Trotsky himself as head of the Red Army). And the economic concessions to the peasantry through the NEP did not change the basic "proletarian" (albeit with bureaucratic deformations) character of the Soviet power. But these questions are beyond the scope of the book, which deals with 1905–1907 and not with the October Revolution.

Shanin's conclusion is a passionate plea for a *dialectical method* in history inspired by German critical philosophy, Marx's "Theses on Feuerbach," Max Weber, Sartre, and Gramsci. Rejecting determinism, fatalism, and reductionism, which perceive only structural determinants but omit *choice*, this method is able to grasp the interdependence between material circumstances and individual or collective decisions. In this context, Shanin offers two methodological remarks that are of utmost importance and combine to make his work an outstanding contribution not only to the history of turn-of-century Russia, but to history as a social science.

1. We need a historiography that centers on potentials, alternatives, and diversities, an approach that is open to *alternativity* ("to build some flexibility into a stubborn English noun") in history. During well-patterned, repetitive stages, when historical processes behave themselves in a nicely predictable manner, the "alternativity" of history is low. But, once in a while comes a period of major crisis, a revolution: the constraints of rigidly patterned behaviors, self-censored imaginations, and self-evident stereotypes are broken. At such moments, the "alternativity" of history, the significance of consciousness, and the scope for originality and choice increase dramatically.

2. We are living through a paradigmatic change—the collapse of (or at least a major challenge to) the theory of progress as an arch-model of historical time. What is slowly taking its place is a conceptualization of no agreed label, which substitutes for the models of linear rise models of multidirectionality and unevenness of related changes.

11

Marcuse and Benjamin: The Romantic Dimension

Although the affinity between Marcuse and Benjamin has been noticed frequently, there has been no systematic attempt to examine the nature of their spiritual kinship. Scholem once wrote in his "Reflections on Jewish Theology" that Benjamin and Marcuse are among "the most important ideologists of revolutionary messianism . . . whose acknowledged or unacknowledged ties to their Jewish heritage are evident."[1] This is certainly accurate for Benjamin, but much less evident for Marcuse.

Jewish messianism is clearly one of the main sources of Benjamin's *Weltanschauung*; in its apocalypse, catastrophic, destructive dimension, and in its hope for absolute redemption, it is intimately linked to the utopian anarchism of Benjamin's political writings of the 1920s. Yet, both Jewish messianic and utopian anarchist tendencies were rooted in the same cultural foundation: German romanticism, in its antibourgeois aspect and its nostalgia for the precapitalist society and culture. Neoromantic cultural criticism of industrial capitalist society, in the name of *Kultur* against *Zivilisation*, or *Gemeinschaft* against *Gesellschaft*, was one of the main themes in German literature, philosophy, and the social sciences at the end of the nineteenth and the beginning of the twentieth centuries. Even a rationalist such as Weber was not immune to it. Benjamin's first writings, including his 1919 doctoral thesis on German romanticism, as well as his famous 1922 essay on Goethe's *Wahlverwandschaften*, clearly fall into this context: in his *Dissertation* he discovers the idea of messianism in Schlegel and Novalis, as he found it in the Jewish tradition.

Marcuse, on the contrary, has hardly any links to messianism, Jewish or Christian, nor to religion in general. His attitude toward religion is that of an *Aufklärer* and his worldview is utterly secular and atheistic. What he does have in common with Benjamin is not so much Jewish messianism as German romanticism, with its nostalgia for precapitalist communities and its counterposing of artistic *Kultur* to prosaic bourgeois society. There is a great similarity between his 1922 dissertation, "Der deutsche Künstlerroman" (The German Artist Novel), and Benjamin's "Der Begriff der Kunstkritik in der Deutschen Romantik" (The Concept of Art Criticism in German Romanticism). Marcuse's recently published doctoral thesis is essential for understanding his intellectual evolution from this youthful work to his later writings. The central theme of the book is the contradiction between the world of Idea and empirical reality, art and bourgeois life—a contradiction painfully perceived and expressed by the romantics. Some of them, particularly Novalis, tried to overcome this duality by ignoring the empirical world, replacing it with an ideal reality—an imaginary new world dominated by love and peace, Eros and Freya. Others, like Goethe in the *Sorrows of the Young Werther*, show how the artist's idealist subjectivity leads him to a radical conflict with the *zweckhaft-rationellen* order of reality—a conflict that cannot but end with his surrender or death. And some later romantics, like E. T. A. Hoffmann, are attracted to the ancient, dark, and dissolving forces of passion that threaten to explode the existing world.[2] For Marcuse, most of the artist novels (i.e., novels whose central hero is an artist) contain a critical dimension against the growing industrialization and mechanization of economic and cultural life, as a process that destroys or marginalizes all spiritual values. He stresses the burning aspiration of many romantic or neo-romantic writers for a radical change of life, breaking the narrow limits of bourgeois-philistine materialism, and he compares them with contemporary utopian socialists such as Fourier.[3] Some of these ideas of *Der deutsche Künstlerroman* reappear, almost unchanged, in *Eros and Civilization* and *One Dimensional Man*.

There is a striking parallel between the intellectual evolution of Marcuse and Benjamin: both begin with German romanticism and the problems of art; both move towards Marxism during the 1920s, under the influence of Lukács and Korsch, and both become linked to the Frankfurt Institute of Social Research during the 1930s; both are highly critical of social democracy, hope for a socialist revolutionary transformation, but refuse to join the Communist party; and they probably met in Germany or in Paris (1933). Nevertheless, to the best of our knowledge, during Benjamin's lifetime, there is no mention of him in Marcuse's writings.[4] Why this silence? One possible hypothesis is that after the short Heideggerian interlude of 1928–32, Marcuse moved increasingly away from romanticism and toward an interpretation of Marxism linking it to the tradition of Western rationalism, from Plato to Descartes, and from the *Aufklärung* to Hegel.

During his whole life, Marcuse's Marxism moved between two poles: the romantic and the rationalist. For him, these poles are not contradictory. They have a common element, which is the constant substance of his thought: *negation*, the opposition between the idea and the given reality.

There is a remarkable passage in Marcuse's 1960 new preface to *Reason and Revolution* where this is explicitly stated: "Dialectic and poetic language meet . . . on common ground. The common element is the search for . . . the language of negation as the Great Refusal."[5] For Marcuse, another link between rationalism and romanticism is their commitment to *qualitative* human values, cultural or ethical, as opposed to mere quantitative values of the capitalist market. But Reason is conceived as *substantial*, not purely formal and instrumental, which also can be found in capitalist industry, even in concentration camps. This unity of the two poles is the unity of Marcuse's oeuvre beyond the particular (romantic or rationalist) emphasis of different periods of his intellectual evolution.

During the 1930s and 1940s, the rationalist pole becomes predominant in Marcuse's thought. After 1925, when he published an annotated bibliography of Schiller's works, the problems of art, literature, and culture and their opposition to reality tend to disappear from his writings for the next three decades. Although in 1937 he published an essay on "The Affirmative Character of Culture," this text, far from being a restatement of his 1922 ideas, is precisely their *most radical negation*. According to it, traditional culture—in particular literature, by preserving an ideal world above and opposed to the vulgarity of daily life, plays an ideological and conservative role; the beauty of the "soul" (*Seele*) is extolled as a compensation for the wretchedness of the material world: "The freedom of the soul was used to excuse the misery, martyrdom and enslavement of the body. It serves the ideological surrender of existence to the economy of capitalism. . . . The soul has a tranquilizing effect . . . the joys of the soul are cheaper than those of the body and less dangerous." Marcuse seems to believe that there is a basic difference between philosophy and literature, in their relation to the established state of affairs: "The beauty of art—in contrast to the truth of theory—is compatible with the existing evil."

Therefore, to this "affirmative" cultural sphere, with its illusory freedom and happiness, Marcuse opposes the tradition of rational philosophy—Descartes, Kant, Hegel—which is alien to the concept of "soul" and committed to the critical rationality of *spirit*. While the concept of *Seele* is typical of irrationalist tendencies, from romantic historicism (Herder) to modern authoritarian doctrines (a euphemism for fascist ideology), "Hegel does not fit in the authoritarian states. He was for the spirit; the new ones are for the soul and for sentiment." Of course, Marcuse is aware of the one-sided character of this indictment of traditional art and literature in the bourgeois era; he recognizes that they "contain not only the justification of established forms of existence, but also the pain of its existence; not only the reconciliation with that which is, but also the memory of that which could be. Great bourgeois art, because it . . . painted the beauty of people and things and a supra-earthly happiness with the bright colors of this world . . . deposed at the foundation of bourgeois life not only false consolation . . . but also true nostalgia (*Sehnsucht*)." This insight will become decisive in Marcuse's late writings. In 1937, however, it is integrated as a subordinate element in the general conception of culture as "affirmative": "Culture becomes a servant of the existent. The rebellious idea becomes a level for its justification. . . . Since art depicts the beautiful as present, it brings rebellious nostalgia to a halt." Needless to say, such a theoretical framework could not but alienate Marcuse from Benjamin's aesthetic and cultural preoccupations.[6]

This rationalist orientation, which runs through most of Marcuse's 1930s essays, culminating in 1941 with *Reason and Revolution*, may explain why he ignored Benjamin's works. Conversely, Marcuse's increasing move toward the romantic pole in the fifties and sixties may be one of the reasons why he rediscovered Benjamin at that time. One can trace the development of this new turn in Marcuse's thinking through the various prefaces to *Reason and Revolution*, from 1941, 1954, and 1960. In 1941 Marcuse still praised the "American rationalist spirit." This had a direct political translation in his activity as an (antifascist) adviser for the American Office of Strategic Services during the war. But in the 1950s, after the Cold War and McCarthyism, and after a deeper study of American society, Marcuse grew increasingly critical of industrial civilization and its instrumental rationality. In the "Epilogue" written in 1954 for the second edition of the book, Marcuse recognized the *contradictory* character of the Western rationalist tradition: "From the beginning, the idea and the reality of Reason in the modern period contained the elements which endangered its promise of a free and fulfilled existence: the enslavement of man by his own productivity . . . the repressive mastery of nature in man and outside."[7] At the same time, he rediscovered the subversive virtues of imagination and art, that is, the problematic of his early 1920 writings.

This new "romantic" period began with *Eros and Civilization* (1955) where, reinterpreting Freud, Marcuse contraposed erotic sensuousness to the rationality of the performance principle. Art was then conceived in a completely different light than in the 1937 essay (which had opposed the truth of theory to the illusory beauty of artistic imagination): "Fantasy is cognitive in so far as it preserves the truth of the Great Refusal, or, positively, in so far as it protects, against all reason, the aspirations for the integral fulfillment of man and nature which are repressed by reason." The great German writer on whom he had worked in 1925 comes once more into the fore: Friedrich Schiller, whose aesthetic essays attain an "explosive quality" by showing that "freedom would have to be sought in the liberation of sensuousness rather than reason," or at least that "the laws of reason must be reconciled with the interests of the senses." Moreover, according to

Marcuse, "Herder and Schiller, Hegel and Novalis developed in almost identical terms the concept of alienation. As industrial society begins to take shape under the rule of the performance principle, its inherent negativity permeates the philosophical analysis" (a quote from Schiller follows). This remark is highly significant: it combines in the same socio-cultural "front" artists and philosophers, romantics and rationalists, and in particular two thinkers Marcuse had counterposed in 1937 as representatives of the *Seele* (Herder) and of the *Geist* (Hegel).[8]

It is no accident that in *Eros and Civilization*, the first work where the romantic dimension of Marcuse's thought reemerges, is also to be found Marcuse's "rediscovery" of Walter Benjamin. He quotes, comments on, and praises an important passage from the *Theses on the Philosophy of History* (1940). When Marcuse wrote the book, Benjamin's main essays had not yet been republished (Marcuse quotes the *Theses* from a 1950 publication in *Die neue Rundschau*). It is well known that Adorno's edition of the *Schriften* in 1955 became the starting point for a general reception of Benjamin by the Western radical intelligentsia. But Marcuse's interest in him precedes and is not related to it. It flows, rather, from the inner dynamics of his own spiritual development.

In the passage quoted by Marcuse, Benjamin writes: "The wish to break the continuum of history belongs to the revolutionary class in the moment of action." In connection with this passage and the whole content of Benjamin's *Theses*, Marcuse argues: "Remembrance is no real weapon unless it is translated into historical action. Then, the struggle against time becomes a decisive moment in the struggle against domination." The memory of the past as a weapon in the fight for the future: one could hardly imagine a more striking and precise formulation of the romantic revolutionary perspective, which is common to Marcuse and Benjamin and pervades both their political and their aesthetic views.[9]

From 1955 to his last writings, Marcuse was attracted once more to art and the romantic artistic ideal of a world dominated by Eros and peace. This ideal is one of the central features of *One Dimensional Man* (1964), where he stressed its critical potential: "The traditional images of artistic alienation *are indeed romantic* in as much as they are in aesthetic incompatibility with the developing society. *This incompatibility is the token of their truth.* What they recall and preserve in memory pertains to the future: images of a gratification that would dissolve the society which suppresses it. The great surrealist art and literature of the 1920s and 1930s has still recaptured them in their subversive and liberating function."[10] Similar statements on the contradiction between the artistic or poetic universe and the given reality, as well as on the revolutionary dimension of surrealism are also to be found in Marcuse's subsequent books. For instance, in *An Essay on Liberation* (1969), he hails the absolute nonconformism of surrealist poets who find "in the poetic language the semantic elements of the revolution."[11] Benjamin was also a great admirer of surrealism, precisely for its romantic revolutionary and libertarian character. In his essay on French surrealism (1929), he wrote: "Since Bakunin, Europe has been lacking a radical concept of liberty. The surrealists have it. . . . To win the forces of Rausch for the revolution, that was the aim of surrealism in all its books and enterprises."[12]

Marcuse insists—in *Counterrevolution and Revolt* (1972)—that in the most important works of art and literature since the nineteenth century "a thoroughly *anti-bourgeois* stance is prevalent: the higher culture indicts, rejects, withdraws from the material culture of the bourgeoisie. It is indeed separated: it dissociates itself from the world of commodities, from the brutality of bourgeois industry and commerce, from the distortion of human relationships, from capitalist materialism, from instrumentalist reason. The aesthetic universe *contradicts* reality." It is significant that among the great works of literature that represent for Marcuse the most authentic, absolute, and uncompromising form of sublimated Eros, works which, in his view—in *One Dimensional Man*—are "beyond the reaches of the established Reality Principle, which the Eros refuses and explodes" are Goethe's *Wahlverwandschaften* and Baudelaire's *Fleurs du Mal*—two books that are central in Benjamin's aesthetic and philosophical reflection (the first one in the 1920s and the second one during the 1930s).[13]

The relation to Benjamin occupies a very special place in *One Dimensional Man*. As is well known, the book ends with a powerful and moving homage to him: "Critical theory . . . holding no promise and showing no success, remains negative. Thus it wants to remain loyal to those who, without hope, have given and give their life to the Great Refusal. At the beginning of the fascist era, Walter Benjamin wrote: 'Nur um der Hoffnungslosen willen ist uns die Hoffnung gegeben.' It is only for the sake of those without hope that hope is given to us."[14] In its original context, this passage from Benjamin's 1922 essay on Goethe's *Wahlverwandschaften* had a deep religious meaning, while Marcuse gives it a directly political translation (in a way typical of his "secular" reading of Benjamin).

One can find here a *common* element, a peculiar quality of their style of thought, which could be designated as *desperate hope* or *pessimist revolutionarism*. Both Marcuse and Benjamin refuse to believe that the "natural course" of history, the development of productive forces, or inevitable social progress will lead to a rational and liberated society. For them, as Benjamin formulated it in a most remarkable image, the revolutionaries must learn to "brush history against the grain." There is no predestined and irresistible triumph of humanity and reason. Left to itself, "progress" produces only, as in Benjamin's allegory of the angel of history, a "pile of wreckage."

Revolution is not "swimming with the stream" but is a fierce struggle against the blind forces of history, a hard and protracted war whose end result cannot be predicted. In a postscript to a new edition of Marx's *Eighteenth Brumaire*, Marcuse wrote: "the consciousness of defeat, even desperation, belongs to the truth of the theory and its hope." Far from favoring passivity (as does resignation *as well as official optimism* in Kautsky), this brand of voluntarist pessimism is, on the contrary, the most desperate call for action, initiative, and resistance.[15]

In this respect, *One Dimensional Man* owes much to Benjamin's 1940 *Theses*. One can therefore understand why, at the same year as his book appeared (1964), Marcuse felt the need to write an essay on Walter Benjamin himself. This little-known piece is an afterword to a collection of five articles by Benjamin, among them the *Theses on the Philosophy of History* and the *Critique of Violence* (1921). It is not a systematic piece, but clearly reveals the common features between the two—as well as their differences.

First of all both Marcuse and Benjamin stand for an *absolute* negation of the existing social order. Both aspire to a *radical* revolution and recognize the need of oppressed groups to use *violence* against the oppressors. Commenting on Benjamin's essay on violence (1921), Marcuse stresses: "The violence, to which Benjamin's criticism is directed, is not the one . . . employed from below against those above. . . . The violence criticized by Benjamin is that of the existent (*Bestehenden*), which obtained from the existent itself the monopoly of legitimacy, of truth and of right. . . . Benjamin took much too seriously the promise contained in the word 'Peace' to be a pacifist. . . ."[16] Both are irreconcilably opposed to all reformism and gradualism and perceive revolution as *an explosion of the historical continuum*, a totally new beginning, and not an improved version of the existing, or the cumulative result of progressive evolution. At the same time, paradoxically, this new future implies a return to the precapitalist past: as Benjamin puts it in his famous image, resolution is "a dialectical leap of the tiger into the past." These and other leitmotivs of Benjamin's 1940 *Theses* are shared by Marcuse, not only in this essay on Benjamin, but in most of his 1960 and 1970 works.

However, there are also undeniable differences in their understanding of revolution. In his commentaries, Marcuse ignores the anarchist component of Benjamin's early writings and tries to neutralize their religious content by presenting a thoroughly secular and a-theological interpretation of Benjamin's messianism. Thus, he writes: "It becomes clear in Benjamin's critique of violence that messianism is the form of appearance of a historical truth: liberated humanity is only conceivable as the radical (no more the simply 'determinate') negation of the existent, because under the power of the existent even the Good itself becomes powerless and an accomplice.

Benjamin's messianism has nothing to do with traditional religiosity: guilt and expiation are for him social categories."[17] This interpretation may be partly true, but it is one-sided: Benjamin's deep theological dimension, rooted in the Jewish tradition, is linked to social categories, but cannot be reduced to them. Marcuse's remarks are as revealing of his own views as of Benjamin's messianism. While in 1941, in *Reason and Revolution*, he still spoke in terms of a "determinate" negation of the given reality, now, in 1964, he pleads for more total negativity.

The other broad outlook shared by Benjamin and Marcuse is that both criticize not only capitalism but, more generally, all of industrial society, reified technology and alienated productivity, the destruction of nature, and the myth of progress. As Marcuse writes in his essay on Benjamin: "In opposition to the abominable concept of progressive productivity, for whom nature 'exists gratis' to be exploited, Benjamin professes Fourier's idea of a social labor which 'far from exploiting nature, is capable of delivering her of the creations which lie dormant in her womb as potentials.' To liberated humanity, redeemed from oppressive violence, corresponds a liberated and redeemed nature."[18] This is also one of the reasons why both are so critical of the Soviet Union, which failed in their eyes to generate a real alternative to the industrial society of the West, with its productivism and its technological reification.

On the other hand, both Benjamin and Marcuse recognize—each in his own way—the emancipatory possibilities of modern technology. This applies to cinema in the cultural area, for Benjamin, and to automation in the economic sphere, for Marcuse. Both try to grasp the contradictory nature of material progress and industrial technology, even if their conclusions are not the same (Marcuse, like Adorno and Horkheimer, is more critical than Benjamin of the mass production of art and cultural goods).

Benjamin is once more mentioned in Marcuse's last work, *The Aesthetic Dimension* (1977), where the contradiction between art (literature) and established reality, which was the subject matter of his 1922 *Dissertation*, again becomes the main theme of work. Although in 1977 modern and not classic romantic writers are central, Marcuse mentions, as one of the crass errors of dogmatic Marxist aesthetics, "the denigration of romanticism as simply reactionary." *The Aesthetic Dimension* does not oppose "soul" to Reason; it shows that art is committed to the emancipation of sensibility, imagination, *and* reason—a reason distinct from the rationality of the dominant institutions. By its association with Eros against instinctual repression, the aesthetic dimension is a protest against the established world and a promise of liberation. And by preserving the memory of things past, it fulfills a revolutionary role, since "the authentic utopia is grounded in recollection."

The two references to Benjamin in this book reveal Marcuse's affinity with his friend's romantic dimension but also a certain reserve toward his views on the relation between art and politics. It seems as if Marcuse feels closer to the "Baudelairian Benjamin" than to the "Brechtian Benjamin." Although he is an admirer of Brecht's poems (one of them is extensively quoted in *One Dimensional Man*), Marcuse is inclined to believe that, as he puts it, "there may be more subversive potential in the poetry of Baudelaire and Rimbaud than in the didactic plays of Brecht." He criticizes Benjamin's most "Brechtian" writing, "The Author as Producer," for its "identification of literary and political quality in the domain of art." On the other hand, he greatly admires Benjamin's essays on the *poètes maudits*: "the degree to which the distance and estrangement from praxis constitute the emancipatory value of art becomes particularly clear in those works of literature which seem to close themselves rigidly against such praxis. Benjamin has traced this in the works of Poe, Baudelaire, Proust and Valery." Marcuse then adds this commentary: "The 'secret' protest of this esoteric literature lies in the ingression of the primary erotic-destructive forces which explode the normal universe of communication and behavior. They are asocial in their very nature, a subterranean rebellion against the social order."[19]

Both Marcuse and Benjamin were romantic revolutionaries—romantic in the sense of nostalgia for precapitalist *Kultur*, a nostalgia preserved in great art as "remembrance of things past," and revolutionary because they transformed this nostalgia of the past into a radical negation of the present order and into a "desperate hope" for a radically new future society.

This romantic revolutionarism is *not* contradictory with their Marxism, since in Marx and Engels, too, there is a romantic dimension—it is enough to mention their attitude toward certain writers (Carlyle, Balzac, and others). It is, of course, a dimension suppressed by the "one-dimensional" Marcuse of the twentieth century. Finally, this romantic revolutionary orientation is not alien to class struggle, since both Benjamin and Marcuse, each in his way, saw his whole work, life, and thought as ultimately linked to the struggle of the oppressed for their emancipation.

Notes

1. Gershom Scholem, *On Jews and Judaism in Crisis* (New York: Schocken, 1976), p. 287. Scholem mentions also Bloch and Adorno.
2. Referring to E. T. A. Hoffmann, Marcuse notes that in his works "no bridge can be built over the abyss" between passion and the real world; in his essay on Goethe's *Wahlverwandschaften*, also written in 1922, Benjamin advances exactly the same idea: there is in the novel an abyss between passion and "bourgeois

life." See Walter Benjamin, "Goethe's Wahlverwandschaften," 1922, in *Illuminationen* (Frankfurt a.M.: Suhrkamp, 1969), p. 131.

3. Herbert Marcuse, *Der deutsche Künstlerroman*, 1922, in *Schriften*, vol. 1 (Frankfurt a.M.: Suhrkamp, 1978), pp. 43–49, 86, 117–19, 133–43.
4. Benjamin mentions Marcuse in his short article on the Frankfurt Institute of Social Research (1938), and also refers favorably, in a letter to Horkheimer, to Marcuse's contribution to the collective volume *Autorität und Familie*. See Walter Benjamin, "Ein deutsches Institut Freier Forschung," 1938, in *Gesammelte Schriften*, vol. 3 (Frankfurt a.M.: Suhrkamp, 1972), pp. 526, 683.
5. Herbert Marcuse, "Preface," in *Reason and Revolution* (Boston: Beacon Press, 1960), p. x.
6. Herbert Marcuse, "Über den Affirmativen Charakter der Kultur," 1937, in *Kultur und Gesellschaft*, vol. 1 (Frankfurt a.M.: Suhrkamp, 1970), pp. 67–68, 76–81, 89–94. Benjamin knew this essay and mentions it in his notice on the Frankfurt Institute (1938), where he stresses, in reference to Marcuse, the need to oppose a *critical* concept of culture to the "affirmative" one. For him, this "critical culture" is not identified, as for Marcuse, with rationalist philosophy and Hegel: it is made up of cultural elements which, "linked to their early times and to their dreams, do not deny their solidarity with the coming humanity, with humanity herself." Far from rejecting, as did Marcuse, the bourgeois cultural tradition as "ideology," he insists on the need to "salvage the cultural heritage" and, by developing critical insights, to "make room for an authentic tradition." Cf. Benjamin, "Ein deutsches Institut," pp. 525–26.
7. Herbert Marcuse, "Epilogue," in *Reason and Revolution* (Atlantic Highlands, N.J.: Humanities Press, 1954; reprint, 1991), p. 433. Of course, it is probable that Marcuse had also been influenced by Adorno and Horkheimer's criticism of the rationalist tradition in *Dialektik der Aufklärung* (1947), but there is no doubt that he followed his own path to this conclusion.
8. Herbert Marcuse, *Eros and Civilization*, 1955 (London: Sphere Books, 1969), pp. 132, 151, 154.
9. Marcuse, *Eros and Civilization*, p. 186.
10. Herbert Marcuse, *One Dimensional Man* (London: Routledge, 1964), p. 60 (emphasis added).
11. Herbert Marcuse, *An Essay on Liberation* (Boston: Beacon Press, 1969), p. 33.
12. Walter Benjamin, "Der Sürrealismus," (1929), in *Angelus Novus* (Frankfurt a.M.: Suhrkamp, 1966), p. 212.
13. Herbert Marcuse, *Counterrevolution and Revolt* (Boston: Beacon Press, 1972), p. 86; Marcuse, *One Dimensional Man*, p. 77.
14. Marcuse, *One Dimensional Man*, p. 257.
15. Walter Benjamin, "Theses on the Philosophy of History," 1940, in *Illuminations* (London: J. Cape, 1970), pp. 259–61. On Marcuse's "pessimism" see Russell Jacoby's interesting essay "Reversal and Lost Meanings," in *Critical Interruptions, New Left Perspectives on Herbert Marcuse*, ed. Paul Breines (New York: Herder and Herder, 1970), pp. 70–73.
16. Herbert Marcuse, "Nachwort," in Walter Benjamin, *Zur Kritik der Gewalt* (Frankfurt a.M.: Suhrkamp, 1965), pp. 99–100.
17. Ibid., pp. 100–101.
18. Ibid., p. 104.
19. Herbert Marcuse, *The Aesthetic Dimension* (Boston: Beacon Press, 1979), pp. xii-xiii, 6–9, 11, 19–20, 33, 73.

12

Revolution against "Progress": Walter Benjamin's Romantic Anarchism

Walter Benjamin's style of thinking is unique and resists classification, but it can be better understood and explained if related to the cultural atmosphere of *Mittel-Europa* at the beginning of the century, and to certain religious-political undercurrents among German-speaking Jewish intellectuals of this period. *Neo-romanticism*, as a moral and social critique of "progress" and of modern *Zivilisation*—in the name of a nostalgic loyalty to the traditional *Kultur*—became the dominant trend among the German intelligentsia from the end of the nineteenth century to the rise of fascism. It was mainly a reaction to the very forceful, brutal, and rapid process of industrialization of the country during this time, which threatened to dissolve all ancient values and beliefs and replace them with the cold and rational calculations of commodity production. Several German-speaking Jewish writers and philosophers were attracted by this *Weltanschauung* and developed (in a relationship of elective affinity) a romantic version of Jewish messianism and a romantic version of revolutionary (libertarian) utopia. One of the central elements in this affinity was the restorative-utopian character of both spiritual configurations, which can be found in the works of several well-known figures of the Central European Jewish intelligentsia: Martin Buber, Gershom Scholem, Gustav Landauer, Ernst Bloch, Georg Lukács, and so on.[1]

Walter Benjamin is related to this pattern not only by his personal links with most of the members of this complex network, but also because he concentrates in his life and thought all the contradictions, tensions, and oppositions that divided this neo-romantic Jewish-German culture: between Jewish theology and Marxist materialism, assimilation and Zionism, communism and anarchism, conservative romanticism and nihilist revolution, mystical messianism and profane utopia.

The intimate association of messianic and anarchist-utopian themes (against a background of neo-romantic criticism of "progress") is one of the central features of Benjamin's political philosophy. If we examine one of his first works, the speech "On Student Life" (1914), we can already find the seeds of his whole social-religious *Weltanschauung*. Against the "formless" idea of progress he celebrates the critical power of *utopian images*, such as those of the French Revolution and of the messianic kingdom; the real issues for society are not those of technology and science, but the metaphysical problems raised by Plato, Spinoza, the romantics, and Nietzsche, under whose inspiration the student community should become the harbinger of a "permanent spiritual revolution." The anarchist dimension is already suggested by the statement that truly free art and knowledge are "alien to the state, frequently hostile to the state." But it is also present in a more explicit way, in the reference to the Tolstoyan spirit of serving the poor, whose most authentic expressions were "the ideas of the most profound Anarchists and the Christian monastic communities."[2] Utopia, anarchism, revolution, and messianism are alchemically combined and linked to a neo-romantic cultural criticism of "progress" and merely technical-scientific knowledge; the past (the monastic communities) and the future (the anarchist utopia) are directly associated in a characteristically romantic-revolutionary shortcut. This document contains *in nuce* many of Benjamin's future preoccupations, and one can rigorously show its similarity with his last writings. It suggests certain themes and motives that will recur during his life work, sometimes openly, sometimes as a hidden undercurrent. We can see a basic continuity in his spiritual trajectory from 1914 to 1940—which does not mean that there were no changes or transmutations: after 1924 Marxism becomes an increasingly essential ingredient of his worldview. Communism and historical materialism did not replace his former spiritualist and libertarian convictions, but amalgamated with them, forming a distinctive pattern of thought.

For Benjamin—as for many young Jewish intellectuals at the beginning of the century—romanticism was the starting point, the decisive cultural climate, the basic sources of values and feelings. It is important to insist on this, because criticism has (in general) not given sufficient attention to his neo-romantic background and its relevance for his own social, religious, and philosophical-historical views—which represent of course an original perspective, irreducible to classical romantic ideas.

In one of his first publications (under the pseudonym "J. Ardor"), the short notice "Romantik" (1913), Benjamin criticizes the "false Romanticism" taught in school and calls for the birth of a "new Romanticism," stressing that "the Romantic *will* to beauty, the Romantic *will* to truth, the Romantic *will* to action" are "insuperable" (*unüberwindlich*) acquisitions of modern culture.[3] In a little-noticed but highly significant essay in the form of a dialogue, also from 1913 ("Dialog über die Religiosität der Gegenwart"), he writes that "we all still live very deeply immersed in the discoveries of Romanticism" and that we have to thank romanticism for the most powerful insights on "the nocturnal side of the natural." Sharply criticizing the reduction of men to working machines and the debasement of all work to the technical, he insists, in opposition to the illusions of progress and evolution, on the need for a new religion (whose prophets would be Tolstoy, Nietzsche, and Strindberg—i.e., cultural critics of modern civilization) and for a new, "sincere" (*ehrlichen*) socialism, very different from the conventional one.[4]

Enlightenment "Blindness"

Benjamin's first important literary essay (1914–15) was devoted to the revolutionary-romantic Hölderlin, and after 1916, he became fascinated by Friedrich Schlegel's youthful writings, which were to be the *prima materia* of his doctoral thesis. In a letter to Scholem in June 1917, he praised the "infinite deepness and beauty" of the *Frühromantik* (Friedrich and August Wilhelm Schlegel, Novalis, Tieck, and Schleiermacher were mentioned); he was particularly attracted by its ways of uniting religion and history and he significantly concluded that "Romanticism is the last movement that has once again saved tradition for us."[5] At the beginning of 1918, in the essay "Über das Programm der kommenden Philosophie," he sharply criticized the "blindness" not only of the Enlightenment but of *the new times* (*Neuzeit*) in general, precisely in relation to two dimensions of culture that are so essential to romanticism: religion and history. His neo-romantic scorn for the *Aufklärung* went so far that he singled it out as "one of the lowest-situated world-views," and as a cultural era whose experience was "flat and shallow."[6] In 1919 Benjamin presented his thesis "Der Begriff der Kunstkritik in der deutschen Romantik," and it was under the inspiration of this romantic method of literary criticism that he wrote his well-known essay on Goethe's *Elective Affinities*—celebrated by one of the main figures of neo-romanticism, the writer Hugo von Hofmannsthal, as "absolutely incomparable." The correspondence during the twenties gives evidence of his persistent interest in romanticism: he was deeply stimulated by Johann Wilhelm Ritter's "distinctively Romantic esotericism," by Tieck's novel *Eckbert the Blond*, by the medieval fairy tales, and by Grimm's collections of German *Sagen*.[7] He was even sensitive to conservative neo-romantic cultural critics of capitalism: the mystic and esoteric German poet Stefan Georg, the Catholic royalist French novelist Leon Bloy ("has ever a bitterer criticism, or rather satire, been written against the bourgeoisie?"), the Bachofen conservative commentator Ludwig Klages ("without doubt a great philosophical work"), and even—*horribile dictu*—*Action Française*, to which he subscribed in 1924.[8] In 1930 he gave a lecture on E. T. A. Hoffmann and Oscar Panizza, who represented for him "the beginning and the end of the Romantic spiritual movement in Germany in the last century," and whose religious-metaphysical dualism between Life and Automaton he considered as a kind of theology. He saw Hoffmann, with his fantastic story telling, as the follower of an old tradition going back to the Greek and Oriental epic, and he considered that "authentic story-telling (*Erzählen*) has always a conservative character, in the best meaning of the word, and we cannot think of any one of the great story-tellers separated from the oldest spiritual heritage of humanity." He also celebrated Hoffmann's belief in "effective connexions with the most ancient times" (*Urzeit*); as we shall see, this reference to a primeval, archaic, or ancestral era would become central in his later writings, in contradistinction to the usual romantic nostalgia for the Middle Ages.[9]

It is true that in the thirties, with his growing appropriation of historical materialism, the references to romanticism tend to become infrequent; yet some basic elements of the romantic worldview are chemically sublimated in his religious and philosophico-political ideas. One of the last discussions of romanticism in his writings is a review in 1939 of Albert Beguin, *Le romantisme et les rêves*. Benjamin argues that the author was unable to understand romanticism as a reaction to social and industrial development, and he concludes with this illuminating insight: "The Romantic appeal to dream life was an emergency signal; it pointed less towards the way home of the soul to its Motherland, than to the obstacles that already had barred this way."[10]

Romantic Messianism

The link between romanticism and messianism is documented not only by Benjamin's interest in the kabbalist-philosophical writings of the German romantic Ranz Joseph Molitor,[11] but above all in his doctoral thesis, where he insists that the true essence of the *Frühromantik* "must be sought in Romantic Messianism." He discovers the messianic dimension of romanticism, especially in the writings of Schlegel and Novalis, and quotes among others this astonishing statement by the young Friedrich Schlegel: "The revolutionary desire to achieve the Kingdom of God is the beginning of modern history. Anything which is not related to the Kingdom of God is for it just marginal."[12] This theme seems incidental to the main aesthetic subject of the work, but it was essential to his own preoccupations: in a letter to Ernst Schoen, in April 1919, he explains that he cannot deal with "the centre of Romanticism, Messianism," because such questions, though "highly relevant," would prevent the thesis from keeping to a "conventionally scientific" form (which he distinguishes from the authentic one).[13]

Noting in his diary in 1916 a conversation with his friend, Gershom Scholem writes: "The spirit of Benjamin turns . . . around the phenomena of myth, which he approaches from various angles. From history, where he starts from Romanticism, from poetry, where he starts from Hölderlin, from religion, where he starts from Judaism."[14] Benjamin's mind is at this moment a peculiar cultural crucible, in which Hölderlin (or Schlegel) and the Bible, romantic poetry and messianic theology, history and religion are distilled to produce a new and unexpected substance.

Benjamin's libertarian utopia is also grounded in a neo-romantic structure of feeling. There is a very illuminating passage in a letter of 1918 to Gershom Scholem where this connection is explicitly stated. After proclaiming that romanticism is "one of the most powerful movements of the present times," Benjamin argues that "through the reception of social elements" the ideal side of romantic Catholicism (as opposed to its association with political power) "developed into Anarchism (Leonhard Frank, Ludwig Rubiner)."[15] As we have seen, the Catholic-romantic restorative dimension is intimately linked, in Benjamin's speech on students (1914), to its libertarian aspect: monastic communities and anarchist groups are presented as the two most significant models of social action.

In a more general way, Benjamin's social views are influenced by libertarian, anarchist, or anarcho-syndicalist thinkers most akin to romantic anticapitalism and its restitutionist aspirations: Georges Sorel, Gustav Landauer. But his thinking is far from political in the usual sense of the term. Paradoxically he seems to have been attracted neither by the Russian October Revolution nor by the German Revolution of 1918–19; in discussions with Scholem at this time he was more reticent towards the new Soviet power than his friend, who saw it as a kind of "dictatorship of the poor." The sympathies of both went rather to the Socialist Revolutionary (SR) heirs of the Russian "nihilists"—whom they considered to be closer than the Bolsheviks to anarchist ideas.[16] Scholem described as "theocratic anarchism" the conception that was common to both in 1919—the term "theocratic" having a purely religious rather than political significance.[17] According to Werner Kraft, who knew him well at that time, Benjamin's anarchism had a certain "symbolic" quality: it was neither left nor right but "somewhere else."[18] In the twenties Benjamin himself used the term "nihilism" with evident pleasure to designate his own political, or rather antipolitical, ideas.[19] Scholem certainly contributed to the development of such convictions, by providing him with libertarian literature such as the writings of Landauer,[20] but the 1914 speech on students indicates that the tendency already existed before they met.

The key to Benjamin's peculiar form of anarchism lies in its relationship to Jewish messianism—a relationship that can best be analyzed as one of *elective affinity*. Growing out of the same neo-romantic roots, the two cultural outlooks have in common a utopian-restitutionist structure, a revolutionary-catastrophist perspective on history, and a libertarian image of the edenic future.

One of the first occasions on which Benjamin fully expressed his libertarian-revolutionary views was the essay on violence ("Zur Kritik der Gewalt," 1921), directly inspired by Sorel's *Reflections on Violence*. Speaking with harsh contempt of state institutions such as the police ("the most degenerate possible form of violence") or parliament ("miserable representation"), he endorses the "devastating" antiparliamentarian critique of the anarcho-syndicalists and the Bolsheviks (a highly revealing association), as well as the Sorelian idea of the proletarian general strike as an action "whose one and only task is to destroy the violence of the state." This conception, which he explicitly describes as *anarchist*, seems to him "profound, moral and authentically revolutionary," even if it should lead to "catastrophic consequences." However—and here Benjamin parts company with Sorel and moves into the quite different sphere of theological messianism—"pure" and "immediate" revolutionary violence is a manifestation of *divine violence*, the only one capable of "breaking the circle of the mythical forms of law . . . and therefore the violence of the state" and of establishing "a new historical age"; the only one which is "law-destroying" and radically counterposed both to the mythical law-founding violence and to the reactionary law-conserving violence.[21] The sui generis dialectical bond between anarchism and messianism that constitutes the crux of this truly demonic essay (in Goethe's sense of the word) reappears in a particularly intense form in that piece of hermetic quicksilver *The Theologico-Political Fragment*, written more or less at the same time and significantly influenced, in our view, by a reading of Franz Rosenzweig's *Stern der Erlösung*.[22] Although we cannot here attempt the kind of sentence-by-sentence, word-by-word exegesis that this text deserves, a brief outline will give some idea of its content. It starts by drawing a radical distinction between the sphere of historical becoming and the sphere of the Messiah: "nothing historical can relate by itself and from itself to the Messianic." But immediately afterwards Benjamin tries to bridge this abyss through a subtle mediation, a strange passage from earth to heaven: "the profane order of the profane may advance the coming of the Messianic Kingdom. The profane is indeed not a category of this Kingdom, but a category, the most adequate one, for the easiest approach to it."[23] The similarity but not identity with Rosenzweig's thesis—"acts of liberation" which "are not in themselves the kingdom of God" but constitute a "precondition for its coming"—seems undeniable. Concluding the fragment, Benjamin calls for a spiritual and worldly *restitutio in integrum* and assigns this task to a peculiar form of worldly politics "whose method must be called nihilism" (the term *anarchism* perhaps being judged too "profane").

SCHEERBART'S UTOPIA

In 1917, thanks to his friendship with Scholem, Benjamin discovered the work of Paul Scheerbart, who had died in poverty and obscurity in 1915. A bizarre and fantastic utopian, a kind of latter-day offspring of Cyrano de Bergerac and Swift, Scheerbart is generally considered to have been a neo-romantic author, and in an autobiographical note he himself wrote: "Artistically, my main roots must be found in the Romantic age." Although he never published anything directly political, he was a friend of the anarchist poet Erich Mühsam—himself linked to the utopian *Neue Gemeinschaft* movement of which Gustav Landauer was a member—and showed affinities with anarchism in his hostility to imperialism, nationalism, militarism, and the institution of the state. In his "astral utopia" *Lesabendio* (1913) he describes an asteroid "Pallas" whose inhabitants have created a society without any laws, political structures, administration, state, or private property, linked by mutual aid and voluntary common activity. The main theme of the novel is the construction of a gigantic tower to reach a mysterious celestial body. The architectural technique seems to play an important role for the author, but in the final analysis it is an instrument in the service of a "cosmotheism," a religious-astral aspiration. The supreme purpose is "subordination to a Greater One," and a leading character refers to the tower as "what one designates in other stars as religion." In 1918–19 Benjamin wrote a first brief notice on *Lesabendio*, in which he presented its leitmotiv as "the spiritual overcoming of technology" and "the spiritual testimony of a Greater One," identified as "the accomplishment of Utopia." However, the specifically political dimension of Scheerbart's novel was not discussed, although it must have figured prominently in a further review, "The True Politician," that Benjamin wrote in 1919 and lost soon afterwards. In a letter to Scholem from November of that year, he explains that his second essay was designed to show that "Pallas" was "the best of all worlds." At any event, Benjamin's intense interest in Scheerbart—to whom he would frequently refer in his writings of the thirties—is evidence enough of a spiritual kinship with his neo-romantic, religious, and libertarian style of thought.[24]

After Benjamin's simultaneous discovery in 1924 of Marxism (through Lukács's *History and Class Consciousness*) and Bolshevism (thanks to Asja Lacis), communism and later historical materialism became central in his political thought. Aware of the tensions between what he called "the foundations of my nihilism" and Hegelian-Marxist dialectics, as represented by Lukács in 1923, he was nevertheless powerfully attracted by the "political praxis of communism" as an "obligatory attitude" (*verbindliche Haltung*).[25] Two years later, he wrote to Scholem that he was considering joining the Communist party, but he insisted that this did not mean he would "abjure" his former anarchism. (By the way, this letter is the first place where he explicitly refers to his own convictions as *anarchist* rather than just "nihilist.") For him, "anarchist methods are useless and the Communist 'goals' nonsense and non-existent"; however, this does not reduce the value of communist action "because it is the corrective for its own goals and because significant *political* aims do not exist."[26] Anarchist goals, it would seem, are significant because they are not political *aims*, yet the best method to achieve them is provided by communist action. According to Richard Wolin, the meaning of this sybilline formulation is that for Benjamin the only ultimately valuable goals are still messianic.[27] That is a quite perceptive interpretation, but precisely because Benjamin sees anarchist goals and messianic aims as kindred if not identical: in the same letter to Scholem he speaks of an identity between religious and political observance "which shows itself only in the paradoxical conversion (*Umschlagen*) of the one into the other (in any direction whatsoever)." This *Umschlagen* is perhaps one of the keys to Benjamin's complex and subtle social-religious *Weltanschauung*, from the *Political-Theological Fragment* to the *Theses on the Philosophy of History*.

Surrealism

The attempt to combine or articulate communism and anarchism is the leitmotiv of Benjamin's well-known essay on surrealism (1929). Referring to himself ("the German observer") as being "in the most exposed position between anarchist fronde and revolutionary discipline," he celebrates surrealism as the most outstanding heir to the libertarian tradition: "since Bakunin, no radical concept of freedom has existed in Europe. The surrealists do have one." They are also heirs to those other "great anarchists who worked during the years from 1865 to 1875, without knowing each other, in the preparation of their time-bombs": Dostoyevski, Rimbaud, and Lautréamont, whose engines exploded exactly at the same time forty years later, in the upsurge of surrealism. Benjamin praises Breton's "revolutionary nihilism" and draws attention to the passage in *Nadja* where the surrealist poet hails the Parisian days of riot in solidarity with the anarchist martyrs Sacco and Vanzetti.

It is true that Benjamin is concerned about the danger of insisting exclusively on the "anarchist component" of revolution, at the expense of its "methodical and disciplined preparation" (i.e., communism). However, he believes that in relation to the cardinal questions of the time, surrealism and communism are very close; in opposition to the mindless, dilettant optimism of social democracy, they have the same view of the destiny of European humanity: "pessimism all along the line." And if the *Communist Manifesto* requires reality to transcend itself (through a "revolutionary discharge"), "the surrealists are the only ones to have understood its present commands."[28]

From 1929 on, the references to anarchism seem to fade away in his writings, as well as those referring to the messianic era, but one can discover their hermetic presence, as a kind of subterranean fire actively shaping developments on the surface. For instance, it is likely that his sympathy for communism during the years 1929–35 was not unrelated to the distinctly "apocalyptic " orientation of the Comintern during this time: the so-called "Third Period," with its doctrine of the final crisis of capitalism and the imminence of world revolution. In his letter to Scholem of April 1931, he refers to the "Bolshevik revolution in Germany" as a probable event in the near future! In his answer, Scholem sees a danger in Benjamin's intense yearning for community, "even if it is the apocalyptic one of revolution"; Benjamin replies in July 1931 that "it is very unlikely that we will have to wait longer than next autumn for the beginning of the civil war."[29] His 1930 article on theories of fascism contains a famous last paragraph (which Adorno wanted to eliminate from a new edition in the 1960s) calling for the "Marxist trick" of transforming world war into civil war in Germany.[30] Benjamin's peculiar *anarcho-Bolshevism* also included a certain mistrust towards the Soviet Union, which increased after 1935—see, for instance, his notes on the conversations with Brecht in 1938, where the Soviet Union is described as a "workers monarchy," comparable to certain "grotesque sports of nature dredged up from the depths of the sea in the form of horned fish or other monsters."[31] After the German-Soviet Pact in 1939 he definitively broke with Stalinism, and in the *Theses on the Philosophy of History* he described the Stalinist leaders as "politicians in whom the opponents of fascism had placed their hopes" but who "confirm their defeat by betraying their own cause."[32] At the same time, his writings from the late thirties evinced a radical contempt for social democracy, and he remained consistent with his old antiparliamentarism in expressing skepticism about the Popular Front in France. In a letter to Fritz Lieb in July 1937, he complained that the left press in France "sticks to the fetish of the 'left' majority, and is not disturbed by the fact that this majority has a policy which, if operated by the right, would provoke riots."[33]

But there is more direct evidence for the persistence of Benjamin's esoteric anarchist faith during the thirties: in February 1935—during the period when he seemed nearest to the orthodox communist doctrine—he wrote in a letter to Alfred Cohn that on reading Drieu La Rochelle's novel *Le Déserteur*, "I discovered with astonishment the exact presentation of my own political attitude (*Haltung*)."[34] An examination of this novel, published in 1934, can therefore give us a precious clue to his "hidden" political philosophy. Its hero (or antihero) is a French deserter from the First World War exiled in Latin America, a cosmopolitan internationalist and antimilitarist for whom "nationalism is the vilest aspect of the modern spirit." The traveler who is arguing with him (and who probably represents Drieu himself) calls him in turn "an old reactionary," "a wandering Jew," "an anarchist," and "an inoffensive utopian." The deserter answers: "I don't want your European state of war, your general mobilization, your military socialization. You may call this by any name you like; anarchist, if you wish. But I know well that I have nothing to do with theories whose books I never read." But there is a kind of spontaneous libertarian spirit in his antipolitical and antistate philosophy: "Politics is the foulest of all games that this planet offers. All that belongs to the State is the vile task of lackeys."[35] If this literary figure is, in Benjamin's words, *the exact presentation* of his own political position, there is no doubt that this was much nearer to anarchism than his published works from 1935 would suggest.

There is a sad and moving passage in Drieu's piece which one cannot read without immediately thinking of Port-Bou, 1940. The Deserter says: "In 1914 I was one of the rare ones, but there will be thousands like me in the next war. There will be thousands of men who will defend themselves against the earthquake, by running away—or who will choose, between two deaths, the one of the executed protester rather than the one of the resigned subject, bombed or gassed."[36]

No explicit reference to anarchism can be found in the various essays and notes on Baudelaire written by Benjamin in 1938–39; but Rolf Tiedemann has very perceptively grasped that these writings "can be read as a palimpsest: under the explicit Marxism the old nihilism becomes visible, whose road threatens to lead to the abstraction of anarchist practice."[37] The term "palimpsest" is perhaps not accurate enough: the relation between the two messages is not a mechanical one of superimposition, but rather an alchemical one of alloying previously distilled elements.

The same applies to the *Theses on the Philosophy of History* (1940): according to Tiedemann, "Benjamin's representation of political praxis was rather the enthusiastic one of anarchism than the sober one of Marxism."[38] Such a formulation is debatable, not only because Marxism itself is open to an "enthusiastic" reading, but also because the libertarian and the Marxist utopia are not as contradictory as tradition would have it. Habermas too refers to the presence of an "anarchistic conception of *Jetztzeiten*" in the *Theses*—although in another passage of his essay he wrongly argues that from 1930 on, under the influence of Brecht, Benjamin "dissociated himself from his earlier anarchist inclinations."[39] If anarchist ideas are only implicit in the *Theses* of 1940, there is a more direct reference to them in one of the preparatory notes: "Force of hate in Marx. Pugnacity of the working class. To interweave revolutionary destruction with the idea of Redemption (Nechaev. The Devils)." In another note he insists on the need to release the "destructive energies of historical materialism."[40]

The Power of Destruction

Analyzing the regulative ideas governing Benjamin's thought, Scholem shows that "an apocalyptic element of destructiveness is preserved in the metamorphosis undergone in his writing by the messianic idea, which continues to play a patent part in his thought. The noble and positive power of destruction . . . now becomes an aspect of redemption . . . The secularization of Jewish apocalyptic doctrine is plain for all to see."[41] Scholem relates this idea mainly to the essay *Der destruktive Charakter* and to the literary essays of the thirties, but the preparatory notes to the *Theses on the Philosophy of History* are the most arresting expression of such a messianic revolutionary concept of destruction, "interweaving" class struggle and redemption, Marx and Nechaev, historical materialism and Dostoyevski (considered by Benjamin in 1929 as one of the "great anarchists" of the nineteenth century).

Destructiveness is not the only convergence between messianism and libertarian-communist revolution in Benjamin's late writings. The elective affinity between them is grounded in their common restitutionist/utopian structure: the redeemed future as *restitutio in integrum*, reestablishment of a lost paradise, *Tikkun* of the world.[42] The nostalgia for the lost edenic harmony, which is so decisive in Benjamin's early theological writings—for instance, the essay on language (1916) where the expulsion from Paradise is linked to the loss of the "blessed adamite spirit of language" and the subsequent decay into the linguistic chaos of the Tower of Babel[43]—emerges again in the *Theses*. The expulsion is now represented by the dialectical image of a "storm blowing from Paradise," which "irresistibly propels" the angel of history "into the future." The new figure of the Tower of Babel reaching to the heavens is "the pile of debris growing skyward" produced by the storm—a storm which is nothing other than "what we call progress."[44] The criticism of "progress"—defined in the *Theses* as "one single catastrophe which keeps piling wreckage upon wreckage"—is one of the main combustibles with which Benjamin fuels his fire. Of neo-romantic origin, it receives in his work a peculiarly revolutionary and subversive quality. (Soon after his *Theses* were written, technical progress was to be instrumental in adding the two most catastrophic wreckages ever to the pile: Auschwitz and Hiroshima.) It runs throughout his writings, from the speech on the life of students to the end—with the exception of a short period between 1933 and 1935 when, under the influence of Brecht, he experiments with the idea of technological progress as an instrument to forward revolutionary politics.

We find this basic and essential mistrust of "progress" in the dialectical image of *One-Way Street* (1928), which presents the antibourgeois revolution as the act of cutting the burning fuse before it reaches the dynamite "at a certain almost calculable point in economic and technical development," i.e., before the explosion that would put an end to two thousand years of human culture.[45] It is present in the *Storyteller* essay (1936), where Leskov is hailed (through a quotation from Tolstoy) as one of the first men "who pointed out the inadequacy of economic progress," and as the prototype of the storyteller who keeps faith with the lost golden age of harmony between man and nature.[46] It is a crucial argument in the Fuchs essay (1937), where Benjamin shows that positivism—including positivist social democracy—"was only able to see the progress of natural science in the development of technology, but failed to recognize the concomitant retrogression of society." He opposes to this social democratic (Darwinist) evolutionism and its shallow optimistic illusions—which ignore the dangers of technology (particularly in relation to war)—the "vision of emerging barbarism which Engels perceived in *The Condition of the Working Class in England*, and Marx glimpsed in his prognosis of capitalist development."[47] It is also one of the main reasons why Benjamin felt so attracted to Baudelaire. Among his notes on the French poet, there is a remark that probably dates from 1938: "This devaluation of the human environment by the commodity economy had a deep impact on his historical experience. . . . Nothing is more contemptible than to bring into play the idea of progress against this experience. . . . History has since then shown how right he was, not to rely for this reason on technical progress."[48]

In a remarkable essay Irving Wohlfarth argues that Benjamin variously conceived revolution as accelerating the dialectic of historical progress and as pulling its emergency cord.[49] This is a most lucid formulation, but in our view it is necessary to specify that the first variant was a brief intellectual experiment during the mid-thirties, while the criticism of "progress" was an essential component of most of his oeuvre.

How can we explain Benjamin's short-lived experiment in "progressism"? The usual argument is "Brecht's influence"; but influence in general, far from explaining anything, has itself to be explained. We would suggest the following hypothesis: the articles written in 1933–35, in which one can find a highly positive assessment of technological progress, are also characterized by a rather uncritical stand towards the Soviet Union—whose ideology, at the time of the Second Five-Year Plan, was more than ever a blindly industrialist and productivist brand of Marxism. Until 1933 Benjamin, though sympathetic to the Soviet Union, was open to critical views—as one can gather from his reading with "breathless" enthusiasm Trotsky's *My Life* and *History of the Russian Revolution* in 1931–32.[50] The beginning of the "progressist parenthesis" in Benjamin's work coincided with the advent of Hitler in Germany, which made the Soviet Union appear, in the eyes of many leftist intellectuals, as the last bulwark against fascism. The end of it seems to coincide with the first Moscow trials, which filled Benjamin with perplexity and may have stimulated him to take a greater distance from the Soviet Union and its doctrine. Among the recently discovered papers of Benjamin—now deposited at the Bibliothèque Nationale in Paris—there is a short, undated note on Brecht, containing a sharp indictment of the GPU.[51]

After 1936 Benjamin did not, however, simply dismiss science and technology, nor deny that there had been "advances in man's ability and knowledge" (as he explicitly stated in the *Theses*). What he passionately and obstinately rejected was the mortally dangerous myth that technological development in itself would improve the human social and moral condition, and that socialists had only to follow the irresistible movement of material progress in order to establish an emancipated society. He was keenly aware that without a revolutionary interruption of technological progress as it existed under capitalism, the future of mankind itself would be threatened. Moreover, he was increasingly convinced that capitalist industrial "progress" had produced considerable social "regression" and made of human life exactly the contrary of the lost paradise: namely, hell itself. In *Zentralpark* (1938), Benjamin argued that "the concept of progress is to be grounded in the idea of catastrophe. That things 'go like that' *is* the catastrophe. . . . Strindberg's thought: hell is not anything imminent—it is *this life here*."[52] The Second World War was soon to provide a very concrete figure of this profane hell, produced with the help of the most advanced conquests of technology.

The Interruption of History

Against the social democratic and vulgar Marxist myth of progress as an automatic, irresistible, and boundless improvement, Benjamin conceived revolution as a *redemptive interruption* of the continuum of history, a reaching for the emergency brake in the train of history.[53] Blanqui, the legendary revolutionary fighter "whose name was the rallying sound that reverberated through the preceding century," had nothing but scorn for the belief in progress: the basic presupposition of his activity was not this illusory belief but the decision to put an end to present injustice. "This decision, at the last moment to pull humanity out of the impending catastrophe which threatens it, is precisely for Blanqui, more than for any other revolutionary politician of his time, the essential criterion."[54]

Instead of "progress," revolution is "a tiger's leap in the past,"[55] searching for the lost paradise, the archaic golden age of edenic harmony between human beings, as well as between humanity and nature. One finds here again the *restitutio in integrum* suggested by the *Theologico-Political Fragment* (1921–22). Utopia and restitution, future and past are alchemically married and opposed to the present "hell." In a key paragraph of *Paris, Capital of the Nineteenth Century* (1936) Benjamin refers to the dreams of the future as always being "married" (*vermählt*) to elements of prehistoric ages (*Urgeschichte*), "i.e. of classless society"; for him, the experiences from this archaic past stored in the collective memory "produce, by interpenetration with the new, Utopia."[56] As is well known, in his letter to Benjamin of August 1935, Theodor Adorno sharply criticized this formulation, and the whole essay, as being marred by an "overestimation of the archaic," reminiscent of Klages's mythical thought. He refused the association of the archaic past with a "golden age" as well as the identification of the present mercantile era with "hell."[57]

What exactly did this prehistoric, archaic, classless society mean for Benjamin? The main reference here is not Klages, but the great classic which Klages later interpreted in his own reactionary way: Johann Jakob Bachofen. Benjamin's French review of Bachofen (1935) is one of the most seminal, yet still largely neglected, keys to the understanding of his whole philosophy of history. Bachofen's work, writes Benjamin, is "inspired by Romantic sources" and has attracted the interest of both Marxist and anarchist thinkers because of his "evocation of a communist society at the dawn of history." The anarchist Elisée Réclus found in Bachofen's books the ancient "sources of his libertarian ideal" and Engels as well as Lafargue were interested in his studies of matriarchal communities, where there existed a very high degree of democracy and civil equality, as well as forms of primitive communism which "subverted the concept of authority."[58]

This review—together with the contemporaneous mention of Drieu's anarchist "deserter"—points to the continuity of Benjamin's libertarian sympathies. Moreover, it suggests that the primitive communist, antiauthoritarian, and egalitarian communities described by Bachofen are exactly the prehistorical, classless societies defined in *Paris, Capital of the Nineteenth Century* as the source of utopia.

Impressed by Adorno's severe criticism, Benjamin played down the "archaic tendency" in his next Baudelaire essays; yet it is still present, in a subdued form, in the article *On Some Motifs in Baudelaire* (1939), where one can discover, by careful scrutiny, a new version of the opposition between present "hell" and lost "paradise." The central trait of the modern hell is here the degradation of experience that "manifests itself in the standardized, denatured life of the civilized masses," or in the "inhospitable, blinding [experience] of the age of large-scale industrialism"—in particular the life of the unskilled workers whose labor "has been sealed off from experience," degraded, standardized, regimented, and reduced to an automaton by modern machinery.[59]

True experience survives mainly as memory of a collective past, present in "rituals with their ceremonies, their festivals"; it is at the heart of Baudelaire's concept of *correspondances*, which relates to a form of experience "possible only within the realm of the ritual." And here reappears the figure of the edenic age: "The *correspondances* are the data of remembrance—not historical data, but the data of pre-history. What makes festive days great and significant is the encounter with an earlier life. . . . The murmur of the past may be heard in the *correspondances*."[60] As Tiedemann perceptively comments, "the idea of the correspondences is the Utopia through which a lost paradise appears projected in the future." It is a utopia of reconciliation between man and nature—as suggested by Baudelaire's poem itself.[61]

One name is for Benjamin the emblem of this reconciliation: Fourier. In the Jochmann essay (1937) he is mentioned as a dialectician who discovered that "all partial improvements in the social constitution of humanity during 'civilization' are necessarily followed by a deterioration of its general status," and in *Paris, Capital of the Nineteenth Century* he is compared to Benjamin's favorite Paul Scheerbart as a paradigmatic combination of ancient and new in a utopia that gives new life to the primeval symbols of desire. In an unpublished note from the *Passagenwerk* (quoted by Tiedemann), Fourier's *travail passionné* is referred to as the authentic form of a harmonious relation to nature.[62] Finally, in *Über den Begriff der Geschichte*, Fourier's ideas are contrasted to the bourgeois, social democratic, and vulgar Marxist conception of work as "exploitation of nature," and his most fascinating dreams are celebrated as illustrations for a kind of labor that aims at liberating the creativity of nature.[63]

By situating his golden age in the prehistoric past, Benjamin distinguishes himself from the mainstream of German romanticism, whose nostalgic *Heimat* was the Middle Ages. In this he is perhaps closer than he realized to Marx and Engels themselves: in a letter to his friend on March 25, 1868, Marx wrote that the first reaction against the ideology of Enlightenment had a "medieval, Romantic perspective" but that the second reaction, which belonged to the socialist orientation, "consisted in plunging beyond the Middle Ages to the primitive epoch (*Urzeit*) of each people." In such primeval communities one may discover "in the oldest the newest" and in particular "Egalitarians to a degree that would thrill Proudhon."[64] It is highly unlikely that Benjamin knew of this letter, but one cannot but note the striking similarity with his own reference to an egalitarian and libertarian *Urzeit*, where the oldest and the newest are "married."

Ursprung ist das Ziel (origin is the goal): Karl Kraus's epigram serves as motto for Benjamin's Fourteenth Thesis on the philosophy of history, which defines revolution as a "tiger's leap into the past." There is an undeniable affinity between this restitutionist-utopian theory of proletarian revolution and Jewish messianism: in the messianic idea, writes Gershom Scholem, "even the restorative force has a utopian factor, and in utopianism restorative factors are at work. . . . The completely new order has elements of the completely old, but even this old order does not consist of the actual past; rather it is a past transformed and transfigured in a dream brightened by the rays of utopianism."[65]

The elective affinity is not here mere analogy, but active interpenetration and combination of both elements. There exists an intimate link, a *correspondence* in the Baudelairian sense, between each term of the profane revolutionary utopia and of the sacred messianic sphere, between the history of redemption and the history of class struggle: to the Lost Paradise corresponds the prehistoric classless communist society, egalitarian and nonauthoritarian, living in edenic harmony with nature; to the expulsion from the Garden of Eden, or to the tempest blowing men away from Paradise, towards Hell, correspond "progress," industrial civilization, capitalist-commodity society, the modern catastrophe and its pile of wreckage; to the Coming of the Messiah, the proletarian-revolutionary interruption of history; and to the Messianic Age, the reestablishment of Paradise with its edenic adamite language, corresponds the new libertarian-communist classless society and its universal language.[66] *Ursprung ist das Ziel* and *restitutio in integrum* are the spiritual quintessence of this peculiar "theology of revolution."

Many commentators conceive the relation between messianism and revolution in Benjamin's work as one of "secularization," while others (Gerhard Kaiser) speak of a "theologization of Marxism."[67] During the heated *Benjaminstreit* of the sixties in Germany, some insisted on his religious metaphysics, others on his communist materialism. Benjamin himself referred to his thought as "Janus-faced," but it seems that his commentators and partisans choose to look at only one of the faces, ignoring or neglecting the other. In order to supersede this kind of polemic, it might be useful to recall that the Roman god had indeed *two faces* but only *one head*: Benjamin's "faces" are manifestations of one and the same thought, which had *simultaneously* a messianic and a secular expression.

As a matter of fact, Benjamin had already explained in the 1926 letter to Scholem that he was interested in a form of *identity* between religion and politics that showed itself "only in the paradoxical *Umschlag* of the one into the other": the *Theses on the Philosophy of History* are exactly such a paradoxical conversion of Jewish religion into Marxist class struggle, and of revolutionary utopia into apocalyptic messianism.

The first kind of *Umschlag*—from messianism into politics—cannot be grasped strictly as "secularization," for the religious dimension does not disappear. What can be said, however, is that this dimension has *secular implications and consequences*. In the preparatory notes for the *Theses*, Benjamin wrote: "Marx secularized the representation of the Messianic age in the representation of classless society. And rightly so." But, in contradiction to the claims of social democratic philosophy, "classless society is not the final aim of progress in history; it is its frequently unsuccessful but finally accomplished interruption." Therefore, "one must restore to the concept of classless society its true Messianic face, in the interest of the revolutionary politics of the proletariat itself."[68] Criticizing these notes, Tiedemann argues against Benjamin: "Therefore the revolutionary policy of the proletariat should not be implemented in the interest of establishing classless society but, the other way round; the latter is only an occasion to bring into play revolutionary politics, in order to make a revolution for the sake of revolution. . . . Goal and means—classless society and revolution—are confused."[69] But the aim and the means are not "confused"—they are dialectically and inseparably united in Benjamin's thought; there can be no classless society without a revolutionary interruption of the historical continuum ("progress"), and no revolutionary action of the proletariat if the aim (classless society) is not understood in all its messianic explosiveness, as a *breaking point*. Benjamin's aim is not "revolution for the sake of revolution," but for him without revolution there can be no redemption, and without a Messianic-redemptive view of history, no really radical revolutionary *praxis*.

The profane consequence of messianism in his last writings is to increase their explosive charge; it helps to give them that unique subversive quality which makes the *Theses on the Philosophy of History* one of the most radical, path-breaking, and seminal documents of revolutionary thought since Marx's *Theses on Feuerbach*. If we apply to Benjamin's own work the distinction he established between the chemist-commentator and the alchemist-critic, then we should look beyond the "wood" and the "ashes" of his writings and focus on the burning spiritual flame of his oeuvre: the revolutionary redemption of humanity.

Notes

1. We have developed these ideas in the essay "Jewish Messianism and Libertarian Utopia in Central Europe," *New German Critique* 20 (Spring/Summer 1980).
2. Walter Benjamin, "Das Leben der Studenten," in *Illuminationen*, (Frankfurt, 1980), pp. 9, 11, 14, 16.
3. Walter Benjamin, "Romantik," in *Gesammelte Schriften* (hereafter *G.S.*), vol. 2, 1 (Frankfurt, 1977), p. 46.
4. Benjamin, *G.S.*, vol. 2, 1, pp. 22, 24, 25, 26, 34. In another characteristic passage he condemns the reduction of social activity to "an affair of *Zivilisation*, like the electric light" (p. 19).
5. Walter Benjamin, *Briefe*, vol. 1 (Frankfurt, 1966), p. 138.
6. Benjamin, *G.S.*, vol. 2, 1, pp. 158–59.
7. Benjamin, *Briefe*, vol. 1, pp. 342, 381, 383, 394, etc.
8. Benjamin, *Briefe*, vol. 1, pp. 349, 358, vol. 2, p. 515.
9. Benjamin, *G.S.*, vol. 2, pp. 642, 644–45, 647.
10. Benjamin, *G.S.*, vol. 3, p. 560.
11. Benjamin, *Briefe*, vol. 1, p. 134, 136.
12. Friedrich Schlegel, *Seine prosaischen Jugendschriften* (Vienna, 1966), quoted by Benjamin in *Der Begriff der Kunstkritik in der deutschen Romantik*, inaugural dissertation (Berlin, 1920), p. 2. Benjamin mentions also the book by Ch. Pingaud, *Grandlinien der ästhetischen Doktrin Friedrich Schlegels* (Stuttgart, 1914), p. 52, according to which the aspiration to establish the "Kingdom of God" on earth, here and now, is the foundation of F. Schlegel's "new religion."
13. Benjamin, *Briefe*, vol. 1, p. 208.
14. Gershom Scholem, *Walter Benjamin, Geschichte einer Freundschaft* (Frankfurt, 1976), p. 45.
15. Benjamin, *Briefe*, vol. 1, p. 181.
16. Scholem, *Walter Benjamin*, pp. 100, 204, and memorandum of conversation with G. Scholem, December 1979.
17. Scholem, *Walter Benjamin*, p. 108, and memorandum of conversation with G. Scholem, December 1979.
18. Memorandum of conversation with Werner Kraft, January 1980.
19. See, for example, Benjamin, *Briefe*, vol. 1, p. 335, and Scholem, *Walter Benjamin*, p. 155.
20. Scholem, *Walter Benjamin*, pp. 19, 22.
21. Benjamin, *G.S.*, vol. 2, 1, pp. 190, 191, 194, 202.
22. Scholem explains in a letter in 1970 to Maurice de Gandillac, the French translator of Benjamin's writings, that Adorno was wrong to believe this text

was written in 1937: "These pages were composed in 1920–21, and are linked to 'Zur Kritik der Gewalt'; they do not contain any relation to Marxist conceptions. They are situated in the sphere of a metaphysical anarchism, corresponding to the author's ideas before 1924" (Walter Benjamin, *Mythe et violence* [Paris, 1970], p. 149, footnote by the translator). In our opinion it would be more accurate to situate them in 1921–22, because they most probably postdate the publication of Rosenzweig's book.

23. Walter Benjamin, *One-Way Street* (London: New Left Books, 1979), p. 155.
24. See Benjamin, *G.S.*, vol. 2, 2, pp. 618–19, and the notes of the editors in *G.S.*, vol. 2, 3, pp. 1423–25; also *Briefe*, vol. 1, p. 233. Some of Scheerbart's novels (including *Lesabendio*) have been republished in the volume: P. Scheerbart, *Dichterische Hauptwerke* (Stuttgart, 1962). On Scheerbart's worldview see Hubert Bar, *Natur und Gesellschaft bei Scheerbart, Genese und Implikationen einer Kultur Utopie* (Heidelberg, 1977).
25. Letter to Scholem from September 1924, *Briefe*, vol. 1, p. 355.
26. Letter of May 1926, *Briefe*, vol. 1, p. 426.
27. Richard Wolin, *Walter Benjamin, An Aesthetic of Redemption* (Cambridge, 1982), p. 177.
28. Walter Benjamin, "Surrealism," in *One-Way Street*, pp. 225–39. Benjamin carefully distinguishes surrealism from romanticism, and criticizes some "dangerous Romantic prejudices." However, there is, in our view, an unmistakable similarity between neo-romanticism and his own socio-cultural pessimism.
29. Benjamin, *Briefe*, vol. 2, pp. 530, 533, 536.
30. Walter Benjamin, "Theorien des deutschen Faschismus," in *Die Gesellschaft*, vol. 2, (1936) p. 41. Benjamin was very keen on this idea, which had already been censured in one of his former publications. In a 1929 article on a militarist theatrical play he wrote that the only answer to war consisted in "armed insurrection" (*bewaffneter Aufstand*). *Die Literarische Welt* published the article in May 1929—without this passage. (See Benjamin, *G.S.*, vol. 4, 1, p. 463 and *G.S.*, vol. 4, 2, p. 1031.)
31. Walter Benjamin, *Understanding Brecht* (London: Verso, 1983), p. 121.
32. Walter Benjamin, *Illuminations* (New York, 1968), p. 260.
33. Benjamin, *Briefe*, vol. 2, p. 732.
34. Benjamin, *Briefe*, vol. 2, p. 648.
35. Drieu la Rochelle, *Le déserteur* (Paris, 1960), pp. 220, 222, 224, 226.
36. Ibid., p. 223.
37. Rolf Tiedemann, "Nachwort," in Walter Benjamin, *Charles Baudelaire* (Frankfurt, 1980), p. 207.
38. Rolf Tiedemann, "Historischer Materialismus oder politischer Messianismus?" in P. Bulthaup, *Materialen zu Benjamins Thesen "Über den Begriff der Geschichte"* (Frankfurt, 1975), p. 109.
39. Jürgen Habermas, "Consciousness-Raising or Redemptive Criticism: The Contemporaneity of Walter Benjamin," *New German Critique* 17 (Spring, 1979); pp. 51, 55.
40. Benjamin, *G.S.*, vol. 7, 3, pp. 1240–41.
41. Gershom Scholem, "Walter Benjamin," 1964, in *On Jews and Judaism in Crisis* (New York, 1976), pp. 194–95.
42. In Franz Joseph Molitor's book on the Jewish tradition and Kabbala—probably one of the main sources of Benjamin's religious thought—the redemptive

mission of the Messiah is described as the "re-establishment of the former state" before Adam's fall. See Franz Joseph Molitor, *Philosophie der Geschichte oder über die Tradition* (Münster, 1839), part 3, p. 398.

43. Benjamin, *One-Way Street*, p. 121. On the edenic *Ursprache* there is also an interesting chapter in Molitor, *Philosophie der Geschichte*, pp. 329–40.
44. Benjamin, *Illuminations*, pp. 259–60.
45. Benjamin, *One-Way Street*, p. 80. The problem of technological progress is also critically discussed in the final section ("Towards the Planetarium"), which is, in the words of the publisher's note, "perhaps the first and certainly the finest—because most temperate and rational—expression of that rejection of the notion of the mastery of nature by technology that was afterwards to become a hallmark of Frankfurt Marxism." (Ibid., p. 36).
46. Walter Benjamin, "The Storyteller," in *Illuminations*, pp. 92, 97.
47. Walter Benjamin, "Eduard Fuchs, Collector and Historian," in *One-Way Street*, p. 370.
48. Benjamin, *G.S.*, vol. 1, 3, p. 1151–52.
49. Irving Wohlfarth, "On the Messianic Structure of Benjamin's Last Reflections," *Glyph*, 3 (Baltimore, 1978), p. 168.
50. Benjamin, *Briefe*, vol. 2, p. 50. On the various references to Trotsky in Benjamin's correspondence, see the publisher's note in *One-Way Street*, p. 36 n. 13. Already in his *Moscow Journal* Benjamin criticizes the Soviet leadership for "trying to stop the dynamics of the revolutionary process in the life of the state"—exactly the kind of criticism being leveled at the time by Trotsky and the Left Opposition. (*Moscow Journal*, December 30, 1926.)
51. These are self-critical notes, probably from 1939, on his "Commentary on Brecht's Poems," in *Fonds Walter Benjamin* (Paris: Bibliothèque Nationale). In 1937 Benjamin met Pierre Missac, then close to Trotskyist ideas, and one of the things they discussed was Missac's sympathetic review of *The Revolution Betrayed* in the journal *Cahiers du Sud* 196 (August 1937). (Personal communication from Pierre Missac.)
52. Walter Benjamin, "Zentralpark," in *Charles Baudelaire*, p. 179. The term "regression" does not appear in Benjamin, but was coined by the anarchist geographer Elisée Réclus. The contradiction between progress in the control over nature and retrogression in social life is the main theme of Thesis 11 in the "Philosophy of History" (*Illuminations*, pp. 256–57).
53. Benjamin, *G.S.*, vol. 1, 3, p. 1232.
54. Benjamin, *Illuminations*, p. 262, and "Zentralpark," p. 183.
55. Benjamin, *Illuminations*, p. 263.
56. Benjamin, *Charles Baudelaire* (London, 1983), p. 159.
57. Theodor Adorno, in Bloch et al., *Aesthetics and Politics* (London, 1980), pp. 113, 116.
58. Benjamin, *G.S.*, vol. 2, 1, pp. 220, 230–31. Following Bachofen, Benjamin refers to "gynocratic" communities; but there is an obvious contradiction between gynocracy (or matriarchy) on one side, egalitarianism and anti-authoritarianism on the other. Modern anthropology questions the existence of such "gynocratic" societies. Could it not be that "matriarchy" or "gynocracy" is but the mythical expression of patriarchal men's fear and anxiety towards past communities where equality existed among the sexes? "Matriarchy" would in this case simply designate the absence of patriarchal authority.
59. Benjamin, *Illuminations*, pp. 158–59, 178, corrected according to the German

original in *Charles Baudelaire*, pp. 105, 128–29. Benjamin quotes Marx in this context, but one could recall also his essay on E. T. A. Hoffmann in 1930 in which he stressed the religious opposition between Life and Automaton in the stories of the romantic writer.

60. Benjamin, *Illuminations*, pp. 161, 184.
61. Tiedemann, "Nachwort," pp. 205–206. See also Wolin, *Walter Benjamin, An Aesthetic of Redemption*, p. 236: "The correspondences recapture a relation to nature whose lost traces are being extirpated by technical mastery of the environment . . . they hark back to a ur-historical state of reconciliation with nature."
62. Benjamin, *G.S.*, vol. 2, 2, p. 583, and Tiedemann, "Nachwort," p. 205.
63. See Benjamin, *Illuminations*, pp. 261–62. Benjamin does not consider Fourier and Marx as contradictory. In *Paris, Capital of the Nineteenth Century* (p. 160) he quotes Marx's favorable opinion of Fourier's "gargantuan concepts of man."
64. Karl Marx and Friedrich Engels, *Ausgewählte Briefe* (Berlin, 1953), p. 233.
65. Gershom Scholem, *The Messianic Idea in Judaism* (New York, 1971), p. 4.
66. Among the preparatory notes for the *Theses* there is a passage associating the messianic era with the advent of a universal language, able to replace the confusion of the Tower of Babel, a language that everybody will understand "as children on Sunday understand the language of birds." The relation of this idea to his theological reflections of 1914 on the Fall as loss of a primeval, paradisiac language is undeniable. (See on this Irving Wohlfarth's above-mentioned essay on the messianic structure of Benjamin's last reflections.) See also Susan Buck-Morss, "Walter Benjamin—Revolutionary Writer," *New Left Review* 128 (July–August, 1981); p. 37: "Universal language has existed only in Paradise before the Fall. Universal history requires the restoration of Paradise in the form of a revolutionary transformation of society."
67. G. Kaiser, "Walter Benjamin's geschichtsphilosophische Thesen," in P. Bulthup, *Materialien zu Benjamins Thesen*, p. 74.
68. Benjamin, *G.S.*, vol. 1, 3, pp. 1231–32.
69. Tiedemann, "Historischer Materialismus," p. 109.

13

Religion, Utopia, and Countermodernity: The Allegory of the Angel of History in Walter Benjamin

What is modernity? Few concepts are so equivocal, ambiguous, and polysemous. To avoid arbitrary definition, it is best to stick with the current meaning—that of the dictionary. According to the *Petit Robert*, the word comes from the latin *modo*, which signifies *recently* (1361 is given as the original date of reference). The modern therefore would be all that which is "of a relatively recent epoch" or else "present, contemporary." Yet, the present, the recent, and the contemporary are the very movement of time! That which was modern yesterday is today obsolete. . . . The concept thus seems fairly *empty*, a *flatus vocis* (according to the happy expression of medieval theologians), lacking in any concrete and precise content. Nonetheless, the dictionary gives us another, more interesting, indication: modern is that which "benefits from recent progress of technique, of science." The concept of modernity thus would be closely linked to that of *progress*—that is, positive valorization of what is new. Since the eighteenth century, progress par excellence is that which manifests itself in scientific, political, and cultural transformations: urbanization, rationalization, democratization, bureaucratization, reification, secularization, etc.

However, during the two or three centuries of existence of modern, industrial society, religion has constituted one of the principal cultural and symbolic reservoirs of the most diverse forms of resistance (or critique) to progress and to modernity. Habitually, this resistance is addressed in privileged fashion against such and such an aspect of modernity (secularization, for example), but in certain cases it calls its very foundation into question: the idea of progress, faith in the beneficial consequences of industrial, technical, and scientific progress.

The dominant form of religious resistance to modernity is that which manifests itself as *traditionalism* and *conservatism*: rejecting progress, it aspires to *restore the past*, and in particular to reestablish premodern forms of religious life. The countenance it typically presents is that of the counter-revolutionary and intransigent Catholicism of the nineteenth century, with its contemporary prolongations and its equivalents within other confessions.

Nevertheless, there exists another paradigm—minority, less institutional, generally marginal—of religious contestation of modernity: that represented by certain revolutionary utopias. These utopias of religious inspiration may themselves also valorize certain aspects of premodern culture, but their aspiration is less a *return* to the past than a *detour* by the past towards the future, towards a new world. Their critique of modernity and of progress can be profound and radical, but it is a matter here, up to a certain point, of an "internal" critique, founded on values (like democracy, revolution, or social equality) which themselves are given rise to by modern culture. Latin American liberation theology can be considered as a characteristic example of this type of utopia.

Yet, well before the flood tide of the Christian/revolutionary current in Europe or in Latin America, one witnessed the appearance, within certain Jewish intellectual milieux of Central Europe, of vigorous forms of utopico-religious critiques of progress and of modernity, inspired at once by German romanticism and by the Jewish messianic tradition. If this antimodern (or anticapitalist) romanticism tinged with religiosity is one of the principal currents of cultural life in Germany—insofar as it is an expression of the resistance of the academic mandarinate and the traditional intellectual classes to the advent of industrial revolution—it is above all with the Jewish intellectual pariahs that it takes a revolutionary and utopian turn. Walter Benjamin is without doubt the most radical and the most original representative of this Jewish/German "theology of revolution," which does not fail to present certain analogies with that of Gustavo Gutierrez and his friends.

The most important document of the "anti-progress" utopia of Benjamin are his theses *On the Concept of History*, written in 1940, shortly before his death (i.e., his suicide). An enigmatic and fascinating text, a fusion unique within its genre of theology and Marxism, messianism and class struggle, religion and social utopia, it summarizes, in a way that is at once lapidary and allegorical, ideas that had worked upon him for a long time. In a letter to Gretel Adorno (the wife of the Frankfurt philosopher) presenting this document, Walter Benjamin explains: "The war and the constellation which brought it on has led me to put some thoughts down on paper, about which I can say that I have kept them on me—and even of me—for around twenty years."[1] He might have written "twenty-five years": in effect, in one of his first works, the lecture *The Life of Students* (1915), one discovers a number of the themes that are to figure in his 1940 spiritual testament. The remarks that open this early essay already contain a surprising prelude to his messianic philosophy of history and to his critique of progress.

> Confiding in the infinity of time, a given conception of history discerns only the more or less rapid rhythm by which men and epochs advance along the way of progress. Hence the character incoherent, imprecise, lacking in rigour of the demand addressed to the present. Here, on the contrary, as thinkers have always done in presenting utopian images, we are going to consider history in the light of a determined situation which summarizes it as if in a focal point. The elements of the final situation do not present themselves as being of a formless, progressist tendency, but, as creations and ideas in very great peril, highly discredited and mocked, they incorporate themselves, in a profound fashion, into everything present. . . . This situation is not to be grasped except in its metaphysical structure, as the messianic kingdom or as a revolutionary idea in the sense of '89.[2]

The utopian images (messianic and revolutionary) as against "the formless, progressist tendency": here are posed, briefly, the terms of the debate. One need only compare this passage with the "Theses" to appreciate the inanity of any attempt to carve up the work of Walter Benjamin with the guillotine of "epistemological dismemberment" into a period termed theological, Jewish, youthful and another termed materialist, revolutionary, mature.

Nonetheless, it is true that his adherence to Marxism during the 1920s introduces a decisive element that allows one to see in a new light the totality of his vision of history: the struggle of classes. Historical materialism is not going to take the place of his antiprogressist conception (of messianic inspiration), but is going to combine itself with it, thus earning a *critical quality* that distinguishes it radically from the "official" Marxism dominant at that period.

This position manifests itself for the first time in *One-Way Street* (written between 1923 and 1926) where is to be found, under the title "Fire Alarm," this premonition of the menaces of progress: if the overthrow of the bourgeoisie by the proletariat "is not accomplished by an almost calculable moment of scientific and technical evolution (indicated by inflation and chemical warfare) all is lost. One must cut the burning fuse before the spark reaches the dynamite."[3] Shortly thereafter Benjamin drew nearer to the communist movement (a voyage to the Soviet Union in 1926–27) without ever deciding upon total adherence. Not sharing the optimism of those in command of the German workers' movement, Benjamin appeals, in an article from 1929, to a "pessimism all along the line," an "organization of pessimism" (a formula that he takes from the French communist dissident Pierre Naville); he adds ironically: "unlimited confidence only in I. G. Farben and in the peaceable perfecting of the Luftwaffe."[4] These two institutions were very soon going to show, well beyond the most pessimistic expectations of Benjamin, the sinister use that could be made of modern technology. . . .

The political context that presided over the writing of the "Theses" *On the Concept of History* is marked by the German-Soviet Nonaggression Pact and the outbreak of the Second World War. These events constitute the "constellation" of which Benjamin made note in his letter of presentation of the "Theses" to Gretel Adorno. It is not by coincidence that this document signifies at once his rupture with the Soviet variant of Marxism and his most radical and systematic critique of the epistemological foundations of the modern ideology of progress. Yet, nothing could be more false than to reduce this text to a reaction in the face of a desperate historic situation. As has been seen, it forms the summary of a long spiritual trajectory.

Let us try to examine more closely Thesis 9, which summarizes "as in a focal point" the whole of the document and which constitutes a particularly striking example of utopico-religious critique of modernity. We have before us here an *allegorical* text, in the sense that these elements lack significance outside of the role that is intentionally assigned to them by the author. Benjamin was fascinated by religious allegories and in particular by those of German baroque drama—the *Trauerspiel* to which he had dedicated his first major work—in which "the allegory is the *facies hyppocratica* of history which presents itself to the gaze of the spectator as a petrified, primitive landscape."[5] To be able to interpret this allegory one must refer to the other "Theses" *On the Concept of History*, as well as to the whole of the writings of the last period of his life: the essay on *The Narrator*, the article on Fuchs, the works on Baudelaire, the *Passagenwerk*, etc.

Thesis 9 presents itself as the commentary on the painting of Paul Klee entitled *Angelus Novus*, which Benjamin had acquired in his youth. In reality, what he describes has but slight rapport with the painting: essentially, it is a question of the projection of his own sentiments and ideas into the simple and severe image by the Swiss painter. There exists a French translation of this text by Benjamin himself; one loses in grammatical precision, or in elegance of style, but one gains in fidelity to the thought of the author. It reads:

> There is a painting by Klee entitled *Angelus Novus*. One sees therein an angel who has the air of distancing himself from something upon which his regard seems to rest, riveted. His eyes are wide open, his mouth is open and his wings are spread. Such will be the aspect which the Angel of History will present. His face is turned toward the past. There, where to

> our gaze, there seems to be spread out a series of events, there is but one sole [thing] which offers itself to his regard: a catastrophe without modulation nor truce, heaping up the ruins and casting them eternally before his feet. The Angel would very much like to bend down over this disaster, to dress the wounds and resuscitate the dead. But a tempest arises, coming from Paradise; it has swelled the spread wings of the Angel; and he no longer manages to fold them. This tempest carries him off towards the future, to which the Angel does not cease to turn his back while the ruins facing him, mount to heaven. We give the name Progress to this tempest.[6]

Rejecting the modern cult of progress, Benjamin places at the center of his vision of history the concept of *catastrophe*. In one of the preparatory notes to "Theses," he observes "The catastrophe is progress, progress is the catastrophe. The catastrophe is the continuum of history."[7] The assimilation between progress and catastrophe thus, first of all, has a *historical* significance: from the point of view of the oppressed, the past is nothing but an interminable series of catastrophic defeats. Spartacus, Thomas Münzer, June 1848, the Commune of Paris, the German Spartacist uprising of 1919 (these are examples that often appear in the writings of Benjamin): "this enemy has not ceased to vanquish" (Thesis 6). But this equation also has an eminently *contemporary* significance: because "at the hour that it is, the enemy has not yet stopped triumphing" (Thesis 6, Benjamin translation):[8] defeat of republican Spain, the Molotov-Ribbentrop Pact, victorious Nazi invasions in Europe.

In a general fashion, the catastrophes of progress are at the very heart of modernity:

1. The destructive and murderous (*mörderische*) exploitation of nature—instead of the original/utopic harmony dreamed of by Fourier, Baudelaire, and Bachofen.[9]
2. The perfecting of techniques of war whose destructive energies progress without halt. Benjamin insisted, in various writings from the middle of the 1920s, on the terrifying danger represented by *gas* and *aerial bombardments*, without doubting that the future was going to confirm his worst anguishes beyond the imaginable.
3. Fascism. This is not an accident of history, an "exceptional state," something impossible in the twentieth century, an absurdity from the point of view of progress: rejecting dominant illusions from within the left, Benjamin prayed for the coming of "a theory of history on the basis of which fascism might be perceived."[10] This is to say a theory which comprehends that the irrationalities of fascism are but the seamy side of modern (instrumental) rationality. Fascism carries to its final consequences this typically modern combination of technical progress and social regression.

Whereas Marx and Engels have had, according to Benjamin, "the fulgurating intuition of the barbarity to come in their prognostic on the evolution of capitalism,"[11] their twentieth-century epigones have been incapable of understanding—and thus of resisting against efficaciously—a *modern*, dynamic, industrial barbarity, installed at the very heart of scientific and technical progress.

Seeking the roots, the methodological foundations of this catastrophic incomprehension (which contributed to the defeat of the German workers' movement in 1933), Benjamin takes on the ideology of progress, in all its components: Darwinist evolutionist determinism of the scientific-natural sort, blind optimism—the dogma of the "inevitable victory of the party" (just as much the social-democratic as the communist)—the conviction of "swimming with the current" (technical development), in a word, the comfortable belief in an infinite, continuous, automatic progress founded upon quantitative accumulation, the soaring of productive forces, and the growth in the domination of nature. He believes himself to uncover, behind these myriad manifestations, a central strand that he submits to a radical critique: the homogeneous, empty, and mechanical conception (like a clockwork movement) of historical time.

Let us turn again to the text of Thesis 9. The significative structure of the allegory is founded upon a *correspondence*—in the Baudelairean sense—between the sacred and the profane, theology and politics, which traverses each of his images. It is not a question of secularization of the religious in the historic, as the "materialist" school of interpretation of the "Theses" would have it, nor a simple translation into Marxist language of an essentially mystical thought (as Gerschom Scholem suggests): the two dimensions are at once inseparable and distinct, like communicating vessels. Or like the two faces on one single head of the Roman god to which Benjamin refers in a letter defining (allegorically or symbolically?) his thought—Janus. . . .

For one of these images, the two meanings are given to us by Thesis 9: the profane correspondent to the tempest which blows in from paradise is progress, responsible for a "catastrophe without truce" and for heaping up ruins which reach to the sky. But for the others, one must seek their social and political significance in reference to the entirety of the theses *On the Concept of History* and other writings of Benjamin.

What, then, is this paradise lost from which progress draws us further and further away? Various indications seem to suggest that what Benjamin has in mind is a primitive, classless society. In a 1935 article on Bachofen, inspired by a Freudo-Marxist interpretation of matriarchy by Erich Fromm, he makes reference to the profoundly democratic and egalitarian character of primitive, matriarchal communities. If Marxist authors like Engels, or anarchists like Elisée Réclus took an interest in the work of Bachofen, it is because one finds therein "the evocation of a communist society at the dawn of history."[12] In the (1936) essay, *Paris, Capital of the Nineteenth Century*, Benjamin returns to this idea: "the experiences of the classless society of prehistory, deposed in the collective unconscious" in reciprocal liaison with the new "gives birth to utopia."[13]

At the antipodes of paradise, *hell*. There is no mention of it in Thesis 9, but a number of texts by Benjamin suggest a correspondence between *modernity* (or progress) and infernal damnation. For example, in this passage of *Zentralpark Fragments on Baudelaire* (1938): "The concept of progress is to be grounded in the idea of catastrophe. To let things go on like this—that is a catastrophe. . . . Strinberg's thought: hell is not anything immanent—it is *this life here*."[14] In what sense? For Benjamin, the quintessence of hell is the eternal repetition of the same, the most terrible paradigm of which is not to be found in Christian theology but in Greek mythology: Sisyphus and Tantalus condemned to eternal repetition of the same punishment. In this context, Benjamin cites a passage of Engels, comparing the interminable torture of the worker forced to repeat without respite the same mechanical movement, with the infernal punishment of Sisyphus.[15] Elsewhere he describes the vanity, the emptiness, the incompleteness of work in modern factories, founded on automatic gestures. The activity of the worker (like that of the player) is the "eternal recommencement from point zero" and in this sense it dwells in an "infernal time [*höllische Zeit*]," the time "in which unfolds the existence of those who undertake without being able to achieve anything."[16] But, it is not only a question of the worker: the totality of modern society, dominated by merchandise, is submitted to repetition, to "always-the-same [*Immergleichen*] disguised in novelty and fashion: in the kingdom of commodities, humanity cuts a figure of the damned."[17]

The Angel of History would like to stop, to dress the wounds of the victims crushed under the heaps of ruins, but the tempest carries him inexorably towards the future. As long as this tempest lasts, the future will only be a repetition of the past: new catastrophes, new hecatombs, ever more vast and destructive. How to stop the storm, how to interrupt progress in its fatal progression? As always, the response from Benjamin is dual: religious and profane. In the theological sphere, it concerns the task of the *Messiah*; Thesis 17 speaks to us of "the messianic arrest of becoming [*messianische Stillstellung des Geschehens*]" and in one of the preparatory notes one finds the following proclamation: "The Messiah shatters history."[18] His equivalent, or his profane correspondent is none other than *Revolution*: the revolutionary classes, reads Thesis 15, are conscious, at the moment of their action, of "shattering the continuum of history." This same idea is represented (in the notes) by an allegory that turns the traditional Marxist imagery completely around: "Marx has said that revolutions are the locomotive of world history. But, perhaps things are just the other way around. It could be that revolutions are the action, taken by humanity voyaging in this train, to pull the emergency breaks."[19] The messianic/revolutionary interruption of progress is thus Benjamin's response to the menaces resulting from the onslaught of the malefic tempest upon the human species, the imminence of new catastrophes. This was in the year 1940, shortly before Auschwitz and Hiroshima. . . .

These menaces take shape in the demonic figure of the Antimessiah: the Antichrist. Thesis 6 observes: "Let us remind ourselves that the Messiah does not come only as redeemer, but as the vanquisher of the Antichrist."[20] What is the profane and modern face of the Antichrist? The "Theses" *On the Concept of History* indicate nothing, but in an article written in 1938—the review of a book by Anna Seghers on the upsurge of Nazism in Germany—Benjamin gives us the key to this image: the Third Reich, also designated as "the radiating abyss of the Nazi hell [*strahlende Nazihölle*]," mocks socialism as the Antichrist mocks the messianic promise.[21] This image is quite probably inspired by the writings of his friend Fritz Lieb, a Protestant pastor and revolutionary socialist, who wrote in 1938 in an anti-Nazi article: "in a final combat against the Jews, the Antichrist will be vanquished and the Christ will appear to establish the millennial Kingdom."[22]

According to Benjamin, it is only the Messiah who will be able to accomplish what the Angel of History is powerless to bring about: dress the wounds, resuscitate the dead and *bring together all that has been shattered* (*Zerschlagene zusammenfügen*).[23] According to Gershom Scholem, this formula contains an implicit reference to the kabbalistic doctrine of *Tikkun*, the messianic restitution of the original state of divine harmony shattered by the *shevirat hakelim*, the rupture of vases—a doctrine that was known to Benjamin due to the article "Kabbala" published by Scholem in 1932 in the *Encyclopedia Judaica* (in the German language).[24] Rolf Tiedemann observes in this connection that the lurianic idea of *Tikkun*, "the construction of history in dialectical images" is constantly present, like a "fragmentary lightening flash" in the Theses of 1940.[25] This remark seems to me pertinent, despite the fact that the term *Tikkun* does not appear in the "Theses" nor in any other writings of Benjamin. Yet, there is to be found in certain of his texts the concept of *apocatastasis*: which, according to Origene, means the resurrection and redemption of all souls (without exception) and the restitution of the entirety of creation to its original state of perfection. However, in the article by Scholem on the Kabbala in 1932, he explains that the Greek/Christian *apocatastasis* is nothing other than the almost literal translation of the Hebraic *Tikkun*. . . .[26]

What then is the political equivalent of this mystical restitution, of this reestablishment of paradise lost, of this messianic kingdom? The response is to be found in the preparatory notes on "Theses": "One must restore to the concept of classless society its veritable messianic countenance and that in the very interest of the revolutionary politics of the proletariat"; because it is only in taking account of this messianic significance that one can avoid the traps of "progressist ideology" and comprehend that "the classless society is not the final goal of progress, but the accomplishment—if frequently tried in vain—of its definitive interruption."[27] Scholem is thus justified in writing that for Benjamin "Paradise is at once the ancestral origin and past [*Urvergangenheit*] of humanity, and at the same time a utopian image of the future of its redemption," but, it seems to me that he is mistaken in adding that it has to do with a conception of historic process "more cyclical than dialectical."[28] For Benjamin the classless society of the future (the new paradise) is not a pure and simple return to the classless society of prehistory: it contains in itself, as dialectical synthesis, the entire past of humanity. The true *universal history* founded upon the universal remembrance of all the victims, without exception—the profane equivalent of the resurrection of the dead—will only be possible in a future society without classes.[29] As Irving Wohlfarth writes in his remarkable essay on "The Messianic Structure of Walter Benjamin's Last Reflexions," it is more a question here of a "spiral" than of a circle because the messianic future is the *Aufhebung* (in the Hegelian sense) of all past history.[30]

The link which is established here between the messianic era and the future classless society—like that of other "correspondences" present in the Theses of 1940—cannot be understood in terms of secularization. The religious and the political maintain in this type of thought a relationship of reciprocal reversibility, of transposition or mutual translation, which defies any unilateral reduction: in a system of communicating vessels, the fluid needs necessarily to be present in all the branches simultaneously.

The conception of time which is at work in the politico/religious reflection of Walter Benjamin, and which impregnates all the allegories of the "Theses," is not that quantitative, homogeneous, linear, and cumulative one of doctrines of progress. It is a question here of a *qualitative* perception of time, founded on remembrance on the one hand, and the messianic/revolutionary rupture of continuity on the other. In Thesis 15 Benjamin writes: "Thus calendars do not at all mark time in the way that clocks do. They are the monuments of an historic consciousness which, for roughly a century, has become completely foreign to Europe." The last expression of this consciousness manifested itself on the occasion of the Revolution of 1830, when the crowd attacked the clocks. Benjamin cites an anonymous poet, a witness of the period: "New Joshuas, at the foot of each tower. Pulling on the clockfaces to halt the day."[31] Historical time is not empty and homogeneous like that of clocks, but charged with contents by memory and by the "thorns of messianic times" (Thesis 18A) which traverse it.

Few authors of the twentieth century have formulated a utopico-religious critique as radical, dramatic, and totalizing of modernity and of progress as Walter Benjamin. Romantic nostalgia for the premodern (or precapitalist) past was dominant in the German culture of the turn of the century. Even an author as moderate as Max Weber cannot hide, in the conclusion of his *Protestant Ethic,* his anguish and inquietude before the consequences of modernity: the coming of the steel cage and mechanical petrification. But this romantic culture critique generally takes on forms that are conservative, traditionalist, "reactionary" or, for that matter, realist, stoic, and resigned (as in the case of Weber). But it is above all among intellectual Jews belonging to this neo-romantic current (of religious inspiration) that one sees revolutionary and utopian forms of critique of modernity appearing—which is not unrelated to the semipariah condition of the Jewish intelligentsia in Germany (at least until 1918).

The Benjamin case is interesting precisely because he represents an extreme position, by his categorical refusal of the ideology of progress inherited from the Enlightenment. Nonetheless, one cannot help observing that his radical critique of modernity—profoundly impregnated with messianic religiosity—is not thereby any the less inspired by modern values (equality, liberation, democracy) and by revolutionary doctrines (socialism, anarchism, Marxism) resolutely modern: in other words, up to a certain point at least, it is a question of a *modern critique of modernity,* a contest which turns its own weapons against modernity. That is why his vision of history is not the circular one of a return to origins but arises rather from the dialectic between past and future.

Which aspects of modernity are valorized and which others rejected in this type of critique? For Benjamin—but this also goes for many other revolutionary romantics—the positive heritage is that of the *French Revolution,* whereas that of the *Industrial Revolution* is severely called into question. It is not by chance that in his 1915 discourse on the life of students he refers to the Revolution of 1789 and to the messianic kingdom as the two *utopian images* par excellence that he wishes to oppose to the formless myths of progress.[32]

Notes

1. Letter of April 1940, cited in the critical apparatus of *Gesammelte Schriften* (hereafter *G.S.*), vol 1, 3 (Frankfurt: Suhrkamp Verlag, 1980), p. 1226.
2. Walter Benjamin, "La vie des étudiants," in *Mythe et violence,* 1915 (Paris: Denoël-Lettres Nouvelles, 1971), p. 37.

3. Walter Benjamin, *Sens unique* (Paris: Lettres Nouvelles-Maurice Nadeau, 1978), pp. 205–6.
4. Walter Benjamin, "Le surréalisme," in *Mythe et violence*, 1929, p. 312.
5. Walter Benjamin, *Origine du drame baroque allemand* (Paris: Flammarion, 1985), p. 178.
6. Benjamin, *G.S.*, vol. 1, 3, p. 1263.
7. Benjamin, *G.S.*, vol. 1, 3, p. 1244 (preparatory notes to "Theses").
8. Benjamin, *G.S.*, vol. 1, 2, p. 695; and *G.S.*, vol. 1, 3, p. 1262.
9. Walter Benjamin, *Das Passagen-Werk*, vol. 1, (Frankfurt: Suhrkamp, 1983), p. 456.
10. Benjamin, *G.S.*, vol. 1, 3, p. 1244 (preparatory notes).
11. Benjamin, *G.S.*, vol. 2, 2, p. 488.
12. Benjamin, *G.S.*, vol. 3, 1, pp. 220, 230.
13. Walter Benjamin, *Poésie et révolution* (Paris: Denoël-Lettres Nouvelles, 1971), p. 125.
14. Walter Benjamin, *Charles Baudelaire* (Paris: Payot, 1982), p. 242.
15. Benjamin, *Das Passagen-Werk*, vol. 1, p. 162.
16. Benjamin, *Charles Baudelaire*, pp. 183–86: cf. *G.S.*, vol. 1, 2, p. 685.
17. Benjamin, *Das Passagen-Werk*, vol. 1, p. 61.
18. Benjamin, *G.S.*, vol. 1, 2, p. 703; and *G.S.*, vol. 1, 3, p. 1243.
19. Benjamin, *G.S.*, vol. 1, 2, p. 701; and *G.S.*, vol. 1, 3, p. 1232.
20. Benjamin, *G.S.*, vol. 1, 3, p. 1263 (Benjamin translation).
21. Benjamin, *G.S.*, vol. 3, pp. 535, 537.
22. Fritz Lieb, "Der 'Mythos' des nationalsozialistischen Nihilismus," in *Freie Wissenschaft ein Sammelbuch aus der deutschen Emigration* (Strasbourg: S. Brandt Verlag, 1938), p. 110. Cf. Chryssoula Kambas, "Wider den 'Geist der Zeit.' Die antifaschistische Politik Fritz Liebs und Walter Benjamins," in *Der Fürst dieser Welt*, ed. J. Toubes (Paderborn: F. Schoningh, 1983).
23. This expression appears only in the German version of "Theses," cf. *G.S.*, vol. 1, 2, p. 697.
24. Gershom Scholem, *Walter Benjamin und sein Engel* (Frankfurt: Suhrkamp Verlag, 1983), pp. 66, 71.
25. Rolf Tiedemann, "Erinnerung and Scholem," postscript to Scholem, in *Walter Benjamin*, p. 218.
26. Gershom Scholem, "Kabbala," *Encyclopaedia Judaica*, vol. 9 (Berlin: Verlag Eschkol, 1932).
27. Benjamin, *G.S.*, vol. 1, 3, pp. 1231–32.
28. Scholem, *Walter Benjamin*, p. 65.
29. Cf. Benjamin, *G.S.*, vol. 1, 3, pp. 1238–39.
30. Irving Wohlfarth, "On the Messianic Structure of Walter Benjamin's Last Reflections," in *Glyph*, 3 (Baltimore, 1978), p. 186.
31. Benjamin, *G.S.*, vol. 1, 3, p. 1265.
32. I wish to thank Jean Séguy and Danièle Hervieu-Léger, whose criticisms and suggestions have been of great help to me in the writing of this text.

14

Fire Alarm: Walter Benjamin's Critique of Technology

The uncritical approach to technical progress has been the dominant trend in Marxism since the end of the nineteenth century. Marx's own views were less one-sided: one can find in his writing an attempt towards a *dialectical* understanding of the antinomies of progress.

It is true that in some of his works the main emphasis is on the historically progressive role of industrial capitalism. For instance, in the *Communist Manifesto* one can find an enthusiastic celebration of bourgeois technological progress: "The bourgeoisie, during its rule of scarce one hundred years, has created more massive and more colossal productive forces than have all preceding generations together. Subjection of nature's forces to man, machinery . . . steam navigation, railways, electric telegraphs . . . what earlier century had even a presentiment that such production forces slumbered in the lap of social labour?" But even here there are some clear references to the negative consequences of industrial technology: owing to the extensive use of machinery, the work "has lost all individual character, and consequently, all charm for the workman"; the proletarian becomes "an appendage of the machine" and his work becomes increasingly "repulsive" (a term Marx borrows from Fourier).[1]

These two aspects are dealt with extensively in Marx's main economic writings. For instance, in the *Grundrisse* he insists on the "great civilizing influence of capital," but nevertheless recognizes that the machine robs labor "of all independence and attractive character" (another Fourierist category—*travail attrayant*). He has no doubt that capitalist technology means a degradation and intensification of labor: "The most developed machinery thus forces the worker to work longer than the savage does, or than he himself did with the simplest, crudest tools."[2]

In *Capital* the dark side of industrial technology comes very forcefully to the forefront: because of machinery, work in the capitalist factory becomes "a sort of torture," a "miserable routine of endless drudgery and toil in which the same mechanical process is gone through over and over again . . . like the labor of Sisyphus" (here Marx quotes from Engels, *The Condition of the Working Class in England*); the whole labor process is "turned into an organized mode of crushing out the workman's vitality, freedom and independence." In other words: in the present mode of production, the machine, far from improving the condition of labor, "deprives the work of all interest" and "confiscates every atom of freedom, both in bodily and intellectual activity."[3]

Marx seems also to be aware of the *ecological* consequences of capitalist technology: in the chapter on "Great Industry and Agriculture" in *Capital* he observes that capitalist production "disturbs (*stört*) the metabolism (*Stoffwechsel*) between man and the earth" and puts in danger "the eternal natural conditions for the permanent fertility of the soil." As a result, it "destroys both the physical health of the urban worker and the spiritual life of the rural worker." Each step in the progress of capitalist agriculture, each improvement of fertility in the short run, is at the same time "progress in ruining the permanent sources of this fertility. The more a country, like the United States of America for instance, has great industry as the background of its development, the quicker this process of destruction. Therefore, capitalist production only develops the technique and combination of the social process of production, while at the same time undermining the springs of all wealth: the earth and the worker."[4]

Although Marx is far from being romantic, he draws extensively on the romantic criticism of capitalist industrial civilization and technology. Among those who are often quoted in his economic writings are not only utopian communists such as Fourier, but also petty-bourgeois socialists such as Sismondi and even outright Tories like David Urquhart.

However, unlike the romantic economists, Marx does not criticize modern technology itself, but only the way in which *capitalism* uses it. The contradiction and antinomies of machinery do not grow out of machinery itself, but "out of its capitalist use (*Anwendung*)." For instance: "Considered in itself, machinery reduces labor time, while its capitalist use extends the labor day; in itself it makes work easier, its capitalist use heightens its intensity; in itself it is a victory of the human being over the natural force, its capitalist use enslaves man to the natural force; in itself it multiplies the wealth of the producer, its capitalist use pauperizes him, etc."[5]

How then might we understand a postcapitalist, or a *socialist* use of machines and industrial technology? The answer, both in *Capital* and *Grundrisse*, is that mechanization, by shortening the working day, will create free time, which is both idle time and time for higher activity. In a socialist society, technical progress will permit "the general reduction of the necessary labour of society to a minimum, which then corresponds to the artistic, scientific, etc. development of the individuals in the time set free, and with the means created, for all of them."[6]

Does this mean that the modern industrial-technological structure is a *neutral instrument* that can be used either in a capitalist or in a socialist manner? Or is the nature of the present technological system affected by its capitalist origin? This and many other relevant questions are left unanswered by Marx. But much of the *dialectical* quality of his writing on machinery—his attempt to seize the *contradictory* character of its development—has been lost in later Marxist literature, which fell under the spell of technological progress and celebrated its achievements as an unmixed blessing.

Walter Benjamin never dealt systematically with the problems of modern technology, but one can find in his writings remarkable insight which sets him apart as one of the first Marxist thinkers to approach these questions with a critical mind. Rejecting the semipositivist and naively optimistic axioms prevalent in mainstream Marxism (both of the Second and Third Internationals) before World War II, he tried to sound the fire alarm, warning of the dangers inherent in the present pattern of technical progress. His double protest—against technical progress in warfare and against the destruction of nature—has a prophetic ring and an astonishing relevance to our own time.

The roots of Benjamin's attitude towards technology can be found in the romantic tradition. German romantics and neoromantics (at the end of the nineteenth century) criticized *Zivilisation*—soulless material progress linked to technical and scientific development, bureaucratic rationality, quantification of social life—in the name of *Kultur*, the organic body of moral, cultural, religious, and social values. They particularly denounced the fateful results of mechanization, division of labor, and commodity production, nostalgically harking back to precapitalist and preindustrial ways of life. Although much of this romantic anticapitalism was conservative or reactionary, it also expressed a powerful revolutionary tendency. Romantic revolutionaries criticized the bourgeois industrial order in the name of past values, but their hopes were oriented towards a postcapitalist, socialist, and classless utopia. This radical worldview—shared by authors such as William Morris or Georges Sorel, and in Germany by Gustav Landauer and Ernst Bloch—is Walter Benjamin's cultural background and the initial source of his reflections on technology.

In one of his first writings, an essay from 1913 on "The Religiosity of our Times"—wherein he claims that "we all still live very deeply immersed in the discoveries of Romanticism"—Benjamin complained of the reduction of men to working machines and the debasement of all work to its technical form. Directly echoing certain contemporary neoromantic motifs, he believes in the need for a new religion (inspired by Tolstoy and Nietzsche) and rejects the shallow materialism which narrows all social activity to "an affair of *Zivilisation*, like the electric light."[7]

After 1924, Benjamin becomes increasingly interested in Marxism and sympathetic to the Communist movement. His criticism becomes more political and more specific. In an article published in 1925—"The Weapons of Tomorrow"—he draws attention to the usage of modern technology in service of "international militarism." Describing in detail the future battles "with chlorazetophenol, diphenylaminchlorasine and dichlorathysulphide," which are being prepared in chemical and technical laboratories, he argues that the horrors of gas warfare are beyond human imagination. Poisonous gas does not distinguish between civilians and soldiers, and it can destroy all human, animal, and vegetable life in vast expanses of land.[8]

But it is in *One-Way Street* (written before 1926 and published in 1928) that Benjamin really tries to confront the problem of technology in Marxist terms, relating it to *class struggle*. In one of his most impressive illuminations, the paragraph entitled "Fire Alarm," he sees the downfall of the bourgeoisie through proletarian revolution as the only way in which to prevent a catastrophic end to "three thousand years of cultural development." In other words: "if the abolition of the bourgeoisie is not completed by an almost calculable moment in economic and technical development (a moment signalled by inflation and poison-gas warfare), all is lost. Before the spark reaches the dynamite, the lighted fuse must be cut."[9] This argument—surprisingly similar to ideas advanced today by the antinuclear pacifist movement—focuses once more on the mortal danger of war and military technology; moreover, it does not conceive the proletarian revolution as the "natural" or "inevitable" result of economic and technical "progress" (the vulgar semipositivist axiom shared by many Marxists at the time) but as the critical *interruption* of an evolution leading to catastrophe.

The relation between capitalism and the military manipulation of technology is examined in another passage of *One-Way Street*, entitled "To the Planetarium." Technology could have been an instrument for the "marriage" (*Vermählung*) between humanity and the cosmos; but "because the lust for profit of the ruling class sought satisfaction through it, technology betrayed man and turned the bridal bed into a bloodbath" during the world war. Benjamin links the military use of technical progress to the most general issue of the relationship between mankind and nature: technology should not be the mastery of nature—"an imperialist teaching"—but the mastery of the *relation* between nature and man. Comparing the nights of annihilation of the last war to an epileptic crisis of mankind, he sees in the proletarian power "the measure of its convalescence" and the first attempt to bring technology under human control.[10]

It is difficult to know how far the Soviet Union (which Benjamin visited in 1926–27) corresponded with his expectations. In some articles published in 1927 concerning the Soviet cinema—which he defended against various critics—he complains that the Soviet public, because of its passionate admiration for technology, cannot accept grotesque Western movies, whose humor is directed against technology. "The Russians cannot grasp an ironic and skeptical attitude towards technical things."[11]

If he had some hopes in relation to the Soviet experiment, he had none whatsoever for the development of technology in the capitalist world. Following the (oppositionist-Trotskyist) French Communist writer Pierre Naville, Benjamin calls for an *organization of pessimism* and ironically refers to "unlimited trust only in I. G. Farben and the peaceful perfection of the *Luftwaffe*."[12] Both institutions were soon to show, beyond Benjamin's most pessimistic forecasts, the sinister usage that could be made of modern technology.

Benjamin saw in bourgeois society a "gaping discrepancy between the gigantic power of technology and the minuscule moral illumination it affords," a discrepancy which manifests itself through imperialist wars. The increase in technical artifacts and power sources cannot be absorbed and is channeled toward destruction; therefore "any future war will also be a slave revolt of technology." Nevertheless, Benjamin believes that in a liberated society technology will cease to be "a fetish of doom" in order to become "a key to happiness"; emancipated mankind will use and illuminate the secrets of nature thanks to a technology "mediated by the human scheme of things."[13]

In his well-known essay on "The Work of Art in the Age of Mechanical Reproduction" (1936) he again insists that imperialist war is "a rebellion of technology," by which he means the following: "if the natural utilization of productive forces is impeded by the property system, the increase in technical devices, in speed, and in the sources of energy will press for an unnatural utilization, and this is found in war." The "technological formula" of capitalist society can thus be summarized: "Only war makes it possible to mobilize all of today's technical resources while maintaining the property system."[14]

Walter Benjamin becomes increasingly aware that his critical views on technology are radically opposed to the blissfully optimistic approach so characteristic of the dominant ideology in the labor movement—in particular, the positivist-oriented Marxism adopted by Social Democracy from the end of the nineteenth century. In his essay "Eduard Fuchs, Collector and

Historian" (1937) he criticizes the positivist identification of technology with natural sciences: technology is not a purely scientific fact but also a *historical* one, which, in present society, is to a large extent determined by capitalism. Social Democratic positivism—which Benjamin traces back to Bebel—seemed to ignore the fact that in bourgeois society technology serves mainly to produce commodities and to make war. This apologetic and uncritical attitude blinded socialist theoreticians to the *destructive side* of technological development and its socially negative consequences. There is a continuous thread stretching from the Saint-Simonist hymns in glorification of industry to modern Social Democratic illusions concerning the unmixed blessings of technology. Benjamin believes that today the power and capacity of machines is well beyond social needs, and "the energies which technology develops beyond this threshold are destructive—they serve above all for the technical perfection of war. He opposes his pessimistic-revolutionary perspective to the shallow optimism of the modern Marxist epigones and links it to Marx's own prognosis concerning the barbaric development of capitalism.[15]

The negative effects of mechanization and modern capitalist technology on the working class is one of the leitmotivs of Marx's *Capital*. In his essay on Baudelaire (1938), and in his notes for the planned book on the Parisian Arcades, Benjamin articulates Marx's own views with a romantic nightmare: the transformation of human beings into automatons. According to Marx (quoted by Benjamin), it is a common characteristic of capitalist production that the working conditions make use of the worker and not the reverse; but "it takes machinery to give this reversal a technically concrete form." By working with machines, workers learn to coordinate "their own movements with the uniformly constant movements of an automaton" (Marx). While in craftsmanship work required experience and practice, the modern unskilled worker is, writes Benjamin, "sealed off from experience" and "deeply degraded by the drill of the machines." The industrial work process is an "automatic operation," "devoid of substance," wherein each act is the "exact repetition" of the preceding one. He compares the behavior of workers in the factory to that of pedestrians in a big-city crowd (as described by Edgar Allen Poe): both "act as if they had adapted themselves to the machines and could express themselves only automatically"; both "live their lives as automatons . . . who have completely liquidated their memories."[16]

Referring to the "futility," "emptiness," and inability to complete something which is "inherent in the activity of a wage slave in a factory," Benjamin compares industrial time to "time in hell"—hell being "the province of those who are not allowed to complete anything they have started." Like the gambler described by Baudelaire, the worker is forced to "start all over again," performing always the same movements.[17] This is why Engels, in *The Condition of the Working Class in England* (quoted by Benjamin), compared the interminable torture of the worker, who is forced to repeat again and again the same movements, to the infernal punishment of Sisyphus.[18] Considering these views on the "hellish" nature of modern industrial work, it is not surprising that in his last writing, the "Theses on the Philosophy of History" (1940), Benjamin sharply criticizes the German Social Democratic ideology of labor as a new version ("in secularized form") of the old Protestant ethic of work—that is, factory labor is seen by Social Democracy not only as a welcome result of technological progress but even as "a political achievement."[19]

However, Benjamin's criticism of semipositivist "vulgar Marxism" is broader, putting into question its global understanding of technology: "Nothing has corrupted the German working class so much as the notion that it was moving with the current. It regarded technological developments as the fall of the stream with which it thought it was moving."[20] What Benjamin rejects in this Panglossian ideology is both the presupposition that technical progress in itself is leading towards socialism, by laying the economic foundations for a new social order, and also the belief that the proletariat has only to take into its hands the existing (capitalist) technical system and develop it further. Blind to all the dangers and socially negative consequences of modern technology, vulgar (i.e., positivist) Marxism "recognizes only the progress in the mastery of nature, not the retrogression of society; it already displays the technocratic features later encountered in Fascism."[21]

As a matter of fact, Benjamin's critique goes even deeper: it is the very axiom of a "mastery" (*Beherrschung*) over nature, or its "exploitation" (*Ausbeutung*) by technology, which is unacceptable already in his first Marxist writings, as we saw above. For the positivist conception, nature "exists gratis" (a formula used by the Social Democratic ideologist Joseph Dietzgen)—that is, is reduced to a commodity and envisaged only from the viewpoint of its exchange value—and is there to be "exploited" by human labor. Searching for an alternative approach to the relation between mankind and its natural environment, Benjamin refers back to the socialist utopias of the nineteenth century and particularly to Fourier.

This issue is discussed in the notes for the book on the Parisian Arcades (1938): in matriarchal societies, as Bachofen showed, the modern "murderous conception of the exploitation of nature" did not exist—nature was conceived as a *giving mother*. This could again be the case in a socialist society, because the moment production ceases to be founded on the exploitation of human labor, "labor will in its turn lose its character of exploitation of nature by humankind. It will then be accomplished according to the model of children's play, which is in Fourier the paradigm for the *travail passionné* of the *harmoniens*. . . . Such a work instilled with the spirit of play is not oriented to the production of values but to an amelioration of nature."[22] Similarly, in the Theses (1940) he celebrates Fourier as the utopian visionary of "a kind of labour which, far from exploiting nature is capable of delivering her of her creations which lie dormant in her womb as potentials." This does not mean that Benjamin wants to replace Marxism by utopian socialism: he considers Fourier to be complementary to Marx, and in the same passage where he so favorably writes of the French socialist, he also contrasts Marx's insights with the utter confusion of the Social Democratic Gotha Program on the nature of labor.[23]

In his first Marxist work (*One-Way Street*, written in 1923–26) Benjamin sounded the fire alarm: if proletarian revolution does not come in time, economic and technical progress under capitalism may lead to catastrophe. The defeat of revolution in Germany, France, and Spain led to one of the greatest catastrophes in the history of humankind: World War II. As the war began, in 1940, it was too late for ringing the bell. Benjamin had not lost his desperate hopes in revolution, but he redefined revolution through a new version of the allegorical image he used in the 1920s: "Marx said that the revolutions are the locomotives of world history. But perhaps they are something quite different. Perhaps the revolutions are the hand of the human species travelling in this train pulling the alarm brakes."[24]

In conclusion, one can (perhaps) criticize Benjamin for offering images, utopias, and allegories instead of concrete and scientific analysis of modern technology and of the possible alternative. But one cannot deny his importance as a visionary pathbreaker and a revolutionary philosopher. With his critical insight into the dangers and damages of industrial capitalist technology, he renewed Marxist thinking in this area and opened the way for the Frankfurt School's future reflections. He may also be considered a forerunner of the two most important social movements of the end of this century: ecology and antinuclear pacifism. If one reads today his "Fire Alarm" (as well as other writings) it is enough to replace the word "gas" by "nuclear" in order to discover the extraordinary relevance and urgency of his warnings.

Notes

1. Karl Marx, "Manifesto of the Communist Party," in *The Revolutions of 1848*, ed. David Fernbach (New York: Vintage, 1974), pp. 72–74.
2. Karl Marx, *Grundrisse*, trans. Martin Nicolaus (New York: Vintage, 1973) pp. 708–709.
3. Karl Marx, *Das Kapital*, in Karl Marx and Friedrich Engels, *Werke*, vol. 23 (Berlin: Dietz Verlag, 1968), pp. 445–46, 528–29.

4. Ibid., pp. 528–30.
5. Ibid., p. 465.
6. Marx, *Grundrisse*, pp. 706, 712.
7. Walter Benjamin, "Dialog über die Religiosität der Gegenwart," in *Gesammelte Schriften* (hereafter *G.S.*), vol. 2, 1 (Frankfurt a.m.: Suhrkamp Verlag, 1972–85), pp. 16–35.
8. Benjamin, *G.S.*, vol. 4, 1, pp. 473–76.
9. Walter Benjamin, "One-Way Street," in *Reflections*, ed. Peter Demetz, trans. Edmund Jephcott (New York: Harcourt Brace Jovanovich, 1978), p. 84.
10. Ibid., pp. 92–94. Cf. Benjamin, *G.S.*, vol. 4, 1, pp. 147–48.
11. Walter Benjamin, "Zur Lage der russischen Filmkunst" and "Erwilderung an Oscar H. H. Schmitz," in *G.S.*, vol. 11, 2, pp. 750, 753.
12. Walter Benjamin, "Surrealism: The Last Snapshot of the European Intelligentsia," in *Reflections*, p. 191.
13. Walter Benjamin, "Theories of German Fascism," *New German Critique* 17 (Spring 1979): pp. 120–21, 126–28.
14. Walter Benjamin, *Illuminations*, ed. Hannah Arendt, trans. Harry Zohn (Fontana, 1973), pp. 243–44.
15. Walter Benjamin, "Eduard Fuchs, Collector and Historian," *New German Critique* 5 (Spring 1975): pp. 33–34, 45.
16. Walter Benjamin, "On Some Motifs in Baudelaire," in *Illuminations*, pp. 177–80. In an article written several years before (1930) on E. T. A. Hoffmann, Benjamin referred to the romantic writer's metaphysical dualism between Life and Automat and his horror for the diabolical mechanisms that transform men into automatons (Benjamin, "E. T. A. Hoffmann and Oscar Panizza," in *G.S.*, vol. 2, 2, pp. 644–47). Some of this romantic fear is present in Benjamin's remarks on the condition of modern workers and city dwellers.
17. Benjamin, *Illuminations*, pp. 260–61.
18. See Benjamin, *Das Passagen-Werk*, in *G.S.*, vol. 5, 1, p. 162. Marx also compares the gates of the factory to the gates of hell. Benjamin quotes him in *G.S.*, vol. 5, 2, p. 813.
19. Benjamin, *Illuminations*, pp. 260–61.
20. Ibid., p. 260.
21. Ibid., p. 261. This definition of fascism as *technocratic* reveals a significant reevaluation of Benjamin's former views. In an article from 1934, "The Author as Producer"—one of the few of his writings which seems to entertain illusions regarding the benefits of technical progress in itself—he opposes the need for "technical innovations" in cultural production to the call for "spiritual renewal" which he considers typical of fascism—forgetting Marinetti's rapturous hymns to the glory of modern technology (Benjamin, "The Author as Producer," in *Reflections*, p. 228).
22. Benjamin, *Das Passagen-Werk*, in *G.S.*, vol. 5, 1, p. 456.
23. Benjamin, *Illuminations*, p. 261.
24. Benjamin, *G.S.*, vol. 1, 3, p. 1232 (preparatory notes for the "Theses on the Philosophy of History").

15

The Revolution Is the Emergency Brake: Walter Benjamin's Political-Ecological Currency

Walter Benjamin was one of the few Marxists in the years before 1945 to propose a radical critique of the concept of "exploitation of nature" and of civilization's "murderous" relationship with nature.

As early as 1928, in his book *One-way Street*, Benjamin denounced the idea of the domination of nature as "imperialist" and proposed a new conception of art as "the mastery of relations between nature and humanity." In this text there appeared for the first time the concept of revolution as *interruption* of a catastrophic process, closely associated with the technological progress driven by capital: if the overthrow of the bourgeoisie by the proletariat "is not achieved by the time an almost predictable moment of economic and technological development has been reached (inflation and gas warfare point to it), then all is lost. Before the spark hits the dynamite the burning fuse must be cut through."[1] Benjamin was wrong about inflation but not about the war, although he could not foresee that the lethal gas would be used not on the battlefields, as in the First World War, but in the industrial extermination of Jews and Gypsies.

Critical of the ideology of inevitable progress, in his essay on Surrealism (1929) Benjamin argues that revolutionaries need to *organize pessimism*.

We can only trust, he writes ironically, in the IG Farben—the great German capitalist chemicals conglomerate—and the peaceful perfection of the Reich's air force, the Luftwaffe. Benjamin's critical vision allowed him to perceive—intuitively, but with surprising acuity—the catastrophes in store for Europe as a result of the crisis of industrial/capitalist civilization. But not even Benjamin, the most pessimistic of his time, could have foreseen the destruction that the Luftwaffe was to rain down on the civilian populations of Europe's towns and cities, still less could he imagine that IG Farben, just twelve years later, would set up plants in the concentration camps to exploit the prisoners as forced labor.

If Benjamin rejected the doctrines of progress, this did not prevent him from positing a radical alternative to the impending disaster: the revolutionary utopia. Utopias, dreams born of a different future, writing in Paris, capital of the nineteenth century (1935), closely associated with elements coming from prehistory (*Urgeschichte*), that is, a primitive and classless society. Stored in the collective unconscious, these experiences of the past "interact with the new to give birth to [. . .] utopias."[2]

In his 1935 essay on Bachofen, Benjamin develops the reference to prehistory in more specific terms. Friedrich Engels was greatly interested in Bachofen's work on matriarchy, while for the anarchist thinker Élisée Reclus the interest lay in the "evocation of a communist society at the dawn of history," a classless, democratic, and egalitarian society which implied a genuine "subversion of the principle of authority."[3]

Archaic societies also lived in greater harmony with nature. In "The Paris of the Second Empire in Baudelaire" (1938) Benjamin calls into question the "mastery" (*Beherrschung*) of nature and its "exploitation" (*Ausbeutung*) by humans. As Bachofen had already shown, Benjamin insists, "the murderous (*mörderisch*) idea of the exploitation of nature"—a dominant capitalist/modern concept from the nineteenth century on—did not exist in matriarchal societies because nature was perceived as a generous mother (*schenkenden Mutter*).[4]

For Benjamin—as for Engels and the libertarian socialist Élisée Reclus—it was a question not of a return to the prehistoric past but of putting forward the prospect of a *new harmony* between society and the natural environment. The name that sums up for Benjamin the promise of such future reconciliation with nature is Fourier. Only in a socialist society in which production will no longer be based on the exploitation of human labor, "work [...] would no longer be characterized as the exploitation of nature by man. It would be conducted on the model of children's play, which in Fourier forms the basis of the 'impassioned work' of the Harmonians [...] Such work invested with the spirit of play is oriented not towards the production of values but towards the improvement of nature."[5]

In the theses "On the Concept of History" (1940), his philosophical testament, Benjamin once again hails Fourier as the utopian visionary of "a labour that, far from exploiting nature, is capable of extracting from it the virtual creations that lie dormant in her womb" (Thesis XI). This is not to say that Benjamin wanted to replace Marxism with utopian socialism: he regarded Fourier as a supplement to Marx, and in the same passage in which he speaks so highly of the French Socialist invokes Marx's observations on the Gotha Programme's conformist stance on the nature of work. For social-democratic positivism—typified by Joseph Dietzgen—"the new conception of labour amounts to the exploitation of nature, which with naive complacency is contrasted with the exploitation of the proletariat." This is "a conception of nature which differs ominously from the one in the Socialist utopias before the 1848 revolution" and one that "already displays the technocratic features later encountered in Fascism."[6]

We find in the theses of 1940 a *correspondence*—in the sense Baudelaire gives to the term in his poem "Les Correspondences"—between theology and politics: between the lost paradise from which we have been driven by the storm called "progress" and the classless society at the dawn of history, and also between the Messianic age of the future and the new classless society of socialism. But how are we to interrupt the ongoing catastrophe, the accumulation of debris which "grows skyward," the result of so-called "progress" (Thesis IX)? As always in the theses of 1940, Benjamin's answer is both religious and secular. In the theological sphere, it is the task of the Messiah, while the secular equivalent or "correspondence" to Messianic intervention is none other than the *Revolution*. The Messianic/revolutionary interruption of progress is, then, Benjamin's response to the threats posed by the human species by the continuation of evil and impending storm of new catastrophes. We are in 1940, only months away from the start of the Final Solution.

In the theses "On the Concept of History" Benjamin makes frequent reference to Marx, but at one important point adopts a critical distance from the author of *Capital*: "Marx said that revolutions are the locomotive of world history. But perhaps things are very different. It may be that revolutions are the act by which the human race travelling in the train applies the emergency brake."[7] Implicitly, the image suggests that if humanity allows the train follow its course, already laid down by the steel structure of the rails, and nothing stops its vertiginous career, we shall be hurled into catastrophe, the crash or the abyss.

But even so, Benjamin, the most pessimistic of Marxists, could not foresee how far the process of capitalist exploitation and domination of nature—and its bureaucratic double in the countries of the East before the fall of the Wall—would have catastrophic consequences for all humanity.

Some comments on the political-ecological currency of Benjamin's thinking

We are witnessing now in the early twenty-first century the ever faster "progress" of the train of industrial/capitalist civilization into the abyss, an abyss called ecological disaster, the most dramatic expression of which is global warming. It is important to bear in mind the increasing acceleration of the train, the dizzying speed at which it is racing toward disaster.

A few years ago, when one referred to the dangers of ecological catastrophe, it was in the distant future, perhaps at the end of the twenty-first century. Hans Jonas, in *The Imperative of Responsibility*, called on us to protect the lives of generations yet unborn. Now, though, the process of climate change has accelerated to the point that we are discussing what will happen in the next few decades; in fact, the catastrophe has already begun and we are in a race against time to try to impede, slow down, and contain this disastrous process, which will result not only in the raising of the planet's temperature but the desertification of vast areas, the rising of sea levels, and the disappearance under the waves of coastal cities: Venice, Amsterdam, Hong Kong, and Rio de Janeiro.

It is not a matter of the "bad will" of this or that multinational or government but of the *intrinsically perverse* logic of the capitalist system based on unlimited expansion—what Hegel called "bad infinity"—and the unlimited accumulation of goods, capital, profits: a logic that is inevitably destructive of the environment and responsible for climate change.

The United Nations Conference on Climate Change in Copenhagen (December 2009) illustrates the inability or lack of interest of the capitalist powers to address the dramatic challenge of global warming.

Partial reforms are completely inadequate. What is at issue is the need for a revolutionary interruption: to stop the train of modern industrial/capitalist civilization before it reaches the abyss. In other words, it is necessary to replace the microrationality of profits with a social and ecological macrorationality, which requires a shift in the paradigm of civilization.

We need a much more radical and profound vision of what a revolution is. It is a matter of changing not only relations of production, property relations, but the very structure of the forces of production, the structure of the productive apparatus. The same logic must be applied to this apparatus that Marx used in relation to the state apparatus on the basis of the experience of the Paris Commune. According to Marx, workers cannot appropriate the apparatus of the bourgeois state and make it serve the proletariat; they need to destroy it and create a different kind of power. The same logic can be applied to the existing—capitalist—system of production: it has to be, if not destroyed, at least radically transformed. In its current structure and functioning—based on fossil fuels—it is ecologically unsustainable. The socio-ecological revolution implies a profound reorientation of technology that will replace existing energy sources with other, nonpolluting, renewable sources such as wind or solar polar; indeed, some ecosocialists speak of "solar communism," seeing an elective affinity between the (free) energy of the sun and socialism.

The first question to be addressed, then, is that of control of the means of production, and especially decisions about investment and technological change; such means and decisions should be taken away from the banks and venture capitalists to become the communal property of society. Clearly, radical change involves not only production but also consumption. However, the problem of bourgeois/industrial civilization is not, as environmentalists often claim, the "excessive consumption" of the population, and the solution is not a general "limiting" of consumption, first and foremost in the advanced capitalist countries. It is the nature of present-day consumption, based on ostentation and waste, mercantile alienation, and obsessive accumulation that needs to be questioned.

What is needed is the full-scale reorganization of the mode of production and consumption on the basis of criteria other than those of the capitalist market: the real needs of the population (not necessarily the profitable ones) and the safeguarding of the environment. In other words, an economy of transition toward socialism, "adjusted" (as Karl Polanyi would say) to the social and natural environment because it is founded on the democratic selection of priorities and investments decided by the people, not by market forces or an omnipotent Politburo. In other words, democratic planning—local, national, and eventually international—with a view to defining: 1) what products should be subsidized or distributed free of charge; 2) what energy options should be allowed, even if they are not at first sight "profitable"; 3) how to reorganize the transport system according to social and ecological criteria; and 4) what steps can be taken to repair, as quickly as possible, the massive environmental damage left by the "legacy" of capitalism.

This transition will lead not only to a new mode of production and an egalitarian and democratic society but to an alternative way of living, a new civilization, ecosocialist, beyond the realms of money, of patterns of consumption artificially induced by advertising and the infinite production of goods that harm the environment.

Utopia? In the etymological sense ("no-place"), yes: without a doubt. But if we no longer believe, like Hegel, that "all that is real is rational, and all that is rational is real," how are we to think a substantial rationality without referring to utopias? Utopia is indispensable in social change, provided it is based on the contradictions of reality and real social movements.

Among these movements, one of the most important today is that of indigenous communities, particularly in Latin America. It is no accident that 2010 saw the meeting in Cochabamba, Bolivia, convened by President Evo Morales, of the World People's Conference on Climate Change and the defence of Pachamama, Mother Earth. The resolutions adopted at Cochabamba take up, almost literally, Walter Benjamin's argument about of industrial-capitalist civilization's "murderous" relationship with nature, which prehistoric communities regarded as a "generous Mother."

* * *

A revolution is necessary, Benjamin wrote, to halt the race toward catastrophe. Ban Ki-moon, secretary-general of the United Nations, who is far from being a revolutionary, recently (*Le Monde*, 05.09.2009) offered the following diagnosis: "We," he said, referring no doubt to the governments of the world, "have our foot stuck on the accelerator and we are heading towards an abyss."

Walter Benjamin defined the destructive progress that accumulates catastrophes as a "storm." The same word, "storm," appears in the title (which seems to be inspired by Benjamin) of the latest book by James Hansen, a NASA climatologist and one of the world's foremost specialists in climate change. Published in 2009, the title of the book is *Storms of My Grandchildren: The Truth about the Coming Climate Catastrophe and Our Last Chance to Save Humanity* (Bloomsbury). Hansen is no revolutionary, either, but his analysis of the coming "storm"—which is for him, as for Benjamin, an allegory for something much more menacing—is impressive in its lucidity.

Will humanity apply the revolutionary brakes? Every generation, Benjamin writes in "On the Concept of History," has been endowed with a "weak Messianic power," and so has ours. If we do not exercise it "by the time an almost predictable moment of economic and technological development has been reached [...] then all is lost," as Benjamin told us in 1928.

Walter Benjamin was a prophet; not like someone who tries to see the future, like a Greek oracle, but in the Old Testament sense: that is, one who calls the people's attention to future dangers. His predictions were conditional: see what will happen, unless . . . if we do not . . . The future is still open. Every second is the narrow gate through which salvation can come.

Notes

1. Walter Benjamin, *One-way Street and Other Writings,* trans. J. A. Underwood (London: Penguin, 2008), p. 87.
2. Walter Benjamin, "Paris, die Hauptstadt des XIX. Jahrhunderts" (1935), *Gesammelte Schriften* (*GS*), Frankfurt/Main, Suhrkamp Verlag, 1977, V, 1, p. 47.
3. Walter Benjamin, "Johann Jakob Bachofen," (1935), *GS* II, 1, pp. 220–30.
4. Walter Benjamin, "Das Passagen-Werk," *GS* VI, 1, p. 456.
5. "Das Passagen-Werk," I, p. 47.
6. As I quote from "On the Concept of History" in my book *Fire Alarm,* trans. Chris Turner (London: Verso), 2005.
7. Walter Benjamin, *GS* I, 3, p. 1232. This is one of the preparatory notes to "On the Concept of History," which does not appear in the final versions of the document. The passage from Marx to which Benjamin refers appears in *The Civil War in France*: "Die Revolutionen sind die Lokomotiven der Geschichte" (the word "world" does not appear in Marx's text).

16

Capitalism as Religion: Walter Benjamin and Max Weber

Among the unpublished papers of Walter Benjamin, which came out in 1985, in the sixth volume of the *Gesammelte Schriften*,[1] the fragment "Capitalism as Religion" is one of the most intriguing and remarkable. Its relevance for the present state of the world is arresting. It comprises only three or four pages, including notes and bibliographical references. Dense, paradoxical, sometimes hermetic, it was not intended for publication and is not easily deciphered. The commentaries that follow are a partial attempt at interpretation, based more on hypotheses than certitudes, and leaving out some shadow areas that remain impenetrable. They may be read in the vein of biblical or Talmudic exegeses, trying to explore each statement in some detail, and seeking to trace its connections and meanings.

The title of the fragment is directly borrowed from Ernst Bloch's 1921 *Thomas Münzer as Theologian of the Revolution*, which denounces Calvinism for having "completely destroyed Christianity," replacing it with the elements of a new religion, "capitalism as religion [*Kapitalismus als religion*]," or the Church of Mammon.[2] We know that Benjamin read this book, because in a letter to Gershom Scholem from November 27, 1921, he told his friend: "Recently [Bloch] gave me, during his first visit here, the complete proofs of his 'Münzer' and I've begun to read it."[3] This means that the date when the fragment was written is not exactly "at the latest in the middle of 1921," as the editors indicate in a note, but rather "at the earliest at the end of 1921." It should also be noted that Benjamin did not at all share the views of his friend about a Calvinist/Protestant treason of the true spirit of Christianity.[4]

Benjamin's fragment is clearly inspired by Max Weber's *Protestant Ethic and the Spirit of Capitalism*. Weber's book is mentioned twice, once in the body of the text, and then in the bibliographical notes, which include the 1920 edition of the *Gesammelte Aufsätze sur Religionssoziologie*, as well as Ernst Troeltsch's book, *Die Soziallehren der christlichen Kirchen und Gruppen* (1912), which develops, concerning the origins of capitalism, similar theses as Weber's. However, as we shall see, Benjamin's argument goes well beyond Weber, and, above all, it replaces the latter's "value-free [*Wertfrei*]" analysis with a passionate anticapitalist attack.

"One must see capitalism as a religion": it is with this categorical statement that the fragment opens. This is followed by a reference to Weber's thesis, which doubles as a critical annotation: "To demonstrate the religious structure of capitalism—i.e. to demonstrate that it is not only a formation conditioned by religion, as Weber thinks, but an essentially religious phenomenon—would take us today into the meanders of a boundless universal polemic." Further on, the same idea appears again, in a somewhat attenuated form, in fact closer to the Weberian argument: "Christianity, at the time of the Reformation, did not favour the establishment of capitalism, it transformed itself into capitalism." This is not so far from the conclusions of *The Protestant Ethic*. What is new is the idea of the properly religious nature of the capitalist system itself: this goes well beyond Weber, even if it relies on many aspects of his analysis.

Both dimensions of Benjamin's response to Weber are present in his discussion of the main characteristics of the "religious structure of capitalism." Benjamin does not quote Weber in this context, but his presentation is nourished by the ideas and arguments of the German sociologist, giving them however a new meaning, infinitely more critical, more radical—socially, politically, and philosophically (and perhaps theologically)—and one in contradiction to the Weberian thesis of secularization.

The first decisive trait of the capitalist religion is that it is

> a purely cultic religion, perhaps the most extremely cultic that ever existed. Within it, nothing has meaning that is not immediately related to the cult; it has no specific dogma or theology. Utilitarianism acquires in it, from this viewpoint, its religious coloration.

In other words, the utilitarian practices of capitalism —capital investment, speculation, financial operations, stock-exchange manipulations, the selling and buying of commodities—have the meaning of a religious cult. Capitalism does not require the acceptance of a creed, a doctrine, or a theology. What counts are the actions, which take the form, in terms of their social dynamics, of cult practices. Somewhat in contradiction to his argument about Christianity and the Protestant Reformation, Benjamin compares this capitalist religion with pagan cults, which were also "immediately practical" and without "transcendent" aspirations.

But what is it that permits one to assimilate these economic capitalist practices to a religious "cult"? Benjamin does not explain it, but he uses, a few lines later, the word "adorer"; we may therefore suppose that, for him, the capitalist cult includes some divinities that are the object of adoration. For instance: "Comparison between the images of saints in different religions and the banknotes of different states." Money, in the form of paper notes, would therefore be the object of a cult similar to the one of saints in "ordinary" religions. It is interesting to note that, in a passage from *One-way Street* (1928), Benjamin compares the banknotes with the "façade-architecture of Hell [*Fassaden-architektur der Hölle*]," which manifests "the holy spirit of seriousness" of capitalism.[5] Let us also recall that on the gate—or the façade—of Dante's hell stands the famous inscription: "Lasciate ogni speranza, voi ch'entrate." According to Marx, these were the words inscribed by the capitalist at the entrance of the factory, for the instruction of his workers. As we shall see below, *despair* is for Benjamin the religious state of the world under capitalism.

However, banknotes are only one of the manifestations of a much more essential divinity within the capitalist cultic system: *money*, the god Mammon, or, according to Benjamin, "Pluto . . . the god of wealth." In the fragment's bibliography, a violent and desperate attack on the religious power of money is mentioned: it is to be found in the book *Aufruf zum Sozialismus* [Call to Socialism], published by the German-Jewish anarchist Gustav Landauer in 1919, just before his murder by the military after the defeat of the revolution in Munich. In the page mentioned in Benjamin's bibliographic note, Landauer wrote:

> Fritz Mauthner (*Wörterbuch der Philosophie*) showed that the word "God" [*Gott*] is originally identical with "idol" [*Götze*], and both mean "the melted" [or the "cast," the "moulded"] [*Gegossene*].
>
> God is an artefact made by humans, which gains a life of its own, attracting to himself the lives of humans, and finally becoming more powerful than humanity.
>
> The only "cast" [*Gegossene*], the only idol [*Götze*], the only God [*Gott*], to whom human beings gave life is money [*Geld*]. Money is artificial and it is alive, money produces money and more money, money has all the power in the world.
>
> Who does not see, even today, that God is nothing but a spirit begot by human beings, a spirit which became a lively thing [*Ding*], a monster [*Unding*], and that it is the meaning [*Sinn*], which has become meaningless [*Unsinn*], of our life? Money does not create wealth, it is wealth, it is wealth in itself; there is no other wealth than money.[6]

Of course, we do not know how far Benjamin shared Landauer's argument. But we can suppose, at least hypothetically, that this passage, mentioned in the bibliography of Benjamin's fragment, is an example of what he understood by the "cult practices" of the capitalist religion. From a Marxist viewpoint, money is only one of the manifestations—and not the most important—of capital, but Benjamin was nearer, in 1921, to the romantic and libertarian socialism of Gustav Landauer—or of Georges Sorel—than to Marx and Engels. It was only later, in *The Arcades Project* [*Passagenwerk*], that he would use Marxian concepts in order to criticize the fetish cult of the commodity and analyze the Parisian arcades or *passages* as "temples of merchant capital." However, there is also a certain continuity between the 1921 fragment and the great unfinished book from the 1930s. In any case, for the young Benjamin, (gold or paper) money, wealth, and commodities are some of the divinities, the idols of the capitalist religion, and their "practical" manipulation in capitalist life constitutes cult phenomena, beyond which "nothing has any meaning."

The second decisive trait of capitalism, which is intimately linked to its concrete cult nature is that "the duration of the cult is permanent." Capitalism is "the celebration of a cult *sans trêve et sans merci*. There are no 'ordinary days,' no days which are not holidays, in the terrible meaning of the deployment of sacred pomp, of the extreme tension which inhabits the adorer." Once again, Benjamin is probably taking his cue from Weber's *Protestant Ethic*, which emphasizes the methodical rules of behavior imposed by Calvinism/capitalism, the permanent control of conduct, and the "religious valuation of professional work in the world—the activity which is implemented *without pause, continuously and systematically*."[7]

Without pause, *sans trêve et sans merci*: Weber's idea is absorbed by Benjamin, almost with the same words; not without irony however, when speaking of the permanent "holidays": in fact, the Puritan capitalists suppressed most of the Catholic holidays, which they considered a form of idleness. Therefore, in the capitalist religion, every day sees the deployment of the "sacred pomp"—that is, the rituals of stock exchange or finance—while the adorers follow, with anguish and "extreme tension," the rise and fall of the share values. Capitalist practices do not know any pause, they rule over the life of individuals from morning to night, from spring to winter, from the cradle to the grave. As Burkhardt Lindner notes, Benjamin's fragment borrows from Weber the conception of capitalism as a dynamic system in global expansion, an iron destiny to which no one seems able to escape.[8]

Finally, the third characteristic aspect of capitalism as religion is its guilt-producing character: "Capitalism is probably the first example of a cult which is not expiatory [*entsühnenden*] but guilt-producing." One could ask oneself what would be, in Benjamin eyes, an example of expiatory cult, that is one opposed to the spirit of capitalist religion. Since Christianity is considered by the fragment as inseparable from capitalism, it could perhaps be Judaism, whose main religious holiday is, as is well known, Yom Kippur, usually translated as "the Day of Pardon," but whose precise meaning is "the Day of Expiation." But this is only a hypothesis, and nothing in the fragment points toward it.

Benjamin continues his condemnation of the capitalist religion with the following argument:

> In this way, capitalism is thrown into a monstrous movement. A monstrously guilty consciousness which does not know how to expiate takes possession of the cult, not in order to atone for [i.e., expiate] this guilt, but in order to universalize it, to introduce it forcefully into consciousness, and above all, in order to involve God in this guilt, so that he himself finally has an interest in expiation.

Benjamin mentions, in this context, what he calls "the demonic ambiguity of the word *Schuld*"—which means at the same time "debt" and "guilt."[9]

One can find in Max Weber similar arguments, which also play with the connections between economic debt, moral duty, and religious guilt: for the Puritan bourgeois, "what he spends for his *personal* aims is stolen from the service of God's glory"; one therefore becomes at the same time guilty and "in debt" toward

God. Moreover, the "idea that man has *duties* toward the possessions which have been entrusted to him and of whom he is only a devoted administrator . . . weighs over life with all its icy weight. He must . . . increase them by working without respite."[10] Benjamin's expression "forcefully introduce guilt into consciousness" is not so far from the Puritan/capitalist practices analyzed by Weber.

However, I think that Benjamin's argument has a broader, and more general, import. It is not only the capitalist who is guilty and "indebted" toward his capital: guilt is universal. The poor are guilty because they failed to make money and became indebted: since economic success is, for Weber's Calvinist, a sign of election and salvation, the poor are obviously damned. The *Schuld* is also generalized because it is transmitted, in the capitalist epoch, from generation to generation; according to a passage by Adam Müller—a German romantic-conservative, but strongly anticapitalist, social philosopher of the nineteenth century, quoted by Benjamin in the fragment's bibliography—

> economic misfortune, which in the past was only borne . . . by the concerned generation and disappeared with its death, has become, now that all action and behaviour is expressed in gold, a heavier and heavier *mass of debts* [*Schuldmassen*] which weighs on the following generation.[11]

God himself is involved in this generalized guilt: if the poor are guilty and excluded from grace, and if, in capitalism, they are doomed to social exclusion, it is because "such is the will of God," or, according to its equivalent in capitalist religion, the will of the Market. But is it not possible to say, from the viewpoint of the poor and indebted—which is Benjamin's viewpoint—that it is God who is guilty, and with him, capitalism? In either case, God is intimately associated with the process of universal culpability.

So far, we can clearly make out the Weberian starting point of the fragment, in its analysis of modern capitalism as a religion born out of a transformation of Calvinism. However, there is a passage where Benjamin seems to endow capitalism with a transhistoric dimension, which is not shared by Weber—or by Marx:

> Capitalism has developed in the West as a parasite of Christianity—one can demonstrate this not only in relation to Calvinism, but to all the other orthodox currents of Christianity—so that, in the last analysis, the history of Christianity is essentially the history of its parasite, capitalism.

Benjamin does not attempt to argue for this hypothesis, but he quotes in the bibliography a rather obscure book *Der Geist der Bürgerlich-Kapitalistischen Gesellschaft* (1914) whose author, a certain Bruno Archibald Fuchs, tries (in vain) to prove, in a polemic against Weber, that the origins of the capitalist world can already be found in the asceticism of the monastic orders and in the pope's centralisation of power in the medieval Church.[12]

The result of this "monstrous" process of general capitalist culpability is the generalization of *despair*:

> It belongs to the essence of this religious movement which is capitalism to persist until the end, until God becomes completely and definitively guilty, until the world reaches a state of such despair that one can hardly still *hope*. What is historically unprecedented in capitalism is that its religion is not one of reform but of the ruin of being. Despair spreads until it becomes the religious state of the world, whose salvation one should hope for.

Benjamin adds, speaking of Nietzsche, that we witness the "transition of the planet human being, following its absolutely solitary orbit, into the house of despair [*Haus der Verzweiflung*]."

Why is Nietzsche mentioned in this astonishing diagnosis, with its poetical and astrological overtones? If despair is the radical absence of any hope, it is perfectly represented by the *amor fati*, "the love of fate" preached by the philosopher with a hammer in *Ecce Homo*: "My formula for human greatness is *amor fati*, not wanting anything to be different, not forwards, not backwards, not for all eternity. Not just enduring what is necessary . . . but *loving* it . . . ."[13]

Of course, Nietzsche does not speak of capitalism. It is the Nietzschean Max Weber who will acknowledge with resignation—but not necessarily with love—the ineluctable character of capitalism, as the fate of modern times. It is in the last pages of the *Protestant Ethic* that Weber notes, with pessimistic fatalism, that modern capitalism "determines, with overwhelming force, the lifestyle of all individuals born into it—*not only* those directly concerned with economic acquisition." This constraint is compared to a sort of prison, into which individuals are trapped by the rational system of commodity production: "According to Baxter, the concern for material goods should lie upon the shoulders of his saints like 'a lightweight mantle that could be thrown off at any time.' But fate transformed this mantle into an iron cage [*stahlhartes Gehäuse*]."[14] There are several translations or interpretations for the expression *stahlhartes Gehäuse*: for some scholars it is a "cell" (as in a monastery), for others a "shell," like the one carried by the snail on its back. The most plausible hypothesis is, however, that Weber borrowed the image from the "iron cage of despair" invented by the English Puritan poet Bunyan.[15]

Haus der Verzweiflung, Stallhartes Gehäuse, iron cage of despair: from Weber to Benjamin we find ourselves in the same semantic field, which tries to describe the merciless logic of the capitalist system. But why does it produce despair? There are several possible answers to this question:

a) First of all because, as we have seen, capitalism, by defining itself as the natural and necessary form of the modern economy, does not admit any different future, any way out, any alternative. Its force is, writes Weber, "irresistible," and it presents itself as an inevitable *fate* [*fatum*].

b) The system reduces the vast majority of humanity to "damned of the earth" who cannot hope for divine salvation, since their economic failure is the sign that they are excluded from God's grace. Guilty for their own fate, they have no hope of redemption. The God of the capitalist religion, money, has no pity for those who have no money . . .

c) Capitalism is "the ruin of being," it replaces *being* with *having*, human qualities with commodified quantities, human relations with monetary ones, moral or cultural values with the only value that counts, money. This argument does not appear in the fragment, but it is extensively developed by the anticapitalist, romantic-socialist authors mentioned in Benjamin's bibliography: Gustav Landauer and Georges Sorel—as well as, in a conservative variant, Adam Müller. It is interesting that the word used by Benjamin, *Zertrümmerung*, is similar to the one used in Thesis IX of 'On the Concept of History,' to describe the ruins produced by Progress: *Trümmern*.

d) Since humanity's "guilt"—its indebtedness toward Capital—is permanent and growing, no hope of expiation is permitted. The capitalist constantly needs to grow and expand his capital if he does not wish to be crushed by his competitors, and the poor must borrow more and more money to pay their debts.

e) According to the religion of Capital, the only salvation consists in the intensification of the system, in capitalist expansion, in the accumulation of more and more commodities; but this "remedy" results only in the aggravation of despair.

These hypotheses are not contradictory or mutually exclusive, but there are no elements in the fragment that would allow one to draw conclusions and settle for one or the other. Benjamin seems, however, to associate despair with the absence of a way out:

> Poverty, such as that of vagabond monks, does not offer a spiritual—non-material—way out. A state of affairs that offers such few ways out generates guilt. The "worries" are the index of this guilty consciousness of the lack of a way out. The "worries" originate in the fear that there is no way out, neither a material and individual nor a communitarian one.

The ascetic practices of the monks are not a way out, because they do not question the domination of the capitalist religion. The purely individual escapes are an illusion, and a communitarian, collective, or social way out is denied by the system.

However, for Benjamin, a sworn enemy of the capitalist religion, a way out must be found. He briefly examines, or at least mentions, some of the suggestions for "exiting capitalism":

i) A reform of the capitalist religion. This is impossible, because of its complete perversity: "One cannot expect expiation, neither from the cult itself nor from a reform of this religion—since it would be necessary for this reform to ground itself in some definite aspect of this religion—nor in its abjuration." Abjuration is not a way out, because it is purely individual: it does not prevent the gods of Capital from continuing to impose their domination on society. As far as reform is concerned, here is what Gustav Landauer has to say, in the page next to the one mentioned by Benjamin in the bibliography: "The God [Money] has become so powerful and omnipotent that it cannot be abolished by a simple restructuring, a reform of the mercantile economy [*Tauschwirtschaft*]."[16]

ii) Nietzsche and his superman. For Benjamin, far from being an opponent, Nietzsche was

> the first to knowingly take the initiative to accomplish the capitalist religion. . . . The thought of the superman displaces the apocalyptic "leap" not in conversion, expiation, purification and contrition, but in an intensification. . . . The superman is the historical man who has arrived without converting himself, who grew by trespassing heavens. Nietzsche inflicted damage to this explosion of heaven provoked by the intensification of the human, who is and remains, from the religious viewpoint (even for Nietzsche), guilty.[17]

How are we to interpret this rather obscure passage? One possible reading could be the following: the superman only intensifies the *hybris*, the will to power and infinite expansion of the capitalist religion; he does not challenge the guilt and despair of human beings, leaving them to their fate. This is just another attempt by individuals who consider themselves to be exceptional, or by an aristocratic elite, to escape the iron circle of the capitalist religion, but in fact it ends up reproducing capitalism's logic. This is only a hypothesis, and I must confess that this part of Benjamin's critique of Nietzsche remains quite mysterious to me.

iii) Marx's socialism: "In Marx, capitalism which has not converted itself becomes socialism by interest and compound interest, which are a product of the *Schuld* (see the demonic ambiguity of this word)." In effect, at this time, Benjamin did not know much about Marx's work. He is probably taking over Gustav Landauer's critique of Marxism: according to the anarchist thinker, Marx aims at a sort of *Kapitalsozialismus*, where "capitalism brings forward entirely [*ganz und gar*] socialism out of itself; the socialist mode of production 'blooms' [*entblüht*] out of capitalism," above all by the centralization of production and credit.[18] But it is not clear why Benjamin refers, in this context, to the concept of *Schuld*, that is, at the same time "debt" and "guilt." In any case, for him, Marxian socialism remains imprisoned in the categories of capitalist religion, and therefore does not represent a real way out. As we know, Benjamin will radically change his mind in this respect, after reading, in 1924, Georg Lukács's *History and Class Consciousness* (and, of course, meeting the Soviet theater director/activist Asja Lacis).

iv) Erich Unger and the exit out of capitalism: "Overcoming capitalism by *Wanderung*."[19] By *Wanderung*, Benjamin does not mean excursions in the woods—one of the ordinary meanings of the word—but rather *migration*. The expression used by Erich Unger is *Wanderung der Völker*, the migration of peoples. Here is what he writes on page 44 of the book mentioned by Benjamin:

> There is only one logical choice: either traffic without friction, or the migration of peo-

> ples. . . . The attack against the "capitalist system" is eternally doomed to failure in the site of its validity. . . . In order to accomplish something against capitalism, it is necessary, before everything else, to leave [*heraustreten*] its sphere of efficacy [*Wirkungsbereich*], because within itself, the system is able to absorb any contrary action.[20]

The aim is, in the final analysis, to replace civil war by the *Völkerwanderung*.

Benjamin had much interest and sympathy for Erich Unger's "metaphysical Anarchist" ideas, favorably mentioning him in his correspondence with Scholem. However, we do not know if he considered this "exit out of the capitalist sphere" as a valid way out. The fragment does not give us any clue.[21]

v) Gustav Landauer's libertarian socialism, as presented in *Aufruf zum Sozialismus*. In the page next to the one quoted by Benjamin in the fragment, we find the following argument:

> Socialism is the return [or conversion] [*Umkehr*]; socialism is a new beginning; socialism is the restoration of the link [*Wiederanschluss*] with nature, a re-infusion of the spirit, a re-conquest of the [human] relationship. . . . Socialists want once more to assemble in communes [*Gemeinden*].[22]

The strange word used by Landauer, *Umkehr*, is exactly the one Benjamin employs to criticize Nietzsche—whose superman refuses "conversion, expiation [*Umkehr, Sühne*]" and reaches the heavens without conversion [*Umkehr*]; as well as Marx, whose socialism is nothing but "a capitalism that does not convert itself [*nicht umkehrende*]." What can be the precise meaning of this curious theological-political terminology? One may suppose that Landauer's socialism—which requires a sort of "conversion" or "return" to nature, to human relations, to communitarian life—is the escape hatch out of the "house of despair" built by the capitalist religion. Landauer is not far from believing, like Erich Unger, that one has to leave the sphere of capitalist domination in order to create, in the rural areas, socialist communes. But, in his eyes, this program did not contradict the perspective of a social revolution: soon after the publication of his book, he participated, as people's commissar for education, in the short-lived Munich Conciliar Republic of 1919—a courageous commitment that would cost him his life.

In an interesting commentary on the concept of *Umkehr* in Benjamin's fragment, Norbert Bolz has interpreted it as an answer to Weber's argument concerning capitalism as an inescapable destiny. For Benjamin, *Umkehr* means at the same time interruption of history, *metanoia*, expiation, purification, and . . . revolution.[23] Of course, these are all suppositions, since the fragment itself does not indicate any way out; it only analyzes, with horror and obvious hostility, the merciless and "monstrous" logic of capitalist religion.

In Benjamin's writings from the 1930s, foremost in the *Passagenwerk*, this topic of capitalism as religion will be replaced by the critique of commodity fetishism, and of Capital as a mythical structure. One can certainly point to the affinities between both arguments—for instance, the reference to the religious aspects of the capitalist system—but the differences are also evident: the theoretical framework is now clearly a Marxist one.

Weber's problematic seems also to disappear from the theoretical field developed by the later Benjamin. However, in the theses "On the Concept of History" (1940), we can find a last reference—implicit but easily identifiable—to the Weberian argument. Criticizing, in Thesis XI, the cult of industrial labor in German Social Democracy, Benjamin writes: "With the German workers, the old protestant work ethic [*protestantische Werkmoral*] celebrated, under a secularized form, its resurrection."[24]

Inspired by Weber, but going well beyond his sober sociological analysis, Benjamin's 1921 fragment belongs to an intellectual constellation that could be designated as *the anticapitalist readings of Max Weber.* This sort of interpretation must be considered, to a large extent, as a creative "misappropriation": Weber's attitude towards capitalism did not go beyond a certain ambivalence, a mixture of "value-free" science, pessimism, and resignation. Instead, some of his dissident "disciples" will use the arguments of *The Protestant Ethic* in order to develop a virulent anticapitalism, of socialist-romantic inspiration.

The first star in this constellation is Ernst Bloch, who, in the years 1912–14, was in Max Weber's circle of friends that met every Sunday at the latter's home in Heidelberg. As we have seen, it was Bloch who "invented," in his 1921 *Thomas Münzer*, the expression "capitalism as religion [*Kapitalismus als religion*]"—a theological disaster whose responsibility he assigns to Calvinism.[25]

The witness called on to shore up this accusation is none other than . . . Max Weber. Among Calvin's followers, says Bloch,

> thanks to the abstract duty to work, production unfolds in a harsh and systematic way, since the ideal of poverty, applied by Calvin only to *consumption*, contributes to the formation of capital. The obligation of saving is imposed on wealth, conceived as an abstract quantity which is an aim in itself, requiring growth. . . . As Max Weber has brilliantly shown, the capitalist economy in development is totally emancipated, detached, liberated from all the qualms of primitive Christianity, as well as all the relatively Christian aspects of the economic ideology of the Middle Ages.[26]

Weber's "axiologically neutral" analysis of the role of Calvinism in the rise of the capitalist spirit becomes, in the eyes of Ernst Bloch—a *sui generis* Marxist fascinated by Catholicism—a ferocious attack on capitalism and its Protestant origins.

As we saw, Benjamin certainly took inspiration from his friend's book, without however sharing Bloch's sympathy for the "qualms of primitive Christianity" or the "relatively Christian" moments of medieval Catholicism's economic ideology. One can also find, in certain passages of Lukács's *History and Class Consciousness*, quotations from Weber used as arguments in support of his Marxist critique of capitalist reification. A few years later, the Freudo-Marxist Erich Fromm refers, in an essay from 1932, to Weber and Sombart in order to denounce the responsibility of

Calvinism in the destruction of the idea of a right to happiness, typical of precapitalist societies—such as the medieval Catholic one—and its replacement by bourgeois ethical norms: the duty to work, acquire, and save.[27]

Benjamin's 1921 fragment is one of the striking examples of this strain of "inventive" readings—all by romantic-socialist Jewish-German thinkers—which use Weber's sociological research, and, in particular, *The Protestant Ethic and the Spirit of Capitalism*, as ammunition in order to mount a thorough attack on the capitalist system, its values, its practices, and its "religion."[28]

Notes

1. Benjamin 1985. English translation in Benjamin 1996b. Translations of the fragment are by the author.
2. Bloch 1962. In this new edition, Bloch replaced 'Satan's Church' with 'Mammon's Church.'
3. Benjamin 1996a, pp. 212–13.
4. On the relation between Benjamin and Bloch on this issue, see Hamacher 2002, pp. 88–89.
5. Benjamin 2001, p. 139.
6. Landauer 1919, p. 144.
7. Weber 1984, p. 180.
8. Lindner 2003, p. 201.
9. According to Burkhardt Lindner, the fragment's historical perspective is grounded on the premise that one cannot separate, in the system of capitalist religion, "mythical guilt" from economic debt. See Lindner 2003, p. 207.
10. Weber 1984, pp. 177, 178.
11. Müller 1816, p. 58.
12. Fuchs 1914, pp. 14–18.
13. Nietzsche 2007, p. 35.
14. Weber 1984, p. 188.
15. Tiryakian 1981.
16. Landauer 1919, p. 145.
17. Benjamin 1986, p. 102.
18. Landauer 1919, p. 42.
19. Benjamin 1986, p. 103.
20. Unger 1989, p. 44.
21. According to Joachim von Soosten, while Unger looks for an exit out of capitalism in *space*, Benjamin thinks in eschatological *temporal* terms. See von Soosten 2003, p. 297.
22. Landauer 1919, p. 145.
23. Bolz 2003, p. 205.
24. Benjamin 1991, p. 274.
25. Bloch 1962, p. 123.
26. Bloch 1962, p. 119.
27. See Fromm, pp. 59–77.
28. It would be interesting to compare Benjamin's "Capitalism as Religion" with the writings of some Latin-American liberation theologians, who—without having the slightest knowledge of the fragment from 1921—developed, from the 1980s, a radical criticism of capitalism as an idolatrous religion. For instance, according to Hugo Assmann, it is in the implicit theology of the economic paradigm itself, and in daily fetishistic devotional practice, that the capitalist

religion reveals itself. The explicitly religious concepts that can be found in the literature of "market Christianity"—for instance, those produced by neoconservative theologians—only have a complementary function. Market theology, from Malthus to the latest World Bank document, is a ferociously sacrificial theology: it requires from the poor that they offer their lives at the altar of economic idols. See Assmann and Hinkelammert 1989. The analogies (as well as the differences) with Benjamin's ideas are manifest.

References

Assmann, Hugo and Franz J. Hinkelammert 1989. *A Idolatria do Mercado. Ensaio sobre Economia e Teologia*, Sao Paulo: Vozes.

Benjamin, Walter 1985. *Gesammelte Schriften*, volume VI, ed. Ralph Tiedemann and Hermann Schweppenhäuser, Frankfurt: Suhrkamp Verlag.

——1991. *Gesammelte Schriften*, Volume I, 2, Frankfurt: Suhrkamp Verlag.

——1996a. *Gesammelte Briefe*, Volume II, Frankfurt: Suhrkamp Verlag.

——1996b. *Selected Writings, Volume 1, 1913–1926*, Cambridge, MA: Harvard Belknap.

——2001. *Einbahnstrasse*, in *Gesammelte Schriften*, Volume IV, Frankfurt: Suhrkamp Verlag.

Bloch, Ernst 1962 [1921]. *Thomas Münzer als Theologe der Revolution*, Frankfurt: Suhrkamp Verlag.

Bolz, Norbert 2003. "Der Kapitalismus—eine Erfindung von Theologen?," *Kapitalismus als Religion*, edited by Dirk Baecker, Berlin: Kulturverlag Kadmos.

Fromm, Erich 1980. "Die psychoanalythische Charakterologie und ihre Bedeutung für die Sozialpsycholgie" (1932), in *Gesamtausgabe*, volume I, Stuttgart: Deutsche Verlag-Anstalt.

Fuchs, Bruno Archibald 1914. *Der Geist der bürgerlich-kapitalistischen Gesellschaft*, Munich: Verlag von R. Oldenbourg.

Hamacher, Werner 2002. "Guilt History: Benjamin's Sketch 'Capitalism as Religion,'" *diacritics*, 32, 3–4: 81–106.

Landauer, Gustav 1919. *Aufruf zum Sozialismus*, Berlin: Paul Cassirer.

Lindner, Burkhardt 2003. "Der 11.9.2001 oder Kapitalismus als Religion," in *Ereignis. Eine fundamentale Kategorie der Zeiterfahrung. Anspuch und Aporien*, edited by Nikolaus Müller Schöll, Bielefeld: Transcript Verlag.

Müller, Adam 1816. *Zwölf Reden über die Beredsamkeit und deren Verfall in Deutschland*, Leipzig.

Nietzsche, Friedrich 2007. *Ecce Homo*, trans. Duncan Large, Oxford: Oxford University Press.

von Soosten, Joachim 2003. "Schwarzer Freitag: die Diabolik der Erlösung und die Symbolik des Geldes," in *Kapitalismus als Religion*, edited by Dirk Baecker, Berlin: Kulturverlag Kadmos.

Tiryakian, Edward A. 1981. "The Sociological Import of a Metaphor: Tracking the Source of Max Weber's 'Iron Cage,'" *Sociological Inquiry* 51, no. 1: 27–33.

Unger, Erich 1989 [1921]. *Politik und Metaphysik*, edited by Mangred Voigt, Würzburg: Könnigshausen & Neumann.

Weber, Max 1984. *Die protestantische Ethik und der Geist des Kapitalismus*, Hamburg: Guter-sloher Verlagshaus.

17

Revolutionary Dialectics against "Tailism": Lukács's answer to the criticisms of *History and Class Consciousness*

History and Class Consciousness (HCC) is certainly Georg Lukács's most important philosophical work and a writing that influenced critical thinking throughout the twentieth century. Next to the dialectical method, one of the most important aspects of the book is the central place occupied by the *subjective dimension* of the revolutionary struggle: class consciousness. In fact, both dimensions are directly linked: a dialectical understanding of history and of politics leads necessarily to a dialectical approach to the subject/object relation, superseding the one-sided vulgar materialist interpretation of Marxism, where only the "objective conditions," the level of development of the forces of production, or the capitalist economic crisis, play a decisive role in determining the issue of historical processes. No other work of those years was able to offer such a powerful and philosophically sophisticated legitimation of the communist program. However, far from being welcome in official communist quarters, it received an intense fire of criticism soon after its publication in 1923. No exclusions were pronounced—such practices were still impossible in the early twenties—but it was obvious that the kind of revolutionary dialectics represented by *HCC* was hardly acceptable to the dominant philosophical *doxa* of the Comintern. For many years scholars and readers wondered why Lukács never responded to these critical comments. It is true that in the 1930s he would indulge in several "self-critical" assessments of his book, rejecting it has an "idealist" piece. But there exists no evidence that he shared this viewpoint already in the early 1920s: on the contrary, one could assume, for instance from his book on Lenin, in 1924, or his critical comments on Bukharin in 1925, that he did *not* recant his philosophical perspective.

The recent discovery of *Chvostismus und Dialektik* in the former archives of the Lenin Institute shows that this "missing link" existed: Lukács *did reply*, in a most explicit and vigorous way, to these attacks, and defended the main ideas of his Hegelo-Marxist masterpiece from 1923. One may consider this answer as his last writing still inspired by the general philosophical approach of *Geschichte und Klassenbewusstsein*, just before a major turn in his theoretical and political orientation.

The German manuscript was published by the Lukács Archives of Budapest in 1996—and translated into English by Verso (London) in 2000 under the title *Tailism and the Dialectic*. Laszlo Illés, the Hungarian editor of the original version, believes that it was written in 1925 or 1926 "at the same time as the significant reviews of the Lassalle-Edition and Moses Hess writings." I think that 1925 is a more accurate guess, because there is no reason why Lukács would wait two years to answer criticisms published in 1924—the style of the document suggests rather an immediate response. But, above all, I don't believe that it is contemporaneous with the article on Moses Hess (1926), for the good reason that this article is, as I'll try to show later on, strictly opposed, in its basic philosophic orientation, to the newly discovered essay.

Now that we know that Lukács found it necessary to defend *History and Class Consciousness* against his "orthodox" communist critics—he never bothered to answer the Social-Democratic ones—the obvious question, curiously not raised by the editors (both of the Hungarian and the English edition) is *why did he not publish it*? I can see three possible answers to this question:

1) Lukács was afraid that his response could provoke a reaction from Soviet or Comintern bodies, thus aggravating his political isolation. I don't think this is a plausible explanation, not only because in 1925—unlike 1935—there was still room for discussion in the communist movement, but above all considering that in 1925 he published a severe criticism of Bukharin's "Marxist sociology," which has many points in common with *Tailism and the Dialectic*. Of course, Bukharin was a much more important figure in the communist movement than Rudas or Deborin, and still Lukács was not afraid of submitting him to intense critical fire.

2) Lukács tried unsucessfully to publish it but failed. One possible hypothesis is that he sent it to a Soviet publication—for instance *Pod Znamenem Marxisma* (Under the Banner of Marxism), where Deborin had published an attack on him in 1924—but the essay was refused, the editors being rather on the side of Deborin. This would explain why the manuscript was found in Moscow, and also—perhaps—why Lukács used the Russian word *Chvostismus*, known only to Russian readers. It may also be that the essay was too long to be published in a review and too short and polemical to appear as a book.

3) Some time after the essay was written—a few months, or perhaps a year—Lukács began to have doubts and finally changed his mind and did not agree anymore with its political and philosophical orientation. This hypothesis, by the way, is not necessarily contradictory with the former one.

As for Lukács's silence on this document during the following years, it can be explained by the new "realist" orientation, beginning with the Moses Hess article from 1926, which will be discussed later—not to mention his rejection—particularly after the thirties—of *HCC* as an "idealist" and even "dangerous" book.

Tailism and the Dialectic (T&D) is, as its title suggests, an essay in defense of revolutionary dialectics, a polemic answer to his main official communist critics: Lazlo Rudas—a young Hungarian communist intellectual—and Abram Deborin—a former Menshevik and follower of Plekhanov, who had belatedly joined the Bolsheviks; both represented, inside the communist movement, an influential and powerful semi-positivist and nondialectical standpoint.

In spite of its outstanding value in this respect, Lukács's essay has, in my view, some serious shortcomings.

The most obvious is that it is a polemic against second-rate authors. In itself, this is not a significant issue: did not Marx discuss at length the writings of Bruno and Edgard Bauer? However, Lukács did, to a certain extent, adopt the agenda of his critics, and limited his answer to the problems they raised: class consciousness and the dialectics of nature. While the first is certainly an essential issue in revolutionary dialectics, the same can hardly be said of the second. It is difficult to perceive the philosophical/political significance of the many pages of *T&D* devoted to the epistemology of natural sciences, or to the question if experiment and industry are, in themselves—as Engels seemed to believe—a sufficient philosophical answer to the challenge of the Kantian thing-in-itself. Another consequence of this limited agenda is that the theory of reification, which is one of the central arguments of *HCC* and Lukács's most important contribution to a radical critique of capitalist civilization—a theory that was to exert a powerful influence on Western Marxism throughout the twentieth century, from the Frankfurt School and Walter Benjamin to Lucien Goldmann, Henri Lefebvre, and Guy Debord—is entirely absent from *Tailism and the Dialectic*, as it was from the laborious polemical exertions of Rudas and Deborin. Could it be that they agreed with the Lukacsian concept? Or, more likely, they just didn't understand it? In any case, they ignore it, and so does Lukács in his answer . . .

In relation to class consciousness and the Leninist theory of the party—certainly the most interesting part of the essay—there is a problem of a different sort. If one compares the discussion of these issues in *HCC* with those of *T&D*, one cannot avoid the impression that his interpretation of Leninism in the last piece gained a distinct authoritarian slant. While in the opus from 1923 there is an original attempt to integrate some of Rosa Luxemburg's insights in a sort of synthesis between Luxemburgism and Leninism, in the polemical essay Luxemburg appears only, in a rather simplistic way, as a negative reference and as the embodiment of pure spontaneism. While in *HCC* the relationship between the "imputed consciousness" and the empirical one is perceived as a dialectical process in which the class, assisted by its vanguard, rises to the *zugerechnetes Bewusstsein* through its own experience of struggle, in *T&D* the Kautskyan strictly un-dialectical thesis that socialism is "introduced from outside" into the class by the intellectuals—a mechanistic view taken up by Lenin in *What Is to Be Done?* (1902) but discarded after 1905—is presented as the quintessence of "Leninism." While in *HCC* Lukács insisted that "the workers councils are the political/economical overcoming of reification," *T&D* ignores the soviets and refers only to the party, going as far as identifying the dictatorship of the proletariat with the "dictatorship of a real Communist Party."

In spite of these problems, *Chvostismus und Dialektik* has little in common with Stalinism: not only is there no reference to Joseph Vissarionovitch and his writings, or to his new thesis of "socialism in one country," but the whole spirit of the essay runs against the sort of metaphysical and dogmatic doctrines imposed by Stalin and his followers. In fact, it may be considered as a powerful exercise in revolutionary dialectics, opposed to the crypto-positivist brand of "Marxism" that was soon to become the official ideology of the Soviet bureaucracy. The key element in this polemical battle is Lukács's emphasis on the *decisive revolutionary importance of the subjective moment in the subject/object historical dialectics*. If one had to summarize the value and the significance of *Tailism and the Dialectic*, I would argue that it is *a powerful Hegelian/Marxist apology of revolutionary subjectivity*—to a higher degree even than in *History and Class Consciousness*. This motif runs like a red thread throughout the whole piece, particularly in its first part, but even, to some extent, in the second one too. Let us try to bring into evidence the main moments of this argument.

One could begin with the mysterious term *Chvostismus* of the book's title—Lukács never bothered to explain it, supposing that its—Russian?—readers were familiar with it. This Russian word—whose origin is the German term *Schwanz*, "tail"—was used by Lenin in his polemics, for instance in *What Is to Be Done?*, against those "economistic Marxists" who "tail-end" the spontaneous labor movement. Lukács, however, uses it in a much broader historical/philosophical sense: *Chvostismus* means passively following—"tailing"—the "objective" course of events, while ignoring the subjective/revolutionary moments of the historical process.

Lukács denounces the attempt by Rudas and Deborin to transform Marxism into a "science" in the positivist, bourgeois sense. Deborin tries, in a regressive move, to bring back historical materialism "into the fold of Comte or Herbert Spencer" (*auf Comte oder Herbert Spencer zurückrevidiert*), a sort of bourgeois sociology studying transhistorical laws that exclude all human activity. And Rudas places himself as a "scientific" observer of the objective, law-bound course of history, whereby he can "anticipate" revolutionary developments. Both regard as worthy of scientific investigation only what is free of any participation on the part of the historical subject, and both reject, in the name of this "Marxist" (in fact, positivist) science any attempt to accord "an *active and positive* role to a subjective moment in history."

The war against subjectivism, argues Lukács, is the banner under which opportunism justifies its rejection of revolutionary dialectics: it was used by Bernstein against Marx and by Kautsky against Lenin. In the name of anti-subjectivism, Rudas develops a fatalist conception of history, which includes only "the objective conditions," but leaves no room for the decision of the historical agents. In an article—criticized by Lukács in *T&D*—against Trotsky published by *Inprekor*, the official Bulletin of the Comintern—Rudas claims that the defeat of the Hungarian revolution of 1919 was due only to "objective conditions" and not to any mistakes of the communist leadership; he mentions both Trotsky and Lukács as examples of a one-sided conception of politics that overemphasizes the importance of proletarian class consciousness. Apparently Rudas suspected Lukács of Trotskyist leanings; in fact, he was not a partisan of Trotsky, but did not hesitate, until 1926, to mention him in a favorable light in his writings—quite a heresy for the official spokesman.

While rejecting the accusation of "subjective idealism," Lukács does not retract from his "subjectivist" and voluntarist viewpoint: in the decisive moments of the struggle "everything depends on class consciousness, on the conscious will of the proletariat"—the subjective component. Of course, there is a dialectical interaction between subject and object in the historical process, but in the *Augenblick* of crisis, this component gives the direction of the events, in the form of revolutionary consciousness and praxis. By his fatalist attitude, Rudas ignores praxis and develops a theory of passive "tail-ending," *Chvostismus*, considering that history is a process that "takes place independently of human consciousness."

What is Leninism, argues Lukács, if not the permanent insistence on the "*active and conscious* role of the subjective moment"? How could one imagine, "without this function of the subjective moment," Lenin's conception of insurrection as an art? Insurrection is precisely the *Augenblick*, the instant of the revolutionary process where "*the subjective moment has a decisive predominance (ein entscheidendes Übergewicht)*." In that instant, the fate of the revolution, and therefore of humanity "depends on the subjective moment." This does not mean that revolutionaries should "wait" for the arrival of this *Augenblick*: there is no moment in the historical process where the possibility of an *active* role of the subjective moments is completely lacking.

In this context, Lukács turns his critical weapons against one of the main expressions of this positivist, "sociological," contemplative, fatalist—*chvostistisch* in *T&D*'s terminology—and objectivist conception of history: the *ideology of progress*. Rudas and Deborin believe that the historical process is an evolution mechanistically and fatally leading to the next stage. History is conceived, according to the dogmas of evolutionism, as permanent advance, endless progress: the temporally later stage is necessarily the higher one in every respect. From a dialectical viewpoint, however, the historical process is "not an evolutionary nor an organic one," but contradictory, jerkily unfolding in advances and retreats. Unfortunately Lukács does not develop this insight, which point toward a radical break with the ideology of inevitable progress common to Second and—after 1924—Third International Marxism.

Another important aspect related to this battle against the positivist degradation of Marxism is Lukács's critique, in the second part of the essay, against Rudas's views on technology and industry as an "objective" and neutral system of "exchange between humans and nature." This would mean, objects Lukács, that there is an essential identity between the capitalist and the socialist society! In his viewpoint, revolution has to change not only the relations of production but also revolutionize to a large extent the concrete forms of technology and industry existing in capitalism, since they are intimately linked to the capitalist division of labor. In this issue too Lukács was well ahead of his time—eco-socialists began to deal with this argument in the last decade—but the suggestion remains undeveloped in his essay.

Incidently, there is a striking analogy between some of Lukács's formulations in *T&D*—the importance of the revolutionary *Augenblick*, the critique of the ideology of progress, the call for a radical transformation of the technical apparatus—and those of Walter Benjamin's last reflections. Of course, Benjamin was familiar with *HCC*, which played an important role in his evolution toward communism, but he obviously could not know Lukács's unpublished piece. It is therefore by following his own way that he came to conclusions so surprisingly similar to those of this essay.

A few months after writing *Tailism and the Dialectic*—in any case less than one year—Lukács wrote the essay "Moses Hess and the Problems of Idealist Dialectics" (1926), which stands for a radically different political/philosophical perspective. In this brilliant but highly problematic piece, Lukács celebrates Hegel's "reconciliation with reality" as the proof of his "grandiose realism" and his "rejection of all utopias." While this realism permitted him to understand "the objective dialectics of the historical process," the moralist utopianism and subjectivism of Moses Hess and the Left Hegelians led to a blind alley. As I tried to show elsewhere, this essay provided the philosophical justification for Lukács's own "reconciliation with reality," that is, with the Stalinist Soviet Union, implicitly representing "the objective dialectics of the historical process." The sharp and one-sided "anti-subjectivism" of this writing is sufficient proof that—unlike the hypothesis of the Hungarian publishers of *T&D*—Lukács's answer to his critics was written *before* the Moses Hess piece—around 1925—and not at the same time. Soon afterwards, in 1927, Lukács, who had still favorably quoted Trotsky in an essay that appeared in June 1926, published his first "anti-Trotskyst" piece, in *Die Internationale*, the theoretical organ of the German Communist Party.

How to explain such a sudden turn, between 1925 and 1926, leading Lukács from the revolutionary subjectivism of *Tailism and Dialectic* to the "reconciliation with reality" of the essay on Moses Hess? Probably the feeling that the revolutionary wave from 1917–23 had been beaten in Europe and that all that remained was the Soviet "socialism in one country." Lukács was by no means alone in drawing this conclusion: many other communist intellectuals followed the same "realistic" reasoning. Only a minority—among which of course were Leon Trotsky and his followers—remained faithful to the internationalist/revolutionary hope of October.

But that is another story . . .

To conclude: in spite of its shortcomings, Lukács's *Tailism and Dialectic* is a fascinating document, not only from the viewpoint of being his intellectual biography, but in its theoretical and political actuality *today*, as a powerful antidote to the attempts to reduce Marxism or critical theory to a mere "scientific" observation of the course of events, a "positive" description of the ups and downs of the economic conjuncture. Moreover, by its emphasis on consciousness and subjectivity, by its critique of the ideology of linear progress and by its understanding for the need to revolutionize the prevailing technical/industrial apparatus, it appears surprisingly tuned to present issues being discussed in the international radical movement against capitalist globalization.

18

The Marxism of *Results and Prospects*

Trotsky's theory of permanent revolution, as sketched for the first time in his essay *Results and Prospects* (1906), was one of the most astonishing political breakthroughs in Marxist thinking at the beginning of the twenieth century. By rejecting the idea of separate historical stages—the first one being a "bourgeois democratic" one—in the future Russian Revolution, and raising the possibility of transforming the democratic into a proletarian/socialist revolution in a "permanent" (i.e., uninterrupted) process, it not only predicted the general strategy of the October revolution, but also provided key insights into the other revolutionary processes that would take place later on, in China, Indochina, Cuba, and so on. Of course, it is not without its problems and shortcomings, but it was incomparably more relevant to the real revolutionary processes in the *peripheria* of the capitalist system than anything produced by "orthodox Marxism," from the death of Engels until 1917.

In fact, the idea of permanent revolution appeared already in Marx and Engels, notably in their *Address of the Central Committee to the Communist League*, from March 1850, while the German Revolution of 1848–50—in an absolutist and backward country—still seemed to unfold. Against the unholy alliance of the liberal bourgeoisie and absolutism, they championed the common action of the workers with the democratic parties of the petty bourgeoisie. But they insisted on the need of an independent proletarian perspective: "while the democratic petty bourgeoisie want to bring the revolution to an end as quickly as possible . . . it is our interest and our task to make the revolution permanent until all the more or less propertied classes have been driven from their ruling positions, until the proletariat has conquered state power and until the association of the proletarians has progressed sufficiently far—not only in one country but in all the leading countries of the world—that competition between the proletarians of these countries ceases and at least the decisive forces of production are concentrated in the hands of the workers."[1] This striking passage contains three of the fundamental themes that Trotsky would later develop in *Results and Prospects*: 1) the uninterrupted development of the revolution in a semi-feudal country, leading to the conquest of power by the working class; 2) the need for the proletarian forces in power to take anticapitalist and socialist measures; 3) the necessarily international character of the revolutionary process and of the new socialist society, without classes or private property.

The idea of a socialist revolution in the backward periphery of capitalism—although not the term "permanent revolution"—is also present in Marx's late writings on Russia: the letter to Vera Zasulich (1881) and, together with Engels, the preface to the 1882 Russian edition of *The Communist Manifesto*: "If the Russian revolution sounds the signal of a proletarian revolution in the West so that each complements the other, the prevailing form of communal ownership of land in Russia may form the starting point for a communist course of development."[2]

With the exception of Trotsky, these ideas seem to have been lost to Russian Marxism in the years between the end of the nineteenth century and 1917. If we leave aside the semi-Marxists in the populist camp, such as Nicolaion, or the "legal Marxists" such as Piotr Struve, there remain four clearly delimited positions inside Russian social-democracy:

1) The Menshevik view, which considered that the future Russian revolution as bourgeois by its nature and its driving force would be an alliance of the proletariat with the liberal bourgeoisie. Plekhanov and his friends believed that Russia was a backward, "Asiatic," and barbarous country requiring a long stage of industrialism and "Europeanization" before the proletariat could aspire to power. Only after Russia has developed its productive forces and passed into the historical stage of advanced capitalism and parliamentary democracy would the requisite material and political conditions be available for a socialist transformation.
2) The Bolshevik conception also recognized the inevitably bourgeois-democratic character of the revolution, but it excluded the bourgeoisie from the revolutionary bloc. According to Lenin, only the proletariat and the peasantry were authentically revolutionary forces, bound to establish through their alliance a common democratic revolutionary dictatorship. Of course, as we know, Lenin changed radically his approach, after the *April Theses* of 1917.
3) Parvus and Rosa Luxemburg, while acknowledging the bourgeois character of the revolution in the last instance, insisted on the hegemonic revolutionary role of the proletariat supported by the peasantry. The destruction of tsarist absolutism could not be achieved short of the establishment of a workers' power led by social-democracy. However, such a proletarian government could not yet transcend in its programmatic aims the fixed limits of bourgeois democracy.
4) Finally, Trotsky's concept of permanent revolution, which envisaged not only the hegemonic role of the proletariat and the necessity of its seizure of power, but also the possibility of a growing over of the democratic into the socialist revolution.

Curiously enough, Trotsky does not mention in *Results and Prospects* any of the above mentioned pieces by Marx and Engels. He probably ignored the *Address* of March 1850: the reissue of 1885 in Zurich, in German, was not well known in Russia. His immediate source for the term "permanent revolution" in 1905 seems to have been an article by Franz Mehring on the events in Russia, "Die Revolution in Permanenz," published in the *Neue Zeit*, the theoretical organ of German Social-Democracy. Mehring's article was immediately translated in 1905 in Trotsky's paper *Nachalo* in Petrograd and in the same issue appeared also the first article in which Lev Davidovitch used the term "permanent revolution": "Between the immediate goal and the final goal there should be a permanent revolutionary chain." However, a close reading of Mehring's piece shows that the German Marxist used the words, but was not really a partisan of permanent revolution in the same sense as Trotsky in 1905–06. The vital kernel of the theory, its concept of the uninterrupted going-over of the democratic toward the socialist revolution, was denied by Mehring. This was well understood by Martov, the great Menshevik leader, who, in a work written many years later, recalled Trotsky's piece as a disturbing "deviation from the theoretical foundations of the Program of Russian Social-Democracy." He clearly distinguished between Mehring's article, which he considered acceptable, and Trotsky's essay, which he repudiated as "utopian," since it transcended "the historical task which flows from the existent level of productive forces."[3]

The ideas suggested in some of Trotsky's articles in 1905—particularly in his preface for the Russian translation of Marx's writings on the Paris Commune—were then developed, in a more systematic and coherent way, in *Results and Prospects* (1906). However, this bold piece of writing remained for a long time a forgotten book. It seems that Lenin did not read it—at least before 1917—and its influence over contemporary Russian Marxism was desultory at best. Like all forerunners, Trotsky was in advance of his time, and his ideas were too novel and heterodox to be accepted, or even studied, by his party comrades.

* * *

How was it possible for Trotsky to cut the gordian knot of Second International Marxism—the economicist definition of the nature of a future revolution by "the level of productive forces"—and to grasp the revolutionary possibilities that lay beyond the dogmatic construction of a bourgeois-democratic Russian revolution that was the unquestioned problematic of *all* other Marxist propositions?

There seems to exist an intimate link between the dialectical method and revolutionary theory: not by chance, the high period of revolutionary thinking in the twentieth century, the years 1905–1925, are also those of some of the most interesting attempts to use the Hegelo-Marxist dialectics as an instrument of knowledge and action. Let me try to illustrate the connection between dialectics and revolution in Trotsky's early work.

A careful study of the roots of Trotsky's political boldness and of the whole theory of permanent revolution reveals that his views were informed by a specific understanding of Marxism, an interpretation of the dialectical materialist method, distinct from the dominant orthodoxy of the Second International and of Russian Marxism. The young Trotsky did not read Hegel, but his understanding of Marxist theory owes much to his first lectures in historical materialism, namely, the works of Antonio Labriola. In his autobiography he recalled the "delight" with which he first devoured Labriola's essays during his imprisonment in Odessa in 1893.[4] His initiation into dialectics thus took place through an encounter with perhaps the least orthodox of the major figures of the Second International. Formed in the Hegelian school, Labriola fought relentlessly against the neo-positivist and vulgar-materialist trends that proliferated in Italian Marxism (Turati!). He was one of the first to reject the economistic interpretations of Marxism by attempting to restore the dialectical concepts of *totality* and *historical process*. Labriola defended historical materialism as a self-sufficient and independent theoretical system, irreducible to other currents; he also rejected scholastic dogmatism and the cult of the textbook, insisting on the need for a *critical* development of Marxism.[5]

Trotsky's starting point, therefore, was this critical, dialectical, and anti-dogmatical understanding that Labriola had inspired. "Marxism," he wrote in 1906, "is above all a method of analysis—not analysis of texts but analysis of social relations." Let us focus on five of the most important and distinctive features of the methodology that underlies Trotsky's theory of permanent revolution, in distinction from the other Russian Marxists, from Plekhanov to Lenin and from the Mensheviks to the Bolsheviks (before 1917).

1. From the vantage point of the dialectical comprehension of the unity of the opposites, Trotsky criticized the Bolsheviks' rigid division between the socialist power of the proletariat and the "democratic dictatorship of workers and peasants," as a "logical, purely formal operation." This abstract logic is even more sharply attacked in his polemic against Plekhanov, whose whole reasoning can be reduced to an "empty syllogism": our revolution is bourgeois, therefore we should support the Kadets, the constitutionalist bourgeois party. Moreover, in an astonishing passage from a critique against the Menshevik Tcherevanin, he explicitly condemned the *analytical*—that is, abstract-formal, pre-dialectical—character of Menshevik politics: "Tcherevanin constructs his tactics as Spinoza did his ethics, that is to say, geometrically."[6] Of course, Trotsky was not a philosopher and almost never wrote specific philosophical texts, but this makes his clear-sighted grasp of the methodological dimension of his controversy with stagist conceptions all the more remarkable.
2. In *History and Class Consciousness* (1923), Lukács insisted that the dialectical category of totality was the essence of Marx's method, indeed the very

principle of revolution within the domain of knowledge.[7] Trotsky's theory, written twenty years earlier, is an exceptionally significant illustration of this Lukacsian thesis. Indeed, one of the essential sources of the superiority of Trotsky's revolutionary thought is the fact that he adopted *the viewpoint of totality*, perceiving capitalism and the class struggle as a world process. In the preface to a Russian edition (1905) of Lassalle's articles about the revolution of 1848, he argues:

> Binding all countries together with its mode of production and its commerce, capitalism has converted the whole world into a single economic and political organism (. . .) This immediately gives the events now unfolding and international character, and opens up a wide horizon. The political emancipation of Russia led by the working class (. . .) will make it the initiator of the liquidation of world capitalism, for which history has created the objective condition.[8]

Only by posing the problem in these terms—at the level of "maturity" of the capitalist system in its *totality*—was it possible to transcend the traditional perspective of the Russian Marxists, who defined the socialist-revolutionary "unripeness" of Russia exclusively in terms of a *national* economic determinism.

3. Trotsky explicitly rejected the un-dialectical economicism—the tendency to reduce, in a non-mediated and one-sided way, all social, political, and ideological contradictions to the economic infrastructure—which was one of the hallmarks of Plekhanov's vulgar materialist interpretation of Marxism. Indeed, Trotsky's break with economicism was one of the decisive steps toward the theory of permanent revolution. A key paragraph in *Results and Prospects* defined with precision the political stakes implied in this rupture: "To imagine that the dictatorship of the proletariat is in some way automatically dependent on the technical development and resources of a country is a prejudice of 'economic' materialism simplified to absurdity. This point of view has nothing in common with Marxism."[9]
4. Trotsky's method refused the un-dialectical conception of history as a predetermined evolution, typical of Menshevik arguments. He had a rich and dialectical understanding of historical development as a contradictory process, where at every moment alternatives are posed. The task of Marxism, he wrote, was precisely to "discover the 'possibilities' of the developing revolution."[10] In *Results and Prospects*, as well as in later essays—for instance, his polemic against the Mensheviks, "The Proletariat and the Russian Revolution" (1908), he analyzes the process of permanent revolution toward socialist transformation through the dialectical concept of *objective possibility*, whose outcome depended on innumerable subjective factors as well as unforeseeable events—and not as an inevitable necessity whose triumph (or

defeat) was already assured. It was this recognition of the open character of social historicity that gave revolutionary praxis its decisive place in the architecture of Trotsky's theoretical-political ideas from 1905 on.

5. While the Populists insisted on the peculiarities of Russia and the Mensheviks believed that their country would necessarily follow the "general laws" of capitalist development, Trotsky was able to achieve a dialectical synthesis between the universal and the particular, the specificity of the Russian social formation and the world capitalist process. In a remarkable passage from the *History of the Russian Revolution* (1930) he explicitly formulated the viewpoint that was already implicit in his 1906 essays: "In the essence of the matter the Slavophile conception, with all its reactionary fantasticness, and also Narodnikism, with all its democratic illusions, were by no means mere speculations, but rested upon indubitable and moreover deep pecularities of Russia's development, understood onesidedly however and incorrectly evaluated. In its struggle with Narodnikism, Russian Marxism, demonstrating the identity of the laws of development for all countries, not infrequently fell into a dogmatic mechanization discovering a tendency to pour out the baby with the bath."[11] Trotsky's historical perspective was, therefore, a dialectical *Aufhebung*, able to simultaneously negate-preserve-transcend the contradiction between the Populists and the Russian Marxists.

It was the combination of all these methodological innovations that made *Results and Prospects* so unique in the landscape of Russian Marxism before 1917; dialectics was at the heart of the theory of permanent revolution. As Isaac Deutscher wrote in his biography, if one reads again this pamphlet from 1906, "one cannot but be impressed by the sweep and boldness of this vision. He reconnoited the future as one who surveys from a towering mountaintop a new and immense horizon and points to vast, uncharted landmarks in the distance."[12]

A similar link between dialectics and revolutionary politics can be found in Lenin's evolution. Vladimir Ilyich remained faithful to the orthodox views of Russian Marxism until 1914, when the begining of the war led him to discover dialectics: the study of Hegelian logic was the instrument with which he cleared the theoretical road leading to the Finland Station of Petrograd, where he first announced "All the power to the soviets." In March–April 1917, liberated from the obstacle represented by predialectical Marxism, Lenin could, under the pressure of events, rid himself in good time of its political corollary: the abstract and rigid principle according to which "the Russian revolution could only be bourgeois, since Russia was not economically ripe for a socialist revolution." Once he crossed the Rubicon, he applied himself to studying the problem from a practical, concrete, and realistic angle and came to conclusions very similar to those announced by Trotsky in 1906: what are the measures, constituting in fact the transition toward socialism, that could be made acceptable to the majority of the people, which is, the masses of the workers and peasants? This is the road which led to the October Revolution . . .

Notes

1. In Marx and Engels, *The Revolutions of 1848* (Penguin, 1973), p. 323–24.
2. Marx and Engels, *The Russian Menace to Europe* (London, 1953), p. 217.
3. Martov, *Geschichte der Russischen Sozialdemokratie* (Berlin, 196), pp. 164–165.
4. Trotsky, *My Life* (New York, 1960), p. 119.
5. See A. Labriola, *La concepcion materialista de la historia (1897)* (La Habana, 1970), p. 115, 243.
6. Trotsky, "The Proletariat and the Russian Revolution," and "Our Differences" in *1905* (London, 1971), p. 289, 306–12.
7. G. Lukacs, *History and Class Consciousness* (London, 1971), ch. 1.
8. Quoted in Trotsky, *Results and Prospects* (London, 1962), p. 240.
9. Trotsky, *Results and Prospects*, p. 195.
10. *Ibid.*, p. 168.
11. Trotsky, *History of the Russian Revolution* (London, 1965), vol. I, p. 427.
12. I. Deutscher, *The Prophet Armed* (London, 1954), p. 161.

About the Author

Michael Löwy was born in Brazil. He is Emeritus Research Director at the CNRS (National Center for Scientific Research) in Paris. He was awarded the Silver Medal of the CNRS in 1994, and is a lecturer at the Ecole des Hautes Etudes en Sciences Sociales in Paris.

His publications include: *Georg Lukács: From Romanticism to Bolshevism* (Verso, 1981), *Redemption and Utopia: Libertarian Judaism in Central Europe* (Stanford University Press, 1992), *Romanticism against the Current of Modernity* (with Robert Sayre, Duke University Press, 2001), *The Theory of Revolution in the Young Marx* (Haymarket Books, 2005), *Fire Alarm: Reading Walter Benjamin's 'On the Concept of History'* (Verso, 2005), and *Franz Kafka, rêveur insoumis* (Stock, 2004). His books and articles have been translated into twenty-nine languages.